Folk Songs of Old New England

COLLECTED AND EDITED BY
ELOISE HUBBARD LINSCOTT

WITH AN INTRODUCTION BY
JAMES M. CARPENTER

SECOND EDITION

DOVER PUBLICATIONS, INC.
NEW YORK

Copyright

Published in Canada by General Publishing Company, Ltd., 30 Lesmill Road, Don Mills, Toronto, Ontario.
Published in the United Kingdom by Constable and Company, Ltd., 3 The Lanchesters, 162–164 Fulham Palace Road, London W6 9ER.

Bibliographical Note

This Dover edition, first published in 1993, is an unabridged republication of the second edition, 1962, published by Archon Books, Hamden (CT) and London. The second edition added the editor's Preface and the concluding Addenda and Corrigenda to the original publication by The Macmillan Company, 1939. A few errors in rhythmic notation have been corrected for the Dover edition.

Library of Congress Cataloging-in-Publication Data

Folk songs of old New England / collected and edited by Eloise Hubbard Linscott ; with an introduction by James M. Carpenter.
p. cm.
Reprint. Originally published: 2nd ed. Hamden, Conn. : Archon Books, 1962.
Contents: Singing games—The country dance—Sea chanteys and fo'castle songs—Ballads, folk songs, and ditties.
ISBN 0-486-27827-1 (pbk.)
1. Folk music—New England. 2. Folk songs, English—New England. 3. Games with music. 4. Folk dance music—New England. I. Linscott, Eloise Hubbard. II. Carpenter, James M.
M1629.F6856 1993 93-34662
CIP
M

Manufactured in the United States of America
Dover Publications, Inc., 31 East 2nd Street, Mineola, N.Y. 11501

To

ELIZABETH WHEELER HUBBARD

and

JENNIE HARDY LINSCOTT

TWO GRANDMOTHERS

who made possible
this book for

JOHN

PREFACE
TO THE SECOND EDITION

It is gratifying to know that there has been enough demand for this book to warrant a reprinting. The steady requests show a genuine and growing interest in the whole field of folk song and music. For many reasons it was not feasible to recast the entire work, and therefore only a few corrections and additions have been possible, to be found in the back of the book.

An important inclusion in the collection would have been the songs of the New England Indians, a music vastly different in cadence and tonal structure which sets their customs and rituals in sharp contrast to those of the white settlers. The *Wampanoag Lullaby* and *Song of the Wild Rice Gatherers* as sung by Metosanya, the last royal princess of the Wampanoag tribe; the *Snake Dance*, the *War Chant*, and *The Capture of Machiasport*, sung by Neptune and Sam Sabat, chiefs of the Micmac tribe; *Lighting the Council Fire* and the impressive *Death Chant*, sung by Nee-Dah-Beh- of Oldtown, Maine — all of these Algonquin Indians — are a chapter in themselves.

If we could move a little further on in time we would include the songs of the Shakers, whose humble hymns were acted out by the faithful, and the songs of the Portuguese, who came to serve in the crews of the whalers and fishing fleets of Gloucester and New Bedford and Maine. From there it is only a step to the era of the railroads and the Civil War, with the thread of Elizabethan ballads and phrases faintly discernible throughout.

The original appearance of this book jogged many a memory, and we were led a merry way to a rich harvest of Yankee music. One of the prolific singers was Mrs. Carrie B. Grover of Gorham, Maine. What she didn't sing she played on her fiddle from a repertoire of more than

400 family songs. She put a lively touch to *Hoodle But and Hoodle Ben* on her violin. And when Aunt Carrie would not finish singing *The Oaks of James Dearing* because "it ain't fitten' ", her husband willingly concluded!

William J. Sherrard of Munsonville, New Hampshire, was born in Limerick, Ireland, the son of the Governor General of the Channel Islands. At the age of twelve, he went to sea, creditably apprenticed, for his first voyage which lasted two years. A deep-water man of thirty years and first mate of square-rigger days, he recalls tales, yarns, and songs of the windjammers as they sailed the oceans of the world. The Chanteys he sings come alive with a roar and meaning that cannot be put on paper. He flings the whiplash of the cat o'nine tails into the rhythm, and one hears the wild scream of the wind as the crew scramble to don their "souls and bodies". His chanteys are not those of the glee club nor of the barbershop quartet, but the heartbeat of a great ship as she rolls while the wind sighs in the rigging.

So we could name the singers and players, one after another, who have remembered their music for us to hear, enjoy, and pass along.

Within the last two decades, a general movement toward the pleasures of folk music has been gathering momentum until once again it is enjoyed unashamed. Many of the airs of today have their roots in the old melodies, perhaps with a change of rhythm, a twist to the words, but still recognizable. Ballad singers still linger over *I Gave my Love a Cherry* (page 267) and hundreds of groups of various tastes and ages are dancing once more to the old tunes and patterns. I realize that the musician will arrange his own accompaniment for more formal cadence and harmony or both. The task has been to set the music down exactly as it was given. If the *Ballad of the Perfect Knight* becomes *How High the Moon* to our modern singer, we have not lost, but kept alive our heritage. The wealth of melody in old New England lies at hand for all to enjoy.

E.L.H.

INTRODUCTION

A songbook that you can take to the piano when the family gather round and sing—such was the ideal of Eloise Hubbard Linscott in the preparation of *Folk Songs of Old New England.* And as you turn the pages, you will begin to realize how well she has succeeded in her aim. For here are tinkling fiddle tunes that have sent thousands of merry feet dancing down the rough pioneering paths of New England—despite lurking Redskin or Puritan divine. Here are nursery songs and singing games that you—and half the English-speaking world besides—have laid by with broken toy or faded doll. In brief, here are songs to suit almost every palate: semipopular songs treasured up by past generations; comical songs; songs of the read-'em-and-weep variety; quaint old minstrels; lumbermen's songs; sea chanteys; songs with a strictly New England flavor—one can all but hear the Yankee nasal twang; and finally, a fair number of Child ballads, "the aristocrats of folk song."

As may be seen, then, the volume is distinctive in more ways than one. In the first place, it is a collection of folk songs from New England. There have been ballads from Maine, from Virginia, from South Carolina, from the southern Appalachians; cowboy ballads and lumbermen's songs from the West. But here is *Folk Songs of Old New England.* In the second place, as indicated above, the collection includes not only ballads and songs, but a valuable group of children's singing games; and in its large number of old country dances—with directions, tunes, and in some cases even the calls—it is almost a pioneer.

SINGING GAMES

The twenty-eight singing games with diagrams and directions will, I know personally, be welcomed by a great number of people. This division was the nucleus out of which the entire collection grew—as will be sensed from the stimulating headnote preceding each game. Here as elsewhere the editor has assembled, in brief terse sentences, pertinent facts that link the songs to historic places and events. The list includes your favorites,

"London Bridge," page 34
"How Many Miles to London Town?" page 18
"Here Come Three Dukes a-Riding," page 13
"Did You Ever See a Lassie?" page 6
"Poor Mary Sits a-Weeping," page 47
"On the Green Carpet," page 46

COUNTRY DANCES

The thirty-five country dances, with directions, charts, calls, and fiddle tunes, will be equally welcome to a great many people. The picturesque titles remind one of the names of sailing ships or race horses:

"Boston Fancy," page 69
"Devil's Dream," page 72
"Fishers' Hornpipe," page 76
"Haymakers' Jig," page 83
"The White Cockade," page 115
"The Portland Fancy," page 108
"The London Lanciers," page 89
"Maid in the Pump Room," page 94
"Money Musk," page 97
"Morning Star," page 98

An ageless antiquity shrouds the origins of some of the older ones. And as the merry dancers execute the intricate figures, weaving in and out in endless mazes, borne onward by the pulsing sea of silvery fiddle notes, something of the mystery, something of the carefree joy from the long past slips down to them.

SEA CHANTEYS

If you want to feel the charm of the chanteys, turn to them and *sing* them:

"Haul Away, Joe!" page 138
"Homeward Bound," page 140
"Reuben Renzo," page 144
"Rio Grande," page 146

The chanteys were the worksongs of deep-sea sailing-ship seamen, used on board merchant ships in hoisting sails and heaving anchors. Their charm lies in their droll humor and indomitable spirit.

FOLK SONGS AND BALLADS

The seventy-seven folk songs and ballads should, however, interest far the greatest number of people. For instance, among the semi-popular songs and broadsides many of the "read-'em-and-weep" variety are priceless in their unintentional humor. In "Willikins and his Dinah" the young damsel is thwarted in love by a cruel father. Her lover, walking in the garden, spies her on the ground

With a cup of cold pizon all down by her side,
So he knew 'twas from pizon that Dinah she died.

Then he kissed her cold corpus a thousand times o'er,
And called her his Dinah, though she was no more,
Then he swallowed up the pizon and sung a short stave,
And Willikins and his Dinah were laid in one grave.

The old minstrel "Julia Grover" is spirited. So is another beginning,

The monkey married the baboon's sister,
Smacked his lips and then he kissed her,
Kissed so hard he raised a blister.

In "Tittery Nan" one senses drama in the opening stanza:

On Saturday night the wind blew west,
Tittery Nan tum tario,
There was a husking in the east,
Fairy nay, tory no, Tittery Nan tum tario.

And the second stanza plumps right into the middle of the melee:

And Old Joe Dimsey, he was there,
. . . .
He stole Josiah's tansy mare.

Jostling elbows with the comics, humorous songs, and "strouds," such as "Go Tell Aunt Rhody," is the plaintively beautiful poem, "Ocean Burial," telling of a dying sea voyager who begs, in a refrain running through the poem, "Oh, bury me not in the deep, deep sea." The last stanza describes the closing of the dark waters above him,

> Where to dip her light wings, the sea bird rests,
> Where the blue waves dance with their foaming crests,
> Where the billows bound, and the wind blows free,
> They have buried him there in the deep, deep sea!

Western cowboys used the poem as a pattern for their folk song, "Oh, bury me not on the lone prairie."

The pretty nursery song "Too-ril-te-too" illustrates the custom of the folk of humanizing the animal world about them:

> Oh! Too-ril-te-too was a bonny cock robin,
> He tied up his tail with a piece of blue bobbin.
> His tail was no bigger than the tail of a flea,
> Too-ril-te-too thought it pretty as a tail could be.
>
> Oh! Too-ril-te-too was so proud of his tail,
> To show it off better, he stood on a rail;
> An old gray cat came over the wall,
> And she ate up poor Too-ril-te-too, tail and all.

The grim swiftness of ballad drama is illustrated in "Tyburn Hill":

> A beggar man laid himself down to sleep,
> Rumsty-O, Rumsty-O!
> A beggar man laid himself down to sleep,
> On the banks of the Mersey so wide and steep,
> Rumsty-O, Rumsty-O!

Two thieves steal the beggar's wallet and staff; then the swift finale:

> As I was going down Newgate stairs,
> I saw those two thieves saying their prayers.
>
> As I was going up Tyburn Hill,
> I saw those two thieves hanging there still.

In the comic song "I'll Not Marry at All," a maiden, running through the whole category of men, discards them all, as,

> I'll not marry a man that's old,
> He'll come home to fret and scold;
>
> I'll not marry a man that's young,
> He'll come home with a flatt'ring tongue.

The song, very popular in this country and in Britain, is in striking contrast to a Scottish bothy song in which the lad repeats:

> I dearly love to marry!

"Springfield Mountain," redolent of New England homespuns, is a quaint piece. You will enjoy it. "The Brookfield Murder" also belongs here. These gory tales will make you relish, as a comic relief, "In Good Old Colony Times" and "The Old Man Who Lived in the Wood." Both are well known in England and Scotland.

The lumbermen's songs, "The Jam on Gerry's Rocks," "The Sawmill Song," and "Jack Haggerty," add a dash of color to the collection. In "The Jam on Gerry's Rocks" tragedy begins brewing

> When six Canadian shanty boys
> Did volunteer to go,
> To break the jam on Gerry's Rocks
> With the foreman young Munroe.

The "boss" warned them to be on their guard, but

> He had no more than spoke those words
> When the jam did heave and go
> And carried away those six brave youths
> And their foreman, young Munroe.

In "Jack Haggerty" the woodsman, like the cowboy singer, is not slow in taking you into his confidence:

> My occupation—I'm a river driver
> Where the white waters roar;

My name it is engraved on
The rocks on the sand' shore.
I'm a lad that stands happy
Where the white waters roll;
I'm a-thinking of Hannah,
She's a-hauntin' my soul.

"The Sawmill Song" goes into graphic detail:

The fireman gets her a-turning,
The sawyer rolls up his sleeves;
When he pulls back the lever,
The marker don't have time to breathe.

The marker cuts slabs for the fireman,
While the roller thinks of his past,
Wishing that the teamsters
Wouldn't pull logs in so fast.

. . . .

Last of all comes the board job,
When the ice it will be so thin;
The fish will have horsemeat for dinner,
And plenty of lumber thrown in.

Among the most delightful of the Child ballads is "The Devil and the Farmer's Wife." Turn to it and sing it. It goes far back in English history for its origin. The farmer's wife is so bad that the devil comes for her and carries her off bodily, as told in the ballad story:

The devil he got her right onto his back,
And down into hell he went snappety-crack.

. . . .

"Oh, now," says the devil, "we'll h'ist her up higher."
She up with her foot and kicked nine in the fire.

Two of the most beautiful tunes are "Frog in the Well" and "The Rolling of the Stones." The latter is as lovely as an organ prelude.

All in all, then, the collection—with its singing games, country dances, chanteys, and folk songs—is unique, and should be popular.

Many of these folk creations are stamped with the local color of New England, and are clearly indigenous. But the greater number of the singing games, chanteys, and folk songs are traditionally related to English and Scottish material that I found during six years of research in Britain. It is a bit astounding to find that so many of these songs and ballads, seemingly peculiar to New England, were, centuries ago, equally at home in England, Scotland, Ireland, Norway, Sweden, and who knows where! But, after all, herein lies much of the charm of folklore—to find quaint, disjointed memory patterns from the long past creeping down, down the centuries to our very door.

JAMES M. CARPENTER

September 17, 1939

FOREWORD

The descendants of the colonial settlers in New England still preserve in the quiet of their living one heritage that touches many persons throughout the whole of our country. This simple and homely treasure is their music, the charm of which lies in its simplicity and significant history.

Some of this music is generally known and found in many other parts of the United States; some of it is indigenous to New England and has not been collected before. Unlike many other sections of this country, New England continues its folk music in this generation.

The songs and games (except those of the kissing parties) in this book are found in use today and with few exceptions have been taken down directly from the singers; the dance tunes, unless otherwise noted, have been transcribed from the fiddlers and prompters, and many of them have been recorded. The manuscript of Elizabeth Foster Reed, from which some material has been taken, has not heretofore appeared in print, but has been in the possession of her descendants continuously for over a hundred and fifty years.

It is necessary to realize that folk music cannot be tampered with; it must be recorded from each individual as accurately as possible. Thus rules and regulations that govern other kinds of music and musical technique must wait upon the transcription of the folk song.

In setting these melodies to piano accompaniments I have tried to keep in mind the background of the song and the personality of the singer.

I have not discussed the points under scholarly dissension, the definition of folk music, the derivation of the word "chantey" as applied to sea songs, and various other questions; it has been my sole purpose to preserve the music that abounds in New England. Much of this will be found of some British claim, but much there is that belongs truly to New England of which I have presented a small part.

On pages 319-337 will be found a list of books of interest to those who would survey the general background.

To those who have cherished the music through the generations we extend our most sincere and humble thanks. To Mr. Phillips Barry, who so generously suffered the invasion of his time and his library, who gave most sympathetic encouragement and understanding, and whose assistance in editing this material was invaluable, I am under truly great obligation. I am indebted to Mr. Félix Fox and Miss Marion Fox for their cooperation in arranging the harmonies of these tunes; to Mr. Stewart Holbrook for his supervision of the material pertaining to the songs of the lumberjack; to Miss Lois Lenski for her enthusiasm in our common interest.

I am also indebted to Miss Elizabeth Burchenal and her publishers, G. Schirmer, Inc., for permission to quote from *American Country Dances;* to Mr. Benjamin Lovett for permission to quote from *Good Morning* and *Dance Manual,* both by Mr. and Mrs. Henry Ford; to Miss Lucy Allen for permission to reprint from the *Allen Collection of Family Songs;* and to the Folk Song Society of the North East for permission to quote from their *Bulletin.*

I am deeply appreciative of all that singers, fiddlers, and prompters have done to develop various chapters of this book. The assistance of these fine New England folk has made possible this record of the music that is their own.

Eloise Hubbard Linscott

CONTENTS

SINGING GAMES

Three centuries have passed since the New England colonists first settled on the shores of Massachusetts Bay. They came not as explorers or conquerors to take away some unclaimed treasure but as folk in search of religious security and the warmth of homely living.

Many of the habits and customs of their former homes were naturally transplanted to the new frontier where the new settler, busy forcing a living from the reluctant wilderness, found an outlet for his emotions in the music and songs with which he was already familiar.

Not all the rigid doctrines of strict religion could stamp out the music of centuries of tradition.

The singing games of New England, with all their simple, conservative, and dramatic rituals, reflect the village life of pioneer America. Generation after generation in New England has handed down by oral tradition these singing games which are reminders of the morris and druid dances of earliest times.

The ceremonial morris (thought to be a corruption of Moorish) dances were of a type introduced into England about the time of Edward III. They were performed in costume by men only and usually in the spring and fall. The druid dances were those pertaining to the ancient pagan rituals of the earliest Celts, whose gods ruled the earth and guided human destiny.

Though other nationalities came to mingle and be absorbed in the colonial settlements, the games that flourished in New England were of predominantly British origin.

In transition, though some changes may appear, these singing games have preserved in their melodies fragments of country dance tunes; in their figures of dramatic and imitative action can be traced developments of the country dance; and their themes of love, riddles, and dramatic narrative come from historic, lyric, and ballad sources of oral tradition. All the games that center about a single player begin with a counting-out rhyme, which may be a relic of magical incantations and prayers formerly in common use.

It is among the youngest in a community that tradition remains longest unspoiled, for children are great mimics; they possess highly imaginative and inventive energies, they are intensely dramatic, but above all, they are dyed-in-the-wool conservatives.

All over New England, from Cape Cod to the Green Hills, the youngsters have kept in their singing games the craft songs and country dances of a forgotten background of the New England colonist.

Just as, in England, these dances were commonly performed not by the peasants and least tutored folk but by the intelligent groups of highest ability in the community, so here in New England these are the groups who have kept alive in urban and rural communities the singing games in which are perpetuated ancient traditions.

In the school yard and at home with neighborhood playmates the children learned, not from formal instruction but from associates of their own kind, the games which were their daily recreation. In many communities, the traditions surrounding the people and the settlements were a factor in preserving these old games as much as mere geographical location. And in places slower to feel the inroads of a mechanical age these games remained in favor much longer and were slower to disappear.

Strange as it may seem, the child from the rural district learned from her visit to Aunt Sophia in the city some of the games her country home had quite forgotten just as often as the city child accumulated the traditions of the country life.

The children, however, could not claim as distinctly their own any certain ones of these games. They were almost the only amusement for the young folk of sixteen to twenty-five.

The strict religious principles of the Puritan forbade all dancing, but in spite of some dissension the singing games, many of which were round dances, were accepted for the most part as simple amusement. The games directed by the singing of the players satisfied those trying to establish a new code of manners—as long as they were performed as games. So the young people steadfastly held to this form of pastime, and in time it came to be the wedge by which the country dance as a dance was accepted. The game, played with or without music, answered every rule of propriety, since the kiss that redeemed the forfeit was in honor given and taken before witnesses.

While the children played their games daily, the young people met frequently for diversion at evening parties.

Invitation passed by word of mouth, and as soon as the last chore for the day was done the guests began to arrive at the chosen place, usually a neighbor's kitchen or front room. Here, dressed in clean common clothes of denim and homespun, or calico and gingham, they played "Rimming the Thimble," "Copenhagen," "I am a Rich Widow," "Going to Boston," or any other game that the mood suggested. These evening affairs were known as kissing parties because of the predominance of the favorite games of forfeit. Should a young man's wife refuse to go with him to one of these kissing parties, he was quite likely to skip off to find some excitement without her.

All these singing games were part of the emotional structure of living in New England and their influence today is still an indefinable something which lingers with our generation.

In these singing games, molded by years of use and changed by customs of time, lies a precious heritage of New England.

COUNTING OUT

The counting-out rhyme used to choose the leader for the games requiring a central player is believed to have come from the magical signs and incantations of the dim past and is generally accepted as a just and impartial method of selecting the leader. He is called "it."

The player that counts out—that is, the one who chooses the leader—is the player that first shouts "Count out." He is accepted by the group, who then stand about him as he recites lines of doggerel, allotting one word to each player by pointing to him as he speaks. The rhyme is repeated till the last word spoken eliminates the player spoken to. Finally, only one player remains, and he is "it."

Three familiar counting-out rhymes are:

Inty, minty, tippity, fig,
Delia, dilia, dominig,
Otchy, potchy, dominotchy,
Ah, tah, see,
O-U-T spells out goes she,
Way down in the middle of the dark blue sea!

Eeny, meeny miny, mo,
Catch a nigger by the toe,
If he hollers let him go,
Eeny, meeny, miny, mo,

Intry, mintry, cutry, corn,
Appleseed and applethorn,
Wire, brier, limberlock,
Nine geese in a flock
Ollica, bollica, boo,
Out goes Y-O-U!

One rhyme of German extraction is used in somewhat different manner. The rhyme goes:

Ibbity, bibbity, sibbity, sab,
Ibbity, bibbity, KNABE!

In counting out by this rhyme, all the players stand in a circle with their fists extended, thumbs uppermost. The player who is counting out stands in the center of the players, with his left fist behind his back. As he moves about the circle, he speaks to each player, at the same time hitting the player's right fist with his own right fist. The player thus struck puts his fist behind him. The counter-out repeats the rhyme until all right fists are behind the players, and then proceeds to strike the left fist of each player, still with his own right fist. When both fists have been struck, the player is eliminated and steps out of the circle. As the counter-out reaches the last word of the rhyme, he strikes the last player as hard as he dares. This last player, when he recovers his equilibrium, becomes "it."

DID YOU EVER SEE A LASSIE?

Sung and played by the children of Dr. and Mrs. Frank Allen Hubbard of Taunton, Massachusetts.

This game was usually played by the girls alone and was a great favorite with the less athletic children, for it gave wider scope to the dramatic imagination and required much less energy than some of the other games in which the boys participated.

From the German folksong, "Buy a Broom," comes the air of this singing game, which is a survival of an English country dance. The dance in turn probably came from one of the morris dances performed with handkerchiefs. This game is similar to the old English singing game from Dorset, "When I Was a Young Girl."

THE GAME

The players form a circle and, as they sing "*this* way and *that* way," one player chooses a motion which the others imitate. The actions generally chosen are gestures of grace: curtsying and figures of a dance, powdering, combing the hair, and dramatic figures expressing emotion.

THE FARMER IN THE DELL

Both boys and girls sang and played this game with the children of the Hubbard family of Taunton, Massachusetts.

This game of choosing, which usually followed a more active one, still retains the characteristics of the game in old England, from whence it came.

"The Farmer in the Dell" was a country dance known over the greater part of England, including the Isle of Wight.

THE GAME

The "farmer" is chosen by a counting-out rhyme. He stands in the center of the circle of players, who sing and revolve about him. He slowly turns and leisurely chooses the "wife." The player singled out leaves the ring to stand with him in the center. It is then her turn to choose the "child"; then the "child" chooses the "nurse," the "nurse" the "dog," and so on till the "cheese" is chosen. At this point the other players return to the circle, leaving the "cheese" alone in the center. The "cheese" then becomes the "farmer," and the game begins again.

3

The wife takes the child,
The wife takes the child,
Heigho, the merry-O,
The wife takes the child.

4
The child takes the nurse, etc.

5
The nurse takes the dog, etc.

6
The dog takes the cat, etc.

7
The cat takes the rat, etc.

8
The rat takes the cheese, etc.

9
The cheese stands alone, etc.

GO IN AND OUT THE WINDOWS

The children of Dr. and Mrs. Frank Allen Hubbard of Taunton, Massachusetts, sang and played this game, which was a great favorite with both boy and girl playmates as long as no kiss was required.

In the figure of this game we see the dance of a particular group of craftsmen, the weavers. As a love game, where one might openly show his preference, it was popular in the eighteenth century. Of English origin, it comes probably from Hampshire.

THE GAME

One player is chosen by a counting-out rhyme to be "it." He weaves in front of one, behind the next, and so on around the circle of singing players that stand in place. At the second verse the player walks around the inside edge of the circle. At the third verse, he kneels before his choice, and at the last verse the player and his partner walk around the outside of the circle. A new player is chosen to be "it," and the game begins again.

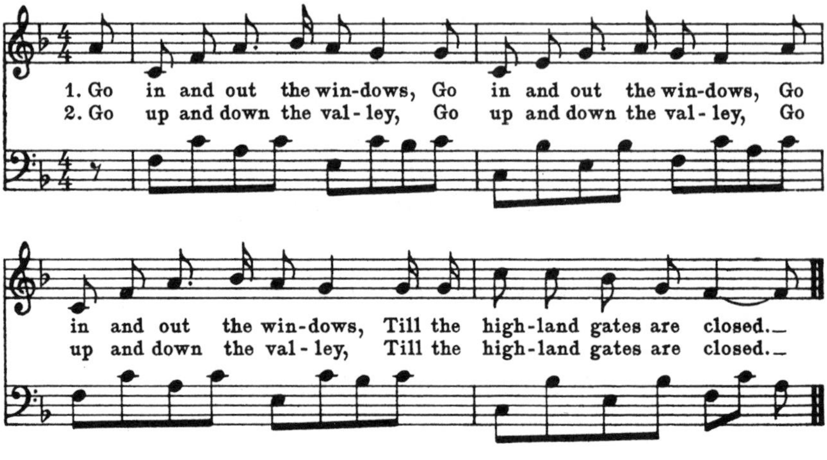

3

Go forth and meet your lover, etc.

4

Kneel down and kiss your lover, etc.

GREEN GRAVEL

This singing game was played by the Misses Mary and Serena Frye of Brookline, Massachusetts, who spent their summers when they were children at Plymouth, Massachusetts, and learned the song from their playmates there. To them it was not a very exciting game and seemed rather silly. It was not played very often because it called for little energy or imagination. As these New England girls played it, it is indeed barely suggestive of the ancient custom of English life from which it came.

The game once was descriptive of the ceremony of washing and burying the dead, in which the whole village took part. All the ceremonial functions attendant upon these rites were performed in dramatic pantomime. The turning back is part of a curious funeral ceremony of ancient times called "Dish-a-loof," in which death was followed by clapping of hands and bell ringing to ward off evil spirits and to call all good men to pray for the departing soul. The final verse that deals with the letter sustains the belief in communion with the dead. The green gravel is the grass; the letter is the communion symbol.

THE GAME

The players join hands in a circle, all facing the center, and move slowly as they sing. At the words "a sight to be seen" all fall to the ground. The last player to scramble to his feet is the one who is "it," and whose name is sung in the second phrase. He faces the outside of the circle and moves with the players as they revolve and sing to him. The game continues till all the players face the outside of the circle.

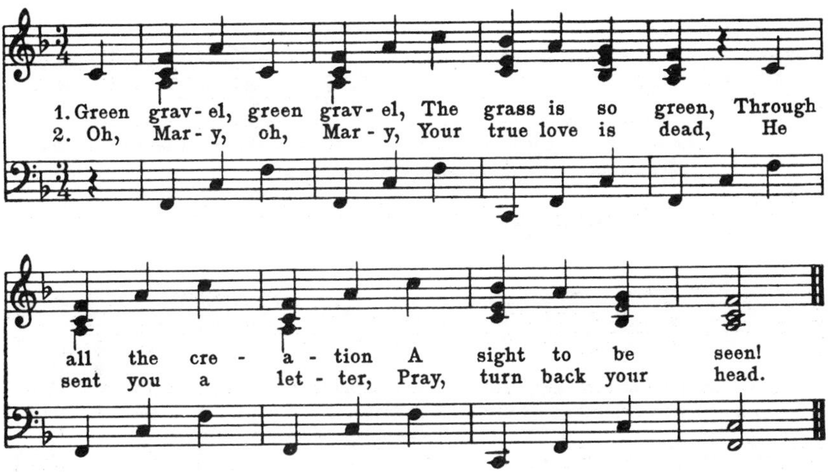

GREEN GROW THE RUSHES, OH!

Sung by Fred Pullen of North Anson, Maine, who remembers playing the game when a young man at the kissing parties in his neighborhood.

This is a kiss-in-the-ring game which is probably a relic of the earliest form of marriage by selection. "Rushes" possibly refers to "bushes" since this game was one common to the spring festivals of olden times. A theory exists that the term "gringo" is a corruption of the title of this song.

THE GAME

The players form two groups, one of boys, the other of girls.

One of these units forms a circle about a single player of the same sex. Then they turn, and as they sing, "Choose your true love," the player in the middle chooses from the group of the opposite sex a player to stand with him in the center. The last verse is acted out, and both players take their places in the circle while one of the circle steps to the middle. The game continues till all the boys and girls are in one big ring.

Another way of singing this game is the following verse:

Green grow the rushes, oh!
Green grow the rushes, oh!
Choose your true love

Now for to be;
Come and stand by the side of me.
Oh, what a wretched choice you have made!
You'd better in your grave be laid.
See that you do no longer stay,
Give her a kiss and send her away.

HERE COME THREE DUKES A-RIDING

Sung and played by Mrs. Helen Dunham Elliott of Avon, Massachusetts, who learned it as a child in Plymouth, Massachusetts. As she remembers it, both boys and girls took part.

This game may involve dukes, kings, or suitors. It is derived from the custom of a group of young men who went from one village to seek wives in another. No element of love is contained in this game that comes from the north of England. The refrain "ransom, tansom tiddy-fi-o" of the Shropshire version presented here may possibly be a war cry of the northern borders.

THE GAME

Two lines of players face each other—one line of dukes, the other a line of ladies. The first verse is sung by the ladies. In the next three verses, the first two lines are sung by the dukes, the second two by the ladies. The dukes step aside for a secret conference to choose a lady, and the girl chosen leaves the group of ladies to join the dukes. The last verse is then sung by all, and the game begins again.

* Substitute a player's name.

3

Boys: You're all too black and dirty, dirty, dirty,
You're all too black and dirty, with a ransom, tansom tiddy-fi-o.

Girls: We're good enough for you, sir, for you, sir, for you, sir,
We're good enough for you, sir, with a ransom, tansom ti.

4

Boys: You're all as stiff as pokers, pokers, pokers,
You're all as stiff as pokers, with a ransom, tansom tiddy-fi-o.

Girls: We can bend as well as you, sir, as you, sir, as you, sir,
We can bend as well as you, sir, with a ransom, tansom ti.

HERE STANDS AN OLD MAID FORSAKEN

At the kissing parties that entertained the young people in New England fifty years ago, this game was sung and played by Fred Pullen of North Anson, Maine. In this singing game New England has preserved the traditions of the English game, "Here Stands the Queen of England," and its historic background. In transition the old English song, "There She Stands a Lovely Creature," may have been fitted to a game of the village ring-dance variety, as such games were played centuries before any other form of dance appeared.

THE GAME

The players form a circle about a single girl in the center, who chooses a boy from the ring; they salute, another girl goes to the middle of the circle, and the game continues.

HERE WE GO GATHERING NUTS IN MAY

This game was commonly played by the children of Dr. and Mrs. Frank Allen Hubbard, of Taunton, Massachusetts, and included both boys and girls. It is remembered as a game that was more fun when there were plenty of players.

This is certainly a dance survival from the May Day festivals of olden days. Parties of young men gathered bundles of may (hawthorn blooms) to decorate the doors of houses and the Maypole at May Day time. The words are a corruption from "knots of may," the game is of English origin, and the tune a variant of the country dance melody, "Nancy Dawson."

THE GAME

There are two opposite rows of players. One side advances and sings; the other side replies. Each side chooses a player, one a "girl" and the other a "boy." At the second verse, the "girl" steps out of line; in the answering verse the "boy" chosen steps out of his line. If the "girl" chosen can be pulled by the "boy" across a line marked on the ground, she must join his side. The game begins again and continues till one side is depleted of players.

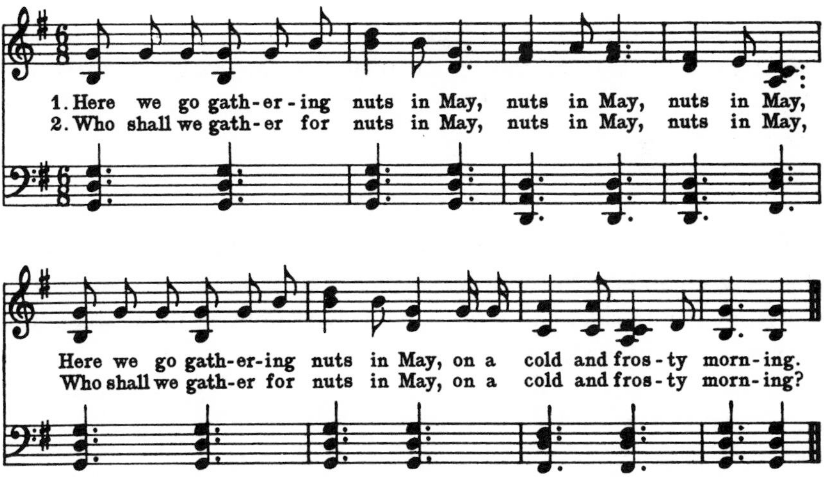

3

Oh, we'll gather Helen Hubbard* for nuts in May, etc.

4

Who shall we gather for nuts in May, etc.

* Substitute a player's name.

HOW MANY MILES TO LONDON TOWN?

Seventy-five years ago, when Mrs. Jennie Hardy Linscott was a little girl in Bremen, Maine, this game was one of her favorites, which she remembers playing with her friends.

This is a dramatic representation of merchandise entering a walled city. One authority states that it is a relic from the Crusades, when the king and queen of Cantilon (Catelon) were traveling with the pilgrims. The game probably dates from Tudor times, as there was a saying, "He went out of town as far as a farthing candle would light him." A Scotch version of this song is

> Open the gates and let me through,
> Not without a beck and boo!

"Beck," meaning curtsy, and "boo," meaning bow, make it still consistent with the idea of toll. Some forms of this song call the town "Babylon," "Barberry," or "Barley Bright"; but our singer recalls the name "London."

THE GAME

The players form two lines, facing each other across a wide space. One player stands in the middle. At the end of the rhyme, the players run from side to side, and those caught by the one in the center must help catch the others until all are caught.

I AM A RICH WIDOW

Sung by Fred Pullen of North Anson, Maine, who remembers playing this kissing game at the young folks' evening parties when he was twenty years old.

This New England singing game recalls the ancient marriage games of selection and may have been derived from the old English game known as "Lady of the Land" or "Widow of Cumberland." The poor widow with daughters to marry off is a familiar European figure lost in transition, to become a well-to-do Yankee mother.

THE GAME

The players form a circle around two girls in the center. The circle sings and revolves around the center figures till the words, "Daughter, oh, daughter, go choose you a man," when the one who is playing the daughter steps out of the circle to choose a boy. He returns to the center as the mother goes back to the circle. All sing, while still keeping the circle form, and in motion. Then, as the players come to the last line, all the boys kiss the daughter.

To continue the game, the daughter becomes the inactive mother and chooses arbitrarily another "daughter" from the circle of players. The boys are always in the ring until one is chosen.

I'LL GIVE TO YOU A PAPER OF PINS

This was one of the games played by the children of Dr. and Mrs. Frank Allen Hubbard of Taunton, Massachusetts. It was usually played by the girls alone, as it did not contain enough action for the boys.

This singing game comes from an old mummer's dance, and as such was highly dramatic for it depicted the offers of the Devil seeking to win an adherent. "The Keys to Heaven" is another form of this same song and game but was not known to those who remember this version. Elsewhere in this collection is still another variant called "The Quaker's Wooing," which was not known as a game to the family in which it is traditional.

In olden times pins were as valuable as jewels, and the outcome of the game, although not flattering to the lady, is consistent with those days when the lady herself was held as so much chattel. The origin of this game is Scotch.

THE GAME

With a counting-out rhyme the lady and the suitor are chosen. The lady stands in the center of the circle, and with each offer the suitor advances a step toward her until as the last verse is sung he stands in the center with her. When she accepts his last offer, he rejects her and she returns to the circle. He chooses another lady, who goes to the center while he returns to the circle. The player on his right then becomes the next suitor, and the game begins again.

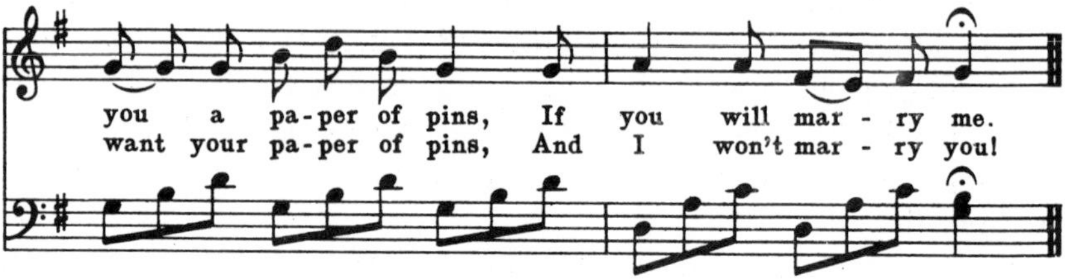

2

Oh, I will give you a coach and six,
And every horse as black as pitch,
Oh, I will give you a coach and six,
If you will marry me.

Answer

Oh, I don't want your coach and six,
Coach and six, coach and six,
Oh, I don't want your coach and six,
And I won't marry you.

3

Oh, I will give you a red silk gown,
With golden laces hanging down,
Oh, I will give you a red silk gown,
If you will marry me.

Answer

(Refusal, as before)

4

Oh, I will give you the key to my heart,
And this will show we'll never part,
Oh, I will give you the key to my heart,
If you will marry me.

Answer

(Refusal, as before)

5

Oh, I will give you the key to my chest,
And you'll have money at your request,
Oh, I will give you the key to my chest,
    If you will marry me.

Answer

Yes, I'll take the key to your chest,
The key to your chest, the key to your chest,
So I'll have money at my request,
    And I will marry you.

6

You shall not have the key to my chest,
The key to my chest, the key to my chest,
Nor any money for your request,
    And I won't marry you.

I PUT MY LITTLE HAND IN

This was perhaps the great favorite played by the children of Dr. and Mrs. Frank Allen Hubbard of Taunton, Massachusetts, as it was thoroughly amusing to everyone and was limited in action only by exhausting the imagination. Mrs. Addie Jackson Morse of Underhill, Vermont, remembers the game as the "Shaker's Dance," but the tune and way of playing it are the same as given here.

The English name for this song was "Hinkum Booby." As a dance, it was done deliberately and with great dignity. In the Scottish form of the game, it was a choral dance and involved the grotesque rites of a deity. "Looby-loo" is a corruption of "lupin," the word for leaping, for the game takes the form of animal antics. It is significant that the word "little" is used in place of the word "right" when designating the right hand, right foot, or other physical feature on the right side of the body. The reason for this is based on the superstition that to call attention to one's strong, or right, feature was to invite the maledictions of evil spirits.

THE GAME

The players form a circle, singing and acting out the words in unison.

(1) "I put my little hand in." The right hand is thrust toward the center of the circle.

(2) "I put my little hand out." The right hand is thrust backward.

(3) "I give my little hand a shake, shake, shake." The right hand is held directly in front and shaken thoroughly.

(4) "And I turn myself about." Each player whirls about in place.

(5) "Here we go looby-loo," to end of chorus. All sing and leap about, keeping in circle formation.

The action is repeated for the second verse, substituting the left hand for the right and naming the left hand; and so forth.

When "both feet" and "whole self" are called, the players jump vigorously toward the center of the circle and then backward, with exaggerated effort.

To make the game last longer, elbows, fingers, ears, knees, and eyes were "put in" and "put out" separately and wholly, till the entire body was completely exhausted.

3

I put my both hands in,
I put my both hands out,
I give my both hands a shake, shake, shake,
And turn myself about.

4

I put my little foot in, etc.

5

I put my left foot in, etc.

6

I put my both feet in, etc.

7

I put my little head in, etc.

8

I put my whole self in, etc.

JENNIA JONES

The children of Dr. and Mrs. Frank Allen Hubbard, of Taunton, Massachusetts, remember that this version of one of the most widely popular singing games was played only by the girls.

This in New England is most significant, for it points to the ancient burial customs of English village life when the girls took an active part in the rites for one of their number.

"Jo" is an old word for sweetheart; in a corrupted form it entered the phrase "Jennia Jones," which may be interpreted as meaning "Jenny, my sweetheart."

The colors chosen and rejected in the chorus of the song may be traced to the Gaelic meanings of each: blue for constancy, green for grief, yellow for gladness, and so forth. In the Yankee interpretation the colors represent the occupations or nationalities, with black and white still standing for the devil and angels respectively. The ghost that arises and chases her disturbers is significant of the sanctity of the dead and the grave. It is interesting to note, in this version, the use of purple for mourners, the color expressing grief in biblical times.

THE GAME

The players form a circle. One of the number is chosen by counting out to be Jennia, and one to be her mother. Jennia sits silently in the center, while the circle sings and her mother replies. As the verses are sung that describe Jennia's failing health and final end, Jennia acts the words in pantomime. When the circle sings the last verse, however, Jennia's corpse suddenly arises with a shriek to disperse the players and interrupt the song. If Jennia catches one of the players that one must be the "mother," and the erstwhile "mother" becomes "Jennia." The game then begins all over again.

Spoken. She's ironing.

3

We're right glad to hear of it,
To hear of it, to hear of it,
We're right glad to hear of it,
And how is she today?

Spoken. She's sick.

4

We're right sorry to hear of it,
To hear of it, to hear of it,
We're right sorry to hear of it,
And how is she today?

Spoken. She's dying.

5

We're right sorry, etc.

Spoken. She's dead.

6

What are we going to bury her in,
Bury her in, bury her in?
What are we going to bury her in,
Now she has passed away?

Spoken. Red.

7

Red is for the firemen,
The firemen, the firemen,
Red is for the firemen,
So that will never do.

Spoken. Green.

8

Green is for the Irish, etc.
So that will never do.

Spoken. Yellow.

9

Yellow is for the dancers, etc.
So that will never do.

Spoken. Blue.

10

Blue is for the sailors, etc.
So that will never do.

Spoken. Purple.

11

Purple is for the mourners, etc.
So that will never do.

Spoken. Black.

12

Black is for the devil, etc.
So that will never do.

Spoken. White.

13

White is for angels, etc.
So that will surely do.

14

I dreamt I saw a ghost last night,
Ghost last night, ghost last night.

I dreamt I saw a ghost last night,
Under the apple tree.

15

The ghost rose up and said to me,
Said to me, said to me,
The ghost rose up and said to me—

Jennia Jones rises and screams, chasing the rest of the players.

KING'S LAND

As sung and played by the children of Dr. and Mrs. Frank Allen Hubbard of Taunton, Massachusetts, this game was noisy and full of action. It seems possible that it survived in this old territory, which was the scene of Indian and Revolutionary activities, through the spirit of Yankee resentment toward hostilities in Colonial settlements. Certainly this game flourished in this particular part of New England, where statesmen and patriots were the main crop.

It is possible that the roots of the game may be found in the Debatable Land on the border between Scotland and England, for in that section, this ancient game was known as the "King of Cantland."

THE GAME

The game requires a large rock, platform, or rise of ground for the King's domain. The King is chosen by a counting-out rhyme. He departs with the first chanting verse and must return as stealthily and as quickly as possible from "Boston" to catch whomever he finds trespassing on his property. All those caught must then go with him to "Boston" and come back unseen to catch other trespassers to add to the King's side. It is a matter of agility to stand shouting on the King's domain and yet be off it when he comes in sight. The game ends when the neighbors rebel at the noise; it has never been known to last to the proper end when all the players are King's men.

LAZY MARY

The children of Dr. and Mrs. Frank Allen Hubbard of Taunton, Massachusetts, played and sang, but infrequently, this very ancient game, which resembles a round of the fifteenth or sixteenth century in which a nun or monk is tempted to dance by various offers. The nun or monk finally succumbs to worldly delights.

THE GAME

The mother and daughter in this game are chosen by a counting-out rhyme. They kneel in the center of the ring, the daughter with her eyes shut. The mother speaks the bribe; then mother and circle sing the bribe to tempt Mary. When Mary yields to the final bribe another mother and daughter are chosen, and the game begins again.

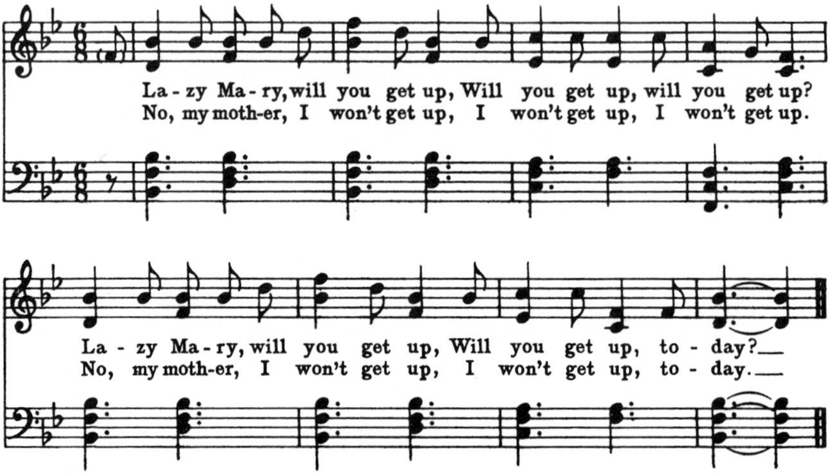

Mary speaks.

What will you give me for my breakfast?

Mother speaks.

A slice of bread and a cup of tea.

3

Mother and chorus sing.

A slice of bread and a cup of tea,
A slice of bread and a cup of tea,
A slice of bread and a cup of tea,
Will you get up today?

4

Mary sings.

No, my mother, I won't get up,
I won't get up, I won't get up,
No, my mother I won't get up,
I won't get up today.

Mary speaks.

What will you give me for my dinner?

Mother speaks.

A roast of goose and a bowl of broth.

5

Mother and chorus sing.

A roast of goose and a bowl of broth,
A roast of goose and a bowl of broth,
A roast of goose and a bowl of broth,
Will you get up today?

Mary sings.

No, my mother, I won't get up, etc.

Mary speaks.

What will you give me for my supper?

Mother speaks.

I will give you a nice young man.

6

Mother and chorus sing.

I will give you a nice young man, etc.
Will you get up today?

7

Mary sings.

Yes, my mother, I will get up,
Yes, my mother, I will get up,
Yes, my mother, I will get up,
I will get up today.

LONDON BRIDGE

When this game was played by the children of Dr. and Mrs. Frank Allen Hubbard of Taunton, Massachusetts, both boys and girls joined in the game.

It was believed in the Middle Ages that the soul separated from the body and, before reaching its final destination, was forced to cross a bridge; succeeding, it was assured of eternal peace.

No edifice, in those early times, was more important than a bridge; hence sanctity was attributed to the builders. It was supposed that the Devil had a certain antipathy toward bridges because of repeated and successful destruction of them. In legends he is finally bought off with offers of all descriptions.

It is known that great erections entailed human sacrifice; but there was no particular code of ethics as to how the sacrifice should be secured. The unwary traveler peacefully going about his own affairs was quite likely to be seized and beheaded for these rites. That would appease a horrid deity.

Of the building of the Tower of London in the twelfth century, Fitzstephen writes that the mortar was mixed with the blood of wild beasts. And it is said the secret of the ancient Irish masons' fine craft was this very mixture of blood and sand. It is well known that men's heads often decorated the bridges and gates of a city, and it is reasonably conjectured that there was other blood in the masonry than that of beasts.

A combination of both explanations makes a very satisfactory background to the singing game, "London Bridge." The seizure of the prisoner is thus explained as foundation rites, and the tug of war that ends the game, the struggle for the possession of the soul.

THE GAME

Two players go away from the group secretly to choose bribes for their respective sides; such as a string of pearls for one side and a diamond necklace for the other side, or a span of black horses and an Arabian charger with gold trappings. The bribes having been chosen, these two leaders return to the group and raise their clasped hands to form an arch with their arms; then the group begins to sing the game and march through the arch. When the words "My fair lady-o" are sung, the two leaders drop their arms quickly around the player just passing through the arch and, while everyone sings the chorus, the prisoner is led away far enough for the offers to be made by the leaders and a choice to be made by the prisoner without being heard by the others. When he has made his selection, he takes his place behind the leader whose gift he has chosen. They return to the group and the game continues till all the players have made their choice. A tug of war ends the game.

3

Build it up with silver and gold,
Silver and gold, silver and gold,
Build it up with silver and gold,
My fair lady, O.

Chorus.

Thieves will steal the silver and gold,
Silver and gold, silver and gold,
Thieves will steal the silver and gold,
My fair lady, O.

4

Build it up with iron bars,
Iron bars, iron bars,
Build it up with iron bars,
My fair lady, O.

Chorus.

Iron bars will last for aye,
Last for aye, last for aye,
Iron bars will last for aye,
My fair lady, O.

LUCY LOCKET

This was a favorite singing game with the children of Dr. and Mrs. Frank Allen Hubbard of Taunton, Massachusetts.

Different versions of the game and the song, when traced back to the British Isles, show from which county the families came. The game as the Hubbard children knew it, comes from Leicestershire, with the Nottinghamshire distinction that the player walks around the outside of the circle. The Dorsetshire rhyme includes "a green and yellow basket."

In New England the figures of the country dance "Hunt the Squirrel" provide the actions of this game, which takes its name from one of the two celebrated courtesans of the court of Charles II, Kitty Fisher and Lucy Locket. It is a pantomime of a cat and mouse, dramatized in music and action.

The air was introduced to America in 1755 and was perhaps the base of "Yankee Doodle." In playing the game the Hubbard children and their playmates many times hummed the verse and chanted the words to the chorus only.

THE GAME

The player chosen by counting out to be "it" circles the outside of the ring, while the others sing the verse. He alone *speaks* the chorus, still moving around the outside of the ring until, with the words, "he will bite you," he drops the handkerchief behind one of the players. For several steps he continues to move around the ring in the same rhythm so that the one chosen will not suspect that the handkerchief lies behind him. When the victim discovers the handkerchief behind him, he seizes it and tries to catch the player who dropped it. The pursued tries to reach the place in the ring left vacant by the second player. If he is caught, he must be "it" again; if not, the second player becomes "it."

Spoken:

I have a little dog at home,
And he won't bite *you*,
And he won't bite *you*,
And he won't bite *you*,
And he *will bite you!*

MULB'RY BUSH

Sung and played by the children of Dr. and Mrs. Frank Allen Hubbard of Taunton, Massachusetts, who remember it as one of the most popular among their playmates. It was usually played by the girls.

The melody of "Mulb'ry Bush," which goes back to the eighteenth century in England, was the tune of a country dance called "Nancy Dawson," after a popular dancer and reigning court favorite and toast of the town. The mulberry bush was sacred to the festivals of marriage. From this lovely little tune have come many variations of other singing games.

THE GAME

The players form a circle and, as each verse is sung, perform the actions of washing, ironing, sweeping, and so forth with dramatic fervor. At the last verse each player makes a quarter-turn in place; then, in circle formation, all sing and promenade sedately around the ring.

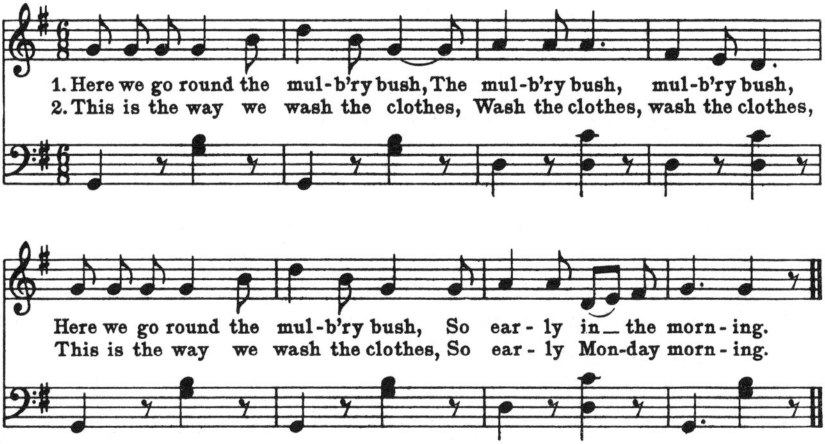

3

This is the way we iron the clothes,
Iron the clothes, iron the clothes,
This is the way we iron the clothes,
So early Tuesday morning.

4

This is the way we mend the clothes, etc.,
So early Wednesday morning.

5

This is the way we sweep the floor, etc.,
So early Thursday morning.

6

This is the way we scrub the floor, etc.,
So early Friday morning.

7

This is the way we bake the bread, etc.,
So early Saturday morning.

8

This is the way we go to church, etc.,
So early Sunday morning.

MY FAIREY AND MY FOREY

Sung by Miss Mary Frye and her sister Miss Serena Frye of Brookline, Massachusetts, who played this singing game with their friends in Plymouth, Massachusetts.

Probably derived from a carol of St. Mary's men (monks), this game was sung in Shetland by guisers, who went from house to house on New Year's Day to collect provisions for a feast. Guisers, or mummers, were masked actors who traveled about playing and singing, particularly at Christmas and Easter.

This New Year's Day custom was a begging expedition of monks in pre-Reformation times.

It suggests the right of entry which mummers and carolers exercised. They, like the bailiffs, could not be ejected without payment of toll, when once they had crossed a threshold.

It seems probable that "Queen Mary" was substituted for "St. Mary"; then "King Henry," "William," or "Arthur," names more related to Protestantism, for Catholicism was under heavy ban at this time. Repeated efforts were made to put down the practice of carol singing, one of the evils complained of at the Scottish Assembly in 1596. These idolatrous songs were strictly forbidden by the Aberdeen Session in 1612, but the practice persisted till the nineteenth century. The carolers tried to rush into a house, with the right of entry sustaining the invasion. The Scottish version, of which the song given here is an example, opens without the request for lodging, or suggestion of territorial usurpation. There is no authority to say that the refrain is not a border war cry, but it looks as if the carol basis can be explained in the refrain as a corruption of monks' Latin and English, a feature of very old English carols. "Mater Redemptoris" is one solution that is not too farfetched for reasonable explanation of the Latin base.

THE GAME

Facing each other, stand two lines of an equal number of players. The first line advances toward the other, singing in a rather blustering, swaggering way; the second line, in reply with dignity and coolness, advances toward the first line. All move in unison and hold hands while in action and singing.

As the words, "A barrel of it you shall not have," are sung, the players stamp their feet with vigor. The next lines, "We are Arthur's walking men," etc., are sung dramatically, and the reply is given with great dignity and emphasis.

The last verse is very spirited and ends with each player in one line seizing the hands of the opposing player of the other and engaging in an individual tug of war.

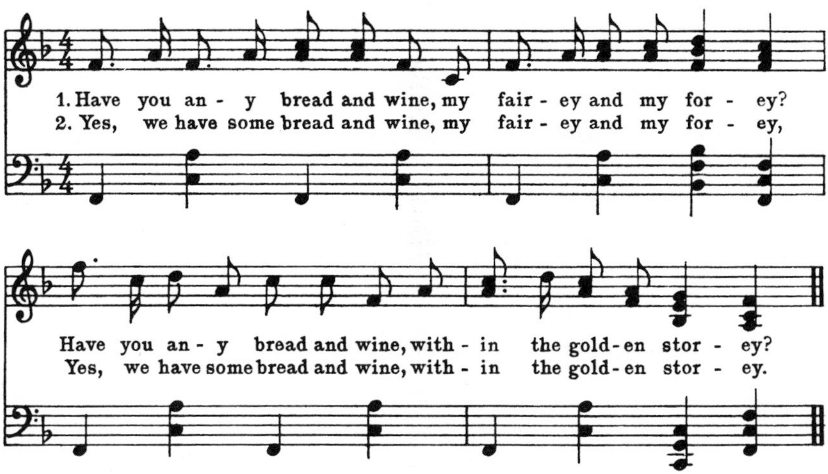

3

Let us have a pint of it, my fairey and my forey,
Let us have a pint of it, within the golden storey.

4

Take your pint and go your way, my fairey and my forey,
Take your pint and go your way, within the golden storey.

5

Let us have a quart of it, etc.

6

Take your quart and go your way, etc.

7

Let us have a gallon of it, etc.

8

Take your gallon and go your way, etc.

9

Let us have a barrel of it, etc.

10

A barrel of it you shall not have, etc.

11

We are Arthur's walking men, etc.

12

We are William's walking men, etc.

13

Are you ready for a fight, etc.

THE NEEDLE'S EYE

Sung by Fred Pullen of North Anson, Maine, who remembers playing the game fifty years ago, when the young people went to kissing parties instead of to dances.

The game is apparently of British origin and is variously known in New England as "Through the Needle's Eye, Boys" or "Threading the Needle."

In France this game was a dance, possibly of invocation, since it was said to be performed "to make the hemp grow." With this rural background the game in New England is reminiscent of the oldest of the sacred dances, executed in the spring of the year to bring fertility to the land.

"The Needle's Eye" may be related to the game of "How Many Miles to London Town?" in that both are possibly derived from the same custom.

THE GAME

Two players, a boy and a girl, stand on chairs facing each other and make an arch with their arms raised and hands clasped, as in "London Bridge." As the song begins, the remaining players walk under the arch (alternately boy and girl) till at the words, "And now it has caught *you,*" the arch drops to hold one player imprisoned. If the one caught is a girl, the boy on the chair leans forward, kisses her as the players sing the refrain. When they have finished, she steps up to take the girl's place on the chair. If the player caught is a boy, the girl in the chair leans forward for her kiss, steps down, and the boy replaces the boy on the chair. The choice of players to be caught is entirely arbitrary.

OLD WOMAN ALL SKIN AND BONE

The children of Dr. and Mrs. Frank Allen Hubbard of Taunton, Massachusetts, who sang and played this game, sometimes reserved it to initiate visiting playmates and newcomers.

The most highly imaginative player usually was chosen for the corpse, for after one really fine screech the game was quite likely to end abruptly with the appearance of a grown-up bringing emphatic requests for less disturbance during the doctor's office hours.

This weird game originally came from Somersetshire and is a dramatization of the belief that the dead return for vengeance on those that disturb them.

THE GAME

Each object and person in the verses is represented by a player chosen by counting out. The one taking the part of the old woman approaches the corpse, which lies at the feet of the sexton. All the players sing as the old woman walks slowly toward the "churchyard," and the eerie, half-moaning chant is broken by the shrill scream of the corpse as it arises suddenly and gives chase to the other players, who add to the effect with shrill cries. If the corpse can catch another player, that one becomes the old woman, the first old woman becomes the sexton, and the game continues.

2

She went to the churchyard all alone. Oo-oo-oo.

3

She looked up and looked down. Oo-oo-oo.

4

She saw a corpse lie on the ground. Oo-oo-oo.

5

"Father, Father," so she said. Oo-oo-oo.

6

"Shall I look so when I am dead?" Oo-oo-oo.

7

The sexton to her made reply. Oo-oo-oo.

8

"Yes, my darling, by and by." *Boo!*

ON THE GREEN CARPET

This choosing game, played by Mrs. Ethel Kidder Fuller when she was a small child in Assonet, Massachusetts, was handed down by her great-grandmother, Abiah Ashley.

The same game, with identical action, is recalled by Fred Pullen of North Anson, Maine, as a very popular one played at kissing parties fifty years ago.

The game is related to the one known as "Oats, Peas, Beans" and comes from the same craft origin, which displays the labor of a farmer and his selection of a wife. The line in earlier versions that mentions the wood is significant of the countryman's hardest chore, for it was very important that the farmer in old England or New England keep a goodly supply of wood on hand.

The tune is a fragment of the country dance, "Faustus."

THE GAME

A player is chosen with a counting-out rhyme. This player stands in the center of a ring of players, and remains silent while the first verse is sung. At the close of this verse the player chooses a second player. They join hands and kneel while the circle sings one couplet to the girl and one to the boy. The two players then salute each other and return to the circle and the game begins again. The players sometimes accompany the words with pantomime representing individual ideas of obedience, kindness, regret, and farewell.

3 (*Optional*)

One version found contained this stanza:

(To the girl). Now you've married you must obey.
You must be true in all you say.

(To the boy). You must be kind and you must be good,
And keep your wife in hickory wood.

POOR MARY SITS A-WEEPING

Played and sung by the children of Dr. and Mrs. Frank Allen Hubbard of Taunton, Massachusetts, with whom it was not a very popular game since it lacked noise, drama, and action.

This is a relic of the ancient marriage ceremony, in which marriage was agreed to in the presence of witnesses, seven years being considered long enough to remain faithful. Verses about the length of time, the marriage cake, and the gift of the cake to the new husband—all of which appeared in the original game—have entirely disappeared in this New England version, which came from Worcestershire, England.

THE GAME

"Mary" is chosen by a counting-out rhyme. She sits alone in the center of the ring of players and sings alternately with them until she makes the choice of her sweetheart, who in turn becomes "Mary" to continue the game.

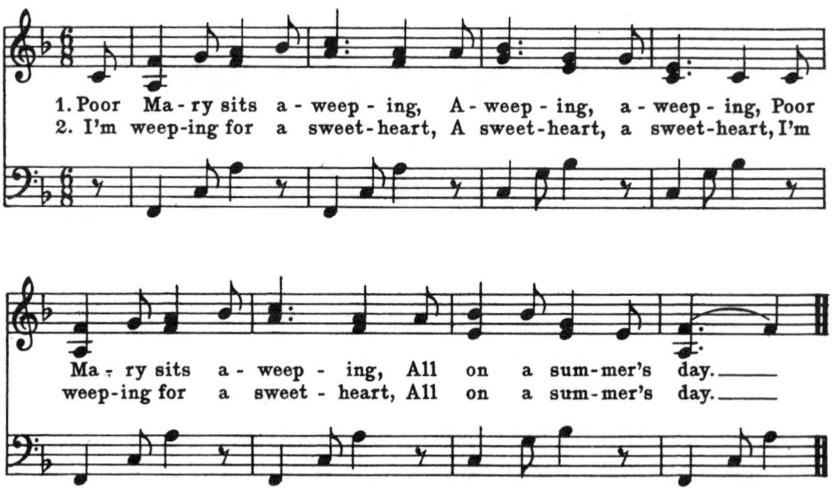

3

Poor Mary, why are you weeping,
A-weeping, a-weeping,
Poor Mary, why are you weeping,
All on a summer's day?

4

I'm weeping for a sweetheart,
A sweetheart, a sweetheart,
I'm weeping for a sweetheart,
All on a summer's day.

5

Pray, Mary, choose a sweetheart,
A sweetheart, a sweetheart,
Pray, Mary, choose a sweetheart,
All on a summer's day.

6

I'll choose Ralph* for a sweetheart,
A sweetheart, a sweetheart,
I'll choose Ralph for a sweetheart,
All on a summer's day.

RING AROUND O' ROSIES

This game was played by the three daughters of Dr. and Mrs. Frank Allen Hubbard, of Taunton, Massachusetts, with their girl playmates, on a hard gravel driveway where the game was fun as long as the pleasure of hard jolts could be suffered.

It is rather well known throughout the British Isles, and shows that the simplest motions have pleasure when put to song. It was probably originally a round dance.

THE GAME

The players form a circle and, keeping the form, move in unison until the last phrase, when amid great merriment all tumble to the ground.

*Substitute a player's name.

SHALL I SHOW YOU HOW THE FARMER?

The children of Dr. and Mrs. Frank Allen Hubbard of Taunton, Massachusetts, sang and played this game with both boys and girls.

It is a survival of the dances sung at festivals in ancient England to bring good fortune to the farmer. It is probably derived from the handkerchief morris dance so common on these occasions.

THE GAME

The players form a circle and sing all the verses in unison as they go through the motions characteristic of sowing, reaping, ploughing, etc.—all the gestures in pantomime representative of farm labor. At the verse "dance and be gay" each player dances slowly and merrily in place. The game then begins again.

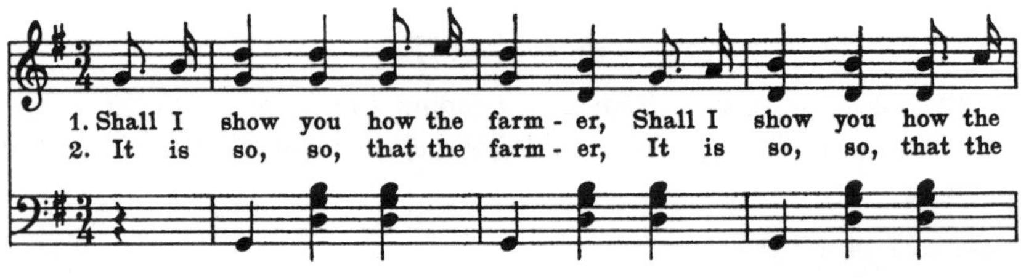

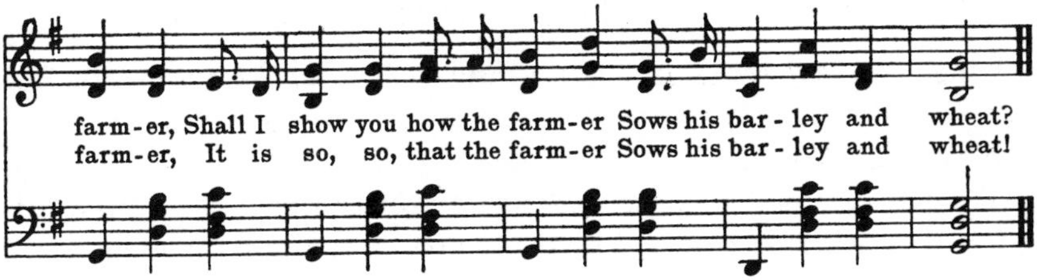

3

Shall I show you how the farmer,
Shall I show you how the farmer,
Shall I show you how the farmer
Hoes his barley and wheat?

4

It is so, so, that the farmer,
It is so, so, that the farmer,
It is so, so, that the farmer
Hoes his barley and wheat.

5

Shall I show you how the farmer,
Shall I show you how the farmer,
Shall I show you how the farmer
Now will dance and be gay?

6

It is so, so, that the farmer,
It is so, so, that the farmer,
It is so, so, that the farmer
Now will dance and be gay.

THE TWELVE DAYS OF CHRISTMAS

Sung and played when she was a child in Assonet, Massachusetts, by Mrs. Ethel Kidder Fuller, who remembers hearing her mother tell of playing the game.

The test of true love once was the number and variety of gifts, the value of which was estimated by the degree of difficulty in attainment.

The twelve days of Christmas are those between Christmas Day and Epiphany, the feasts of which included games of forfeit.

THE GAME

The company is seated around the room. The leader of the game begins with the first line of song. The line is repeated by each of the company in turn. Then the leader repeats the first day, with the addition of the second day; this is repeated by each of the company in turn. The leader then repeats the first day and the second day, and adds the third day; and this goes around the room as before. For every mistake or fault of memory, a forfeit must be given.

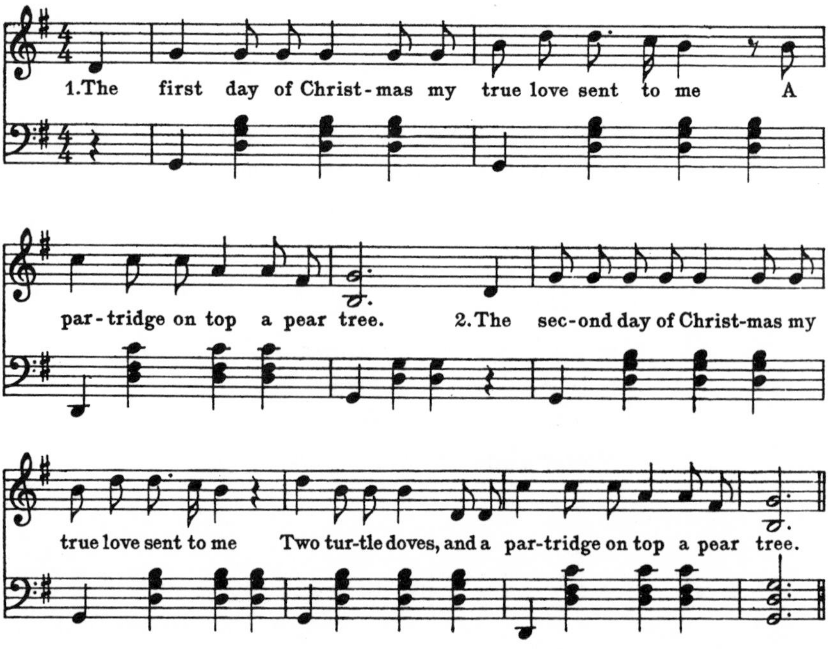

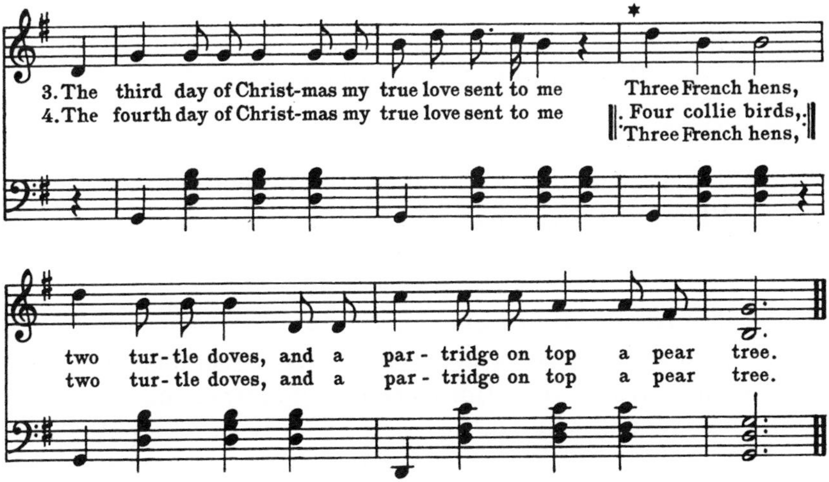

5

The fifth day of Christmas my true love sent to me
Five gold rings, four collie birds, etc.

6

The sixth day of Christmas my true love sent to me
Six geese a-laying, five gold rings, etc.

7

The seventh day of Christmas my true love sent to me
Seven swans a-swimming, six geese a-laying, etc.

8

The eighth day of Christmas my true love sent to me
Eight tars a-running, seven swans a-swimming, etc.

9

The ninth day of Christmas my true love sent to me
Nine lads a-limping, eight tars a-running, etc.

* This measure is sung twice in the third verse, three times in the fourth verse, etc.

10

The tenth day of Christmas my true love sent to me
Ten bulls a-roaring, nine lads a-limping, etc.

11

The eleventh day of Christmas my true love sent to me
Eleven logs a-burning, ten bulls a-roaring, etc.

12

The twelfth day of Christmas my true love sent to me
Twelve bowls a-foaming, eleven logs a-burning, ten bulls a-roaring, nine lads a-limping, eight tars a-running, seven swans a-swimming, six geese a-laying, five gold rings, four collie birds, three French hens, two turtle doves, and a partridge on top a pear tree.

WATER, WATER, WILD FLOWER

From her childhood in Taunton, Massachusetts, Mrs. Mildred Miner Hadley remembers this game, which was played by both boys and girls.

It is a game which reflects the ancient customs of love and marriage in old England. It is possible that "wild flower" is a corruption of wall-flower, a flower widely found on English soil.

THE GAME

The players form a circle and move slowly around to the rhythm of the air. As the name of one player is called, she turns her back to the center of the ring and, as the name of the second player is sung, the two chosen walk to the center of the circle. There the pantomime is acted out: The lady comes down the stairs with a long flowing gown, holding in her hand a flower, which she places in her robe. The boy, with appropriate gestures, arrives at her door and bows low as she curtsies. Then he goes through the motions of showing her a ring, placing it on her finger, and together they walk around the inside of the circle. This ends the game, and new players are chosen for a second round.

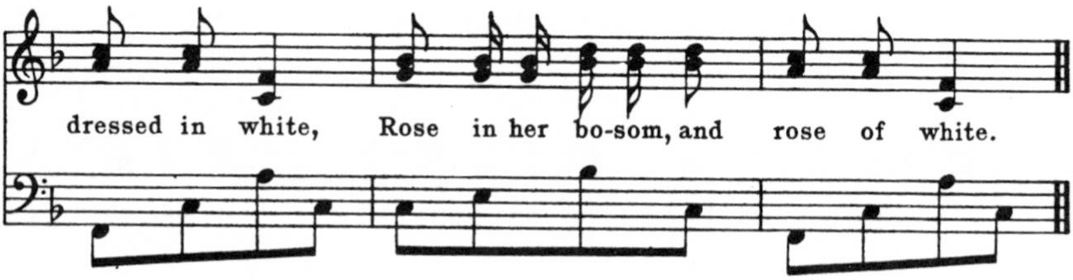

* Substitute a player's name.

THE COUNTRY DANCE

The country dance, reminder of long forgotten traditions, is still a vigorous part of life in many of the little towns and villages scattered throughout New England, where, for one hundred and fifty years, it has survived every attempt to wipe it out and has resisted the strictest disciplinary measures to crush it. The country dance of New England was a direct development of the country dance of England which, through periods of transition from ancient rituals, reached its accepted form in New England by way of the singing games. These games were the dances that pleased the Court long before the settlement of the New England colonies.

But in New England the singing games caused bitter dissension in the church, which ruled the social life, while to the prevailing Puritan spirit the very name of dancing was anathema. As long as the young folk called their pastimes "playing games," these amusements were not prohibited, but they were strictly forbidden to do them as *dances*. Thus the young people preserved in their "games," the dances of the old country.

An excellent example of the fine distinction between *playing a game* and *dancing* is the old singing game of "The Wild Irishman," the figures of which were done to a special tune while verses were sung by the players. "The Wild Irishman," minus the special tune and verses, is known today as the "Ninepin Quadrille."

Gradually, the grown-ups, desirous of setting a new fashion, discarded the singing game. The country dance thus became increasingly popular and, in spite of the most stormy opposition, appeared firmly established *as a dance* in the nineteenth century. In this way, dancing, previously confined to one or two balls a year in the urban areas, spread generally over the countryside.

Though the country dance did not originate in the country nor among the people of the rural districts, and was not confined to season, time, nor place, it has through the years been the social affair of a community, a pastime of any place, any time, and any season. It has been driven into the rural areas as the custom of neighborhood gatherings in the cities has dwindled.

The earliest record of the country dance and its tune is found in John Playford's *The Dancing Master,* printed about 1690. At that period of development, country dance figures were arbitrarily chosen to fit the melody and were usually accompanied by verses of a ballad. Popular usage at last combined certain figures regularly with certain airs to establish the different dances.

Aside from the general background very little is known of the origin, names, and figures of these New England dances; but many, with their tunes, possess the characteristics of the several nationalities which poured into New England territory. There have been few major changes in the country dance, which still retains many of the elements of the transitional phases through which it has passed. Perhaps the most notable change is the elimination of the verses which were sung to the melodies, and which directed the figures. The country dance is performed as of old by the whole community—the school teacher, the carpenter, the selectman, and the man who keeps the general store.

Contra, circle, and square are the names of different formations included in the general designation, country dance. In different localities the country dance may be given the name of one of the formations; thus in some areas the term "square dance," "contry dance," or "line dance" indicates that these formations will predominate on the evening's program.

The *square dance* is usually, but not always, a "quadrille," with the couples forming a square; the *quadrille* is a reel of four couples; the *contry,* as the Yankee calls it (or "line dance"), is rightly termed "contra" and is a dance of opposite lines of couples; the *circle,* or "round," dance arranges all the dancers in a huge ring about the hall. The *waltz* and *polka,* developments on the Continent in the latter part of the nineteenth century, have no definite position for each couple in relation to the other couples.

On the whole, the customs of the country dance have changed but little. In the dance hall, as in Playford's time, the head of the hall is where the orchestra is; and the orchestra, as of old, is usually composed of stringed instruments led by a violin. One dancing master directs the figures of the dances for all to hear. He is known as the "prompter" or "caller." The orchestra leader, usually the fiddler, and the prompter are the two personalities who have probably had most to do with making changes in the country dance, for in their wanderings from village to village they had both time and opportunity for improvisations of their own. A fine example of the manner in which these individuals leave their personalities on music and dance figures is found in the words of the present champion caller of New England, Happy Hale, who says, "Sometimes I think up real good changes of my own—and then, first chance I get—I try 'em out!"

The prompter may move with the dancers or may stand beside the fiddler while singing or calling his changes, sometimes in rhyme, in strong but clear and pleasant tones. The fiddler may be caller, too, but usually the dance challenges the ability of two leaders to direct a crowd through the mazes of an intricate pattern without losing a couple!

Though the country dance orchestra today may include a guitar, clarinet, piano, banjo, or musical saw, the fiddler reigns supreme. He must be ready with the change in melody as the prompter calls the next dance figure.

The best of the tunes played traditionally for certain dances have survived, and in these melodies lies variety for the fiddler. He may start with the traditional tune, mix in a few popular airs, and season the whole effect by returning to the old-time melody. No two fiddlers will play the same tune alike. The tunes presented here are but the most meager suggestions of what a real fiddler can do with his bow. As Edson Cole says, "You can play them any way you've a mind to, but even though I learned my tunes from Uncle Jim I've got a *yank* of my *own*." And it is the "yank of their own" that makes the music of the Yankee fiddlers so irresistible, whether they have been taught by violin instructors or have picked up the melodies by ear.

The dance may be known in another country by another name, but it is almost sure to follow the traditional conservative pattern.

The country dance was the regular pastime of our grandmothers—when piety did not intervene—and was enjoyed usually once a week, unless a special occasion called for celebration. According to the occasion, the dance was held in the kitchen, front room, barn, or town hall, where old and young danced to the strains of "Honest John" and "Hull's Victory." Then, as in some areas today, a corn husking, a harvest, or the laying of the new barn floor, all required due recognition. They came by wagon or shank's mare, sometimes from as far as twenty-five miles, to the kitchen junket and kitchen knockdown of Vermont, the kitchen whang of Maine, the barn dance, or, as some strenuous participants call it, the hog-wrasslin'. These terms are all in present use. When grandmother graduated from playing games to kissing parties, and then later stepped to the lively tune of the "Soldier's Joy," she may have danced on a "spring floor," which once in a while can be found today. This floor was especially constructed to help the dancers keep in step and still provides an aerial sensation to the unsuspecting. In an old tavern today, in an upper room, where dances were held two hundred years ago, is the hall with its wide rock-maple board floor, lined with narrow benches, the fiddler's box at one end, while overhead the high, blue, double-arched ceiling spans the room.

Sometimes butternuts, cookies, apples, or frosted cake were served for refreshments, and quite likely in the fall there would be cider. But food then, as today, was not expected; they came to dance, not to eat!

Tradition persists unspoiled in these country dances of New England, and the radio has not quite usurped the place of the old-time fiddler. Summer and winter, spring and fall, Uncle Ben and all the folks you ever knew dance to the old figures; the painter will ask, "Will you face me?" and as you step into the ring of dancers, your partners will be the leading citizens—the lumberjack, the sheriff, the road commissioner, and the teacher of the district school—*all* the *best* people.

You may dance to a fiddler with a "yank of his own" and a caller who stops the "Paul Jones" in order that you may be his partner; you may balance to the finest swing orchestra in that neck of the woods, or you may keep time to the music of three fifteen-year-old youngsters in straw hats and overalls, or to the rhythm of the homemade instruments of a whole family, and you will find that the entire neighborhood from the age of seven to the spry young grown-ups of eighty-five is there for *social* pleasure *as a community*. The babies sleep peacefully on the benches in the dim light of kerosene lanterns or tucked into a corner of a settle while Mom and Pop, Sis and Bud, and Grandma too, frolic to the old tunes.

The dance swings out to the tune of the fiddler as the changes ring: "Balance and swing below, swing your partner in the center, down the center, cast off, ladies change, balance and swing be-*low!*"

GLOSSARY OF DANCE TERMS

FORMATIONS*

The Circle

The dancers form a circle about the room in couples. This figure may have any number participating.

The Quadrille

A square set of two or four couples facing each other.

Contra

Two lines of dancers face each other; (a) the men on one side and the ladies opposite their partners; or, (b) two lines face each other, partners opposite but alternate gentleman and lady in each line. This is the formation when the dance calls "first, third, fifth," etc., or "every other couple cross over," are given. Six or eight couples participate. Several sets may be formed about the room. When the head couples reach the foot of the line, the lady crosses over to the gentleman's place and the gentleman takes her position.

STEPS*

The dance steps fall on the first and middle beats and the steps used in the dance figures are generally three.

Pivot Step or Swing Step (for turning partner)

Partners stand almost side by side and fit the step to the rhythm of the music. On the count of one, put the right foot down, at the same time stepping on the ball of the left foot, advanced a little. On the count of two, put the right foot down in the *same* place, with the left foot advanced, place the weight on the ball of the left foot. The step is a quick walking, turning step. The emphasis on the right foot accents the turn to the rhythm of the music and it is done vigorously.

Chasse

First measure: Slide right foot forward and bring left foot close to right foot. Slide right foot forward and wait. *Second measure:* Repeat with the left foot. This is the two-step figure and may occur in a forward or side execution.

*From *American Country Dances,* by Elizabeth Burchenal, published and copyrighted by G. Schirmer, Inc. Used by permission of the author and publisher.

Balance

1. *First and second measures:* Walk two steps forward and two steps back, facing partner or partners facing opposite couple.

2. *First measure:* Step forward on right foot, point toe of left foot in front. *Second measure:* Step forward on left foot, point toe of right foot in front.

CALLS FOR THE PROMPTER*

Address . . . . 8 bars

Partners bow to each other and then to their respective corners.

Allemande, Left . . . . 8 bars

Couples link left arms and turn to left.

Allemande All . . . . 4 bars

Gentleman turns lady on his left, with his and her left hands joined, and immediately after gives right hand to partner and executes grand right and left.

Balance Four . . . . 8 bars

Gentleman crosses hands with partner, his right hand above. They promenade to opposite side, each couple passing to the right. Turn (as on a pivot, without the lady changing sides) and return to place, still keeping the lady on the outside.

Balance in Place . . . . 4 bars

Step to side with right foot, point toe of left foot in front. Step to side with left foot, point toe of right foot in front.

Balance and Swing or **Balance Partners** . . . . 8 bars

Partners meet, balance in place, take dance position and turn in place with the pivot step.

Cast Off . . . . 8 bars

Means to go below the next couple.

Chasse All . . . . 8 bars

Face partner, join both hands and slide four steps to right, four to left in circle.

Circle Hands Around . . . . 8 bars

All join hands and circle left or right. *Eight hands around* means that eight dancers circle to the right and back. *Four hands around* means that four dancers circle to the right and back.

*From *Good Morning,* published by Mr. and Mrs. Henry Ford. Used by permission.

Cross Over . . . . 8 bars

Walk directly across, ladies inside, then each turn in place. Repeat to place.

Dos-a-Dos . . . . 4 bars

Lady and gentleman forward, pass to left of each other; having gone one step past each other, take one step to the right, and, without turning, back round each other and walk backward to place.

Down the Center and Back . . . . 8 bars

Partners join hands and go down the center of the set to the foot where they swing half around (make a half turn) and return.

Grand Right and Left . . . . 8 bars

Face partners, salute, then join right hands, gentlemen moving to the right, ladies to the left. Gentleman drops his partner's right hand and takes next lady's left hand in his left, next with right, and so forth.

Half Promenade . . . . 8 bars

Cross hands, and pass to opposite side of the set, as in *Balance Four,* and return to place as in *Right and Left.*

Half Right and Left . . . . 4 bars

By two opposite couples. Couples cross over, ladies inside, gentleman in passing touching lady's right hand.

Ladies Chain (Ladies Change—colloq.) . . . . 8 bars

Ladies cross to opposite places, giving the right hands as they pass each other, and the left hands to the opposite gentlemen; turn around, giving right hand back, left hand to partner, and turn to place.

Ladies Grand Chain . . . . 8 bars

Same as *Ladies Chain,* with all four ladies.

Promenade . . . . 8 bars

March in circle with partners.

Right and Left . . . . 8 bars

By two opposite couples. Couples cross over, ladies inside, gentleman in passing touching lady's right hand. When in opposite couple's place, gentleman takes partner's left hand in his left and turns half around, and repeats back to place.

Reel

Turn your partners or next in line.

Reverse

To prevent the circles from whirling too fast and beyond the prompter's control, this call is used to check the speed of the dancers.

Swing Partners

Take dance position and turn in place with the pivot step.

In the contra dances when the head couple reaches the foot of the line, the lady crosses over to the gentleman's place and the gentleman takes her position while the other couples are swinging partners.

GENERAL TERMS

In Playford's time the top of the room was called the "presence" and was the dais on which the spectators were seated. Today the top of the room is the place where the orchestra sits. This is where the head couple stands, back to the music. The prompter's place is beside the orchestra. The calls or changes, as the dance directions are known, are spoken before the next change of figure. A set is a group of persons required for a dance figure.

The keys in which the dance music is arranged are the standard ones for fast and easy fingering on a fiddle. To vary the monotony of playing, the orchestra will choose one or more melodies of the same rhythm.

The best country dance orchestras are composed of stringed instruments, very often homemade, and the players range in age from four and a half years to eighty years.

DANCE FORMATIONS

Circle Formation

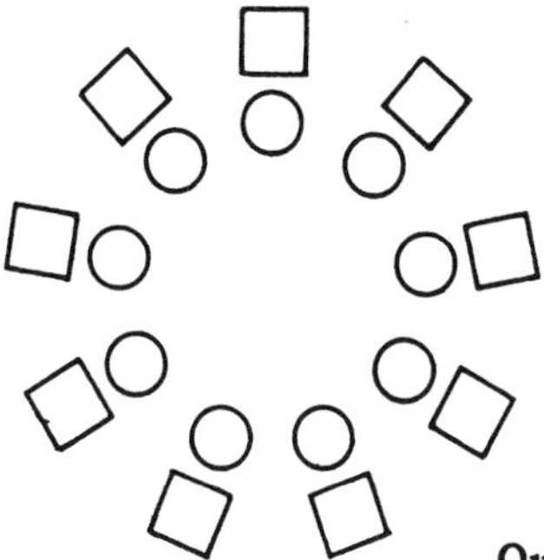

Sicilian Formation

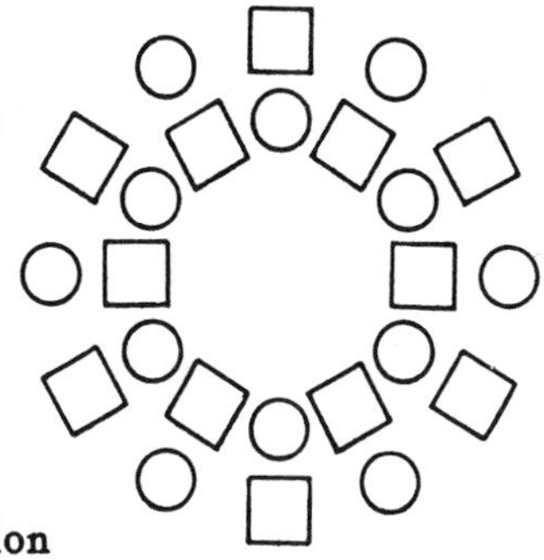

Quadrille Formation

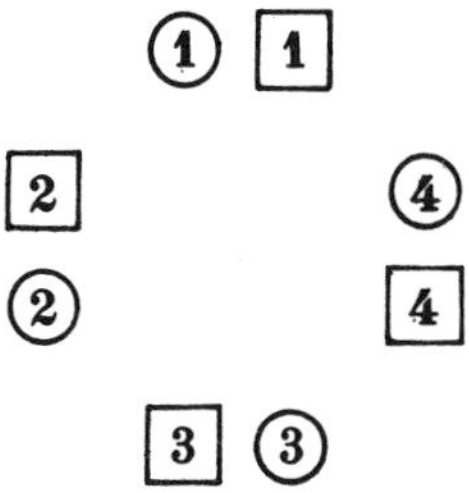

Contra Dance --- A

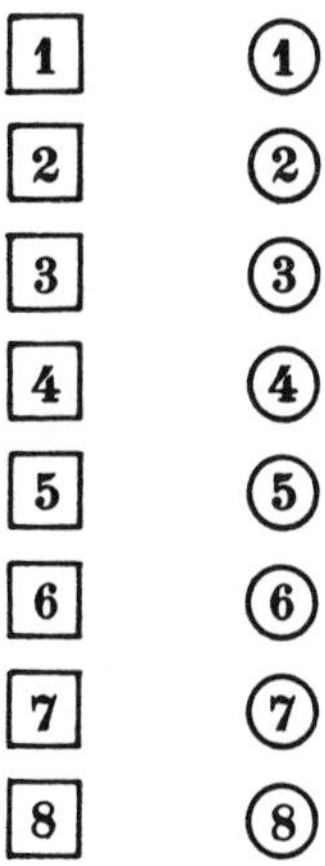

Contra Dance --- B

First, third, and every other couple cross over.

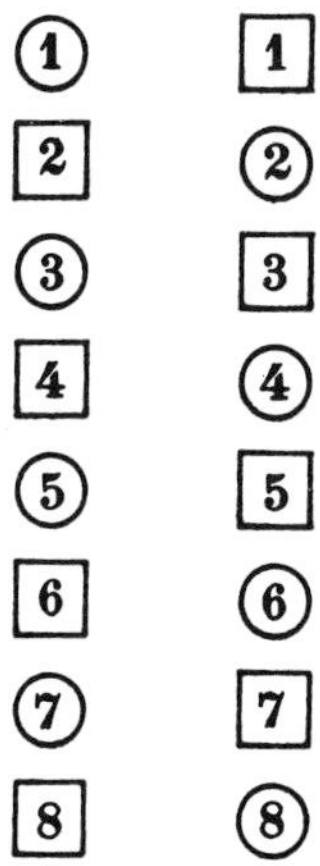

BONAPARTE CROSSING THE RHINE
(MARCH)

The march, "Bonaparte Crossing the Rhine," was a great favorite about 1800. The events of history were recorded in the music of the times. This melody has been taken from the unpublished manuscript of Elizabeth Foster Reed (1796–1823). It is not known just when this book was written, but the manuscript, which contains ballads and dance airs, is in the possession of her descendants today.

BONAPARTE CROSSING THE RHINE

BOSTON FANCY
or
LADY WALPOLE'S REEL

Music: **Opera Reel and Pigtown Fling; Lady Walpole's Reel.**

Played by Smith Paine, Wolfeboro, New Hampshire, and Edson Cole, Freedom, New Hampshire. Each recorded.

Dance changes called by Edson Cole, Freedom, New Hampshire. Recorded.

From the hub city of New England this contra dance takes its name, although it is probably none other than "Lady Walpole's Reel," a dance with its own melody of Scottish origin. It is evidently a variety of Weavers' Dance belonging to the craftsmen of the Weavers' Guild. Since many fiddlers prefer other airs, the tune "Lady Walpole's Reel" is given here as a matter of record only. The air, "Opera Reel," which is played by Smith Paine, was fitted for a contra dance performed on the stage; and the "Pigtown Fling," Edson Cole's favorite tune for this dance, is an Irish reel sometimes known as "Kelton's."

THE DANCE

CONTRA DANCE FORMATION	SIX TO EIGHT TO A SET
First and every other couple cross over	
Balance and swing below	8 bars
Take your partner down the center and back	8 "
Cast off, ladies chain	8 "
Half promenade	4 "
Half right and left	4 "
Balance and swing below to continue dance	

To end the dance, balance your partner, promenade to seat.

OPERA REEL

PIGTOWN FLING

LADY WALPOLE'S REEL

CHORUS JIG

Music: **Chorus Jig.**

Played by Edson H. Cole, Freedom, New Hampshire. Recorded.

Dance changes called by Edson H. Cole.

The "Chorus Jig" has always been a favorite with pipers. It is an Irish melody whose author and date are unknown.

Jigs were originally tunes sung after the play by the clowns. In the seventeenth century everyone sang them, and the dances were danced by persons of all ranks. They are generally thought of as Irish, but jigs were common in England and Scotland. The word "jig" applied to a form of rhyme and is of uncertain derivation.

THE DANCE

CONTRA DANCE FORMATION	SIX COUPLES IN A SET
First couple down the outside and back	8 bars
Down the center and back	8 "
Swing contra corners	8 "
Balance six	4 "
Turn to place	4 "

Couples numbers three and five may dance at the same time.

CHORUS JIG

DEVIL'S DREAM

Nothing is known of the origin of this dance or the melody, but it is probably based on an Irish tune. The dance changes written here are taken exactly as they are called by Happy Hale, who sings the changes.

Music: **Devil's Dream.**
Played by Dennis McClure, Willimantic, Connecticut.
Dance changes called by Happy Hale, Hinsdale, New Hampshire.

THE DANCE

SQUARE FORMATION — FOUR COUPLES IN A SET

Balance partners eight hands around	8 bars
Swing to the corners Head lady swings gentleman on her right. Head gentleman swings lady on his left.	4 "
Join hands and circle eight hands around Back to place	8 "
First lady leads to the right and swings to the corner	4 "
First lady swings to the third gentleman at the same time the first gentleman swings the lady of the second couple	4 "
Dos-a-dos to the corners	4 "
Allemande left. Then right hand to the partner, and swing	8 "
Repeat, with the second couple progressing through the set as did the first couple	

This is the way Happy Hale sings it:

Here we go eight hands around
First lady leads to the right
Grab that gent and hold him up tight
Up to the next and on your toes
Swing that gent with the big long nose
Up to the next who's standing there
Swing that gent with the curly red hair
Up to the next and swing your own
Now—everybody swing
Dosey dos to the corners all
Dosey dos with your own little doll
Allemande left with the lady on your left
Give right hand to your own little doll
(Grand right and left)

Right foot up and left foot down
Hand over hand or you'll never get around
And when you meet her pass her by
Wink at the next as you go by
Kiss the next right on the sly
And swing your own by and by.

DEVIL'S DREAM

THE DUCHESS

Music: **The Duchess.**
Played by Harry E. Brigham, Marlboro, Massachusetts.

The grace of a court dance is in "The Duchess," which is one of the round dances, probably derived from a handkerchief morris dance. It was known as early as the seventeenth century.

The melody is the one which was originally played for the dance in New England and has been used by Harry Brigham for sixty years.

THE DANCE

CIRCLE FORMATION ANY NUMBER MAY PARTICIPATE

Part One

Join hands, separate, face partners. Begin with outside foot for a polka step: gentleman with left foot, lady with right; walk forward three steps and point forward (2 bars); turn, face partner, lady joins right hand to gentleman's right hand and repeat above steps in reverse direction (2 bars).

Part Two

In waltz position, partner: slide, close; slide, close; slide, close; step. Repeat with right foot and toward the right; slide, close; slide, close; slide, close; step (4 bars).

THE DUCHESS

FISHERS' HORNPIPE

Music: **Fishers' Hornpipe.**
Played by Edson H. Cole, Freedom, New Hampshire. Recorded.
Dance changes called by Edson H. Cole.

The hornpipe, an old traditional dance of England and common among the English sailors, was a favorite because of the vigor and liveliness of its execution. Except for the "Sailor's Hornpipe," which is a solo dance, the hornpipes danced in New England are contra dances of comparatively late date.

The melody of the dance is at least two hundred years old, but the actual source is not known. It resembles a tune in ancient Irish folk music known as "Roger MacMum."

THE DANCE

CONTRA DANCE FORMATION — SIX TO EIGHT COUPLES IN A SET

First couple down the outside and back	8 bars
Down the center and back	8 "
Cast off	
Swing six hands around	8 "
Right and left	8 "

The fourth couples may dance at the same time.

FISHERS' HORNPIPE

FRENCH FOUR

Music: **French Four.**

Played by Willie Woodward, Bristol, New Hampshire.

Dance changes called by Willie Woodward.

It is possible that this dance is derived from an old English country dance called "Trenchmore Galliard" or "Westcountry Jigg," the figures of which are somewhat similar to "French Four." In transition the origin of the melody has been lost.

THE DANCE

CONTRA DANCE FORMATION — SIX TO EIGHT COUPLES IN A SET

Head lady balance to the foot gentleman, and	4 bars
Swing whom she please	4 "
Head gentleman balance to the foot lady, and	4 "
Swing whom he please	4 "
Turn partner in center	8 "
Down the center and back	8 "
Cast off	
Right and left to place	8 "

The third and fifth couples may dance at the same time.

The following dance changes are more widely used:

First couple balance and cross over	4 "
Go below one couple	4 "
Balance	4 "
Cross back to place	4 "
First couple down the center, back and cast off	8 "
Right and left	8 "

FRENCH FOUR

THE GIRL I LEFT BEHIND ME

Music: **The Girl I Left Behind Me.**
Played by Dennis McClure, Willimantic, Connecticut.
Dance changes called by Happy Hale, Hinsdale, New Hampshire.

There are many conflicting theories about the exact date and origin of this melody, popular in the eighteenth century and familiarly known as "Brighton Camp." The Irish name, according to Bunting, is "The Spailpin Fanach" or "The Rambling Laborer." The music and words were printed in Dublin in 1791, although it was known much earlier. It is claimed by one authority that this tune originated when Admirals Hawke and Rodney were watching the French fleet off the coast in 1758. Still another opinion asserts that in Queen Elizabeth's time it was very popular and was played when a man-of-war weighed anchor or when a regiment moved in or out of town. Though still a great march favorite, it has always been popular as a country dance throughout New England. These are the dance changes when Happy Hale does the prompting. Sometimes this is used as one of the formations in a plain quadrille.

THE DANCE

SQUARE FORMATION	FOUR COUPLES IN A SET
Circle eight hands around	8 bars
First couple lead to the right halfway round	4 "
Pass right through between the two	4 "
Swing the girl behind you	8 "
Ladies grand chain	8 "
All promenade with the dear little maid, that girl you left behind you	8 "

THE GIRL I LEFT BEHIND ME

GRAND MARCH
followed by
SICILIAN CIRCLE

Used in conjunction with dancing, the march is reminiscent of the processional dances of the festivals of ancient England. The "Grand March" is a march in its most elaborate form and, followed by the "Sicilian Circle," is used to begin the program of country dancing. Various tunes are used for the "Grand March," but the one given here, "Washington's Grand March," is still one of New England's favorites for beginning the country dance.

SICILIAN CIRCLE

Music: **Sicilian Circle (Kinloch).**
Played by Smith Paine of Wolfeboro, New Hampshire. Recorded.
Dance changes called by Edson H. Cole, Freedom, New Hampshire. Recorded.

This dance is one of the few surviving circle dances and was once known as a coronation dance. It is called sometimes "Circassian Circle." The melody is part of a Scotch reel, known as "Over the Water to Charlie," a tune of the time of Charles II.

THE DANCE

"SICILIAN CIRCLE" FORMATION	EVEN NUMBER OF COUPLES
Four hands around	8 bars
Balance partner	8 "
Right and left	8 "
Ladies chain	8 "
Chasse to center and pass through to meet next couple	8 "
Right and left	8 "

WASHINGTON'S GRAND MARCH

KINLOCH

GREEN MOUNTAIN VOLUNTEERS

Music: **Arkansas Traveler.**

Played by Edson H. Cole, Freedom, New Hampshire (Recorded), and the Singing Smiths, South Parsonsfield, Maine.

Dance changes called by Ralph Merrill, Cumberland Mills, Maine.

The dance and tune commemorate the story of the Green Mountain Boys. Organized under Ethan Allen, a small band of settlers in Vermont offered resistance to New York, which claimed Vermont as part of its territory. Allen and his Green Mountain Boys forced the surrender of Fort Ticonderoga on May 10, 1775. They were a valiant band and later played an illustrious part in the Revolution of 1776. The melody used for the dance was once the "Green Mountain Boys," but now the tune is usually the fiddler's choice. The Singing Smiths start the dance to the "Arkansas Traveler," an old melody whose source is unknown. Edson Cole plays an old Irish jig for this dance. The dance itself resembles a column of troops on the march, and the total effect of the combined figures calls to mind the action of firing heavy cannon. The two pieces of music given here for the dance show the wide variety of melodies used in different sections for the same dance.

THE DANCE

CONTRA DANCE FORMATION — SIX TO EIGHT COUPLES IN A SET

Every other couple cross over

Balance and swing below — 8 bars

Down on the left and swing on the right — 8 "

> All the gentlemen that have crossed over promenade with the lady below to the foot and return, while the opposite line turns in place with the one next below.

Down on the right and swing on the left — 8 "

> All the ladies that have crossed over promenade with the gentleman below to the foot and return, while the opposite line turns in place with the one next below.

Ladies chain — 8 "

Cast off

JIG

ARKANSAS TRAVELER

HAYMAKERS' JIG

Music: **Turkey in the Straw.**
Played by Edson H. Cole, Freedom, New Hampshire. Recorded.
Dance changes called by Ralph Merrill, Cumberland Mills, Maine.

The name of this dance suggests the festivals of the harvest time, which was a period of great community rejoicing. "The Hay" was a dance figure and melody known to Shakespeare, but whether or not this dance is derived from it is not known. The characteristics of the dance certainly indicate a festival of the land, and it is very similar to the English "Harvesters' Dance" of today. The tune used for this dance is now the choice of the fiddler. The music used here, "Turkey in the Straw," is popular for many of the contra dances, but particularly fits this one. It is based on the old song, "My Grandmother Lived on Yonder Little Green," the history of which may be found in the ballad section.

THE DANCE

CONTRA DANCE FORMATION — SIX TO EIGHT COUPLES IN A SET

First, third, and every other couple cross over
Swing the next below
First gentleman, first lady, and second lady down the
center and back (and the corresponding dancers
in couples that have crossed over)
Ladies chain
Swing partner (those that have crossed over)
Swing the next below
First gentleman, second gentleman, and first lady down
the center and back
Ladies chain
Swing partner (those that have crossed over)
Swing the next below
Down the center and back (first and second, fourth
and fifth, seventh and eighth, four abreast, down
the center)
Ladies chain
Swing partner

TURKEY IN THE STRAW

HIGH, BETTY MARTIN

Whistled by Cassius Radford of Pembroke, New Hampshire, who played it many times as a fiddle tune for country dances.

The tune and words are traditional and were fitted for a sort of jig that finished off a quadrille. It is a lively reminder to Radford of the days when he was champion fiddler traveling all over New England. He remembers this tune and jig as one that was indulged in by those who felt the need of cutting an extra flourish and was executed with steps similar to the Highland Fling.

These are the words that were sung to the melody:

"High, Betty Martin
Tip toe, tip toe
High, Betty Martin
Tip toe fine
Never found a man
To suit her fancy
Never found a man
To suit her mind."

HIGH, BETTY MARTIN

HULL'S VICTORY

Music: **Hull's Victory.**
Played by Willie Woodward, Bristol, New Hampshire. Recorded.
Dance changes called by Willie Woodward. Recorded.

This dance commemorates Captain Hull's victory. Isaac Hull was commander of the frigate *Constitution,* which engaged the British frigate *Guerrière* in fierce combat in the Gulf of St. Lawrence in 1812. A ballad, "The *Constitution* and the *Guerrière,*" narrates in full the story of this battle. No country dance would be complete without "Hull's Victory."

THE DANCE

CONTRA DANCE FORMATION — SIX TO EIGHT COUPLES IN A SET

First and every other couple take one step forward

Balance four in line crosswise the set	4 bars
Center couples swing half round	4 "
Center couples swing in center	4 "
Down the center and back	8 "
Turn half round, cast off, and right and left	8 "

To end the dance: all forward and back, swing partners, promenade to seats.

When Bill Woodward prompts, the calls sound like this:

Right hand to your partner, left hand to your opposite
Balance four in a line
Turn your opposite with your left hand
Right hand back and balance four
Turn your partner in the center, in the center turn your partner
Down the center with your partner
Back and cast off
Right and left
Right and left
Everyone right and left

HULL'S VICTORY

LADY OF THE LAKE

Music: **Come, Haste to the Wedding.**
Played by Smith Paine, Wolfeboro, New Hampshire. Recorded.
Dance changes called by Smith Paine.

Possibly this dance comes from Walter Scott's heroine, Ellen Douglas; or it may be based on the old tune "Launcelot du Lake," a ballad founded on the romance of Sir Launcelot du Lake. The dance itself seems to have been derived from the Weavers' Guild, although nothing of its origin is definitely known. The tune "Come, Haste to the Wedding," of Gaelic origin, was introduced in the pantomime, "The Elopement," in 1767. This version is known as the Manx tune and was printed by the Percy Society in 1846. It is the basis of the Manx ballad, "The Capture of Carrickfergusby," written by Thurot in 1760. The original tune for the contra dance, "Lady of the Lake," is no longer played, and therefore one of the airs known as "Lady of the Lake" is given here only as a matter of record, as fiddlers in different localities have their favorite tunes.

THE DANCE

CONTRA DANCE FORMATION — SIX TO EIGHT COUPLES IN A SET

First and every other couple cross over	
Balance below (head lady swings gentleman on her right; head gentleman swings lady on his left, and so on down the two lines)	4 bars
Balance partners in center (those that have crossed over)	4 "
Swing partners	
Down the center and back (couples that have crossed over promenade down the center and back)	8 "
Cast off	
Ladies chain	8 "

COME, HASTE TO THE WEDDING

THE LONDON LANCIERS

Music: **The London Lanciers.***
Dance directions called by Edson H. Cole, Freedom, New Hampshire.

From military life have come various contributions to the development of the dance. The Lanciers, a regiment of light cavalry armed with lances, gives its name to this elaborate quadrille. Madam Sacre, in her classes in Hanover Square, London, established the dance as fashionable about 1850. The music used here has been sent by Benjamin Lovett, with the consent of Henry Ford, who is much interested in the revival of the country dance. This dance is found in most programs of country dances.

THE DANCE

QUADRILLE FORMATION — FOUR COUPLES TO A SET

Figure One

Address partners	8 bars
Address corners	8 "
First four forward and back	4 "
First couple chasse across and back while second couple separate, cross over, and return	8 "
Balance corners	4 "
Turn partners	4 "
Second four forward and back	4 "
Second couple chasse across and first couple separate, cross over, and return	8 "
Balance corners	4 "
Turn partners	4 "

*Used by permission of Benjamin Lovett and Henry Ford.

Figure Two

Third couple balance to corners	4 bars
Turn partners	4 "
Third couple chasse across while fourth couple separate, cross over, and return	8 "
Balance corners	4 "
Turn partners	4 "
Fourth couple chasse across while third couple separate, cross over, and return	8 "
Balance corners	4 "
Turn partners	4 "

Figure Three

First four forward and back	4 "
First four forward and address opposite	4 "
Ladies cross right hands in center and swing one-half way around to left while at the same time gentlemen go opposite, then at one-half way (music at slower tempo)	8 "
Ladies reverse, crossing left hands, and swing one-half way round while gentlemen go opposite to place	8 "

Third and fourth couples repeat in same manner

Figure Four

First four lead to right and address	4 "
First four lead to left and address	4 "
First four lead to place and address	4 "

Third and fourth couples repeat in same manner

Figure Five

THE GRAND SQUARE

First four forward, and third and fourth couple step into places of first four	16 bars

Sides forward and first four separate, four steps each way

First couple face up the hall, other couples fall behind

Gentlemen chasse to right, and ladies to left	8 bars
Address partners	4 "
Chasse back again, all still in line	8 "
Gentlemen march left, ladies right, one and one-half around	16 "
All forward and back	8 "
Swing partners to place	4 "

SECOND GRAND SQUARE

Second couple face out and all fall behind	
Chasse right and left	8 "
Address partners	4 "
Chasse back	8 "
Address partners	4 "
Forward and back	4 "
Swing partners, then—	4 "
Grand right and left until each reaches own partner and—	8 "
Promenade to seats	8 "

I

II

III

IV

V

MAID IN THE PUMP ROOM

Music: **Maid in the Pump Room.**
Played by Dennis McClure, Willimantic, Connecticut.
Dance changes called by Dennis McClure.

In England the room or building at a spa or mineral spring where water was dispensed for drinking was called a pump room. In the New England home, the pump room was the "cool pantry," later known as the "butt'ry," and was often used for dairy purposes. It was not uncommon on the New England farm to have the water conveniently brought to the shelter of the house ell, where the well or spring water could be pumped for general use.

This country dance may be related to "Maid in the Mill," a country dance of old England, possibly based on an old English ballad of the same name presented in "The Jovial Crew" in 1731. The tune, however, is unlike ours.

THE DANCE

CONTRA DANCE FORMATION — ANY NUMBER MAY PARTICIPATE

First lady down the center, first gentleman down the outside, and back to places — 8 bars

Lady down the outside, gentleman down the center, and back to places	8 bars
Both down the center, back, and cast off	8 "
Right and left	4 "
Ladies chain	8 "

MAID IN THE PUMP ROOM

THE MERRY DANCE

Music: **The Merry Dance.**

Played by Smith Paine, Wolfeboro, New Hampshire. Recorded.

Dance changes called by Smith Paine. Recorded.

The origin of this lively contra dance can probably be traced to "The Health," sometimes known as "The Merry Wassail," an English country dance; and the tune closely resembles an old Irish air, "The Fairy Dance," from which it probably is derived.

THE DANCE

CONTRA DANCE FORMATION — SIX TO EIGHT COUPLES IN A SET

First and every other couple cross over	
Head couple down the center and back	8 bars

All join hands across	
Down center and back	8 bars
Cast off	
Ladies chain	8 "
Half promenade	4 "
Half right and left to place	4 "

THE MERRY DANCE

MISS BROWN'S REEL

Music: **Miss Brown's Reel.**

Played by the Singing Smiths, South Parsonsfield, Maine.

Dance changes called by Ralph Merrill, Cumberland Mills, Maine.

Nothing is known about the origin of this dance, although the tune is a Scotch reel known as "Coriemonies Rant." It is very old.

THE DANCE

CONTRA DANCE FORMATION	SIX TO EIGHT COUPLES
First and every other couple cross over	
Swing the next below	4 bars
Down the center (the couples that have crossed over join hands and go down the center)	8 "
Half circle back (ladies on the gentlemen's side and gentlemen on the ladies' side)	8 "
Circle four hands around (first two couples)	8 "
Right and left (until the gentleman is opposite a lady and lady opposite a gentleman)	8 "
Swing the next below	4 "

MISS BROWN'S REEL

MONEY MUSK

Music: **Money Musk.**

Played by Lewis L. Jillson, Bernardston, Massachusetts.

Dance changes called by Happy Hale, Hinsdale, New Hampshire.

In the early eighteenth century this tune was known as "The Countess of Airly." It came from the village of Money Musk, in Aberdeenshire, Scotland. The origin of the dance known in New England is not established.

THE DANCE

CONTRA DANCE FORMATION SIX TO EIGHT COUPLES IN A SET

First couple swing once and a half around	8 bars
Each go below one couple and	
Forward six	4 "
Right hand to partner and	
Swing three-fourths around	4 "
Forward six	4 "
Right hand to partner	
Swing three-fourths around to place	4 "
Right and left	8 "

Fourth couple starts dance at same time.

MONEY MUSK

MORNING STAR

Music: **Rakes of Mallow.**
Played by Lewis Jillson, Bernardston, Massachusetts.
Dance changes called by Lewis Jillson.

Where this dance originated is not known, although one similar may be found in *The Dancing Master.* The music is an old Irish reel, and the name of it comes from the local gay blades of the eighteenth century. There is a tune in old Irish folkmusic called "The Morning

Star," but whether a tune derived from this air was ever played in New England for the dance is not known.

THE DANCE

CONTRA DANCE FORMATION — SIX COUPLES IN A SET

Balance partner with right hand and swing to the right in the center
Balance partner with left hand and swing to the left in the center
Down the center and back
Cast off
Right and left to place
Repeat

First, third, and fifth couples start dancing.

RAKES OF MALLOW

NINEPIN QUADRILLE
or
THE CHEAT

Music: **Fiddler's Choice** or **The Cheat.**
Dance changes called by Willie Woodward of Bristol, New Hampshire. Recorded.

This quadrille is one that demands the ingenuity of a talented prompter, for the dance has all the features of a riotous game as the ninepins scramble for partners. "The Cheat," the music here presented, was one of the tunes formerly used. It has been transcribed from the manuscript of Elizabeth Foster Reed. Today the melodies most commonly used for this quadrille are popular tunes in fast tempo. "Darling Nelly Gray" is the air that is played for Bill Woodward.

THE DANCE

QUADRILLE FORMATION — FOUR COUPLES TO A SET

One lady or one gentleman in the center of each set	
Eight hands around your ninepin	4 bars
Now the other way	4 "
Right hand to your partner now in grand right and left (ninepin leaves center and takes part)	
Oh—promenade (lady or gentleman left without partner steps to center of set)	
Eight hands around your ninepin now	4 "
Right hand to your partner now in grand right and left	
Now the other way	4 "
All keep a-goin'	
Now promenade	
Eight hands around your ninepin	4 "
The other way	4 "
Right hand to your partner and grand right and left	
Now all promenade	
Eight hands around your ninepin	4 "
Now the other way	4 "
Now ladies take four hands around the ninepin (ladies step to center, join hands, circle around the ninepin; gentlemen join hands, circle the other way)	
All promenade.	
(This is another favorite figure)	
Eight hands around your ninepin	8 "
Ninepin balance the first gentleman	
Ninepin balance the second gentleman	
Grand right and left	

Form a circle around the hall (all ninepins of all sets go to center)
All balance forward to the ninepins
Balance back to place
Grand right and left (ninepins leave center and join circle)
Promenade
All circle around the ninepin 8 bars
Balance forward to the ninepin
Balance back to place
Promenade

The number of measures for each of these figures except around the ninepins varies according to the mood of the prompter.

THE CHEAT

OLD ZIP COON

Music: **Old Zip Coon.**
Played by Willie Woodward of Bristol, New Hampshire. Recorded.
Dance changes called by Willie Woodward. Recorded.

This contra dance, of vague origin, is only one of the great many varied forms of the dance popular throughout New England and takes its name from the song "Old Zip Coon," a widely known minstrel of the 1800's.

The melody is one derived from the ballad tune "My Grandmother

Lived on Yonder Little Green," the history of which may be found in the ballad section of this book.

THE DANCE

The following dance changes are those which Bill Woodward uses. The more familiar figures are given second. This is an example of how the prompter in a different vicinity pursues the traditions of his own locality.

CONTRA DANCE FORMATION — SIX TO EIGHT COUPLES IN A SET

First, third, and every other couple cross over	
Balance and—	4 bars
Swing your partner once and three-quarters around	4 "
Now balance in line	4 "
Turn your partner in center	4 "
Down the center with your partner	4 "
Now come back and cast off, cast off	4 "
Right and left, oh—right and left—	4 "
Right and left, right and left to as you were	4 "

SECOND VERSION

First couple down the outside, second couple down the center, same time	4 "
First couple up the center, second up the outside	4 "
First couple down the center, second couple down the outside	4 "
First couple up the outside, second couple up the center	4 "
Both couples down the center and back, first couple cast off	8 "
Right and left	8 "

OLD ZIP COON

PETRONELLA

Music: **Petronella.**
Played by Lewis Jillson of Bernardston, Massachusetts
Dance changes called by Lewis Jillson.

The origin of this dance and tune cannot be definitely placed, although the name suggests a French background. The melody is similar to "Tink a tink," an English country dance air of the eighteenth century.

THE DANCE

CONTRA DANCE FORMATION	SIX TO EIGHT COUPLES IN A SET
First couple balance to side	4 bars
Balance to center	4 "
Balance to side	4 "
Balance to center	4 "
First couple down the center and back	8 "
Cast off	
Right and left	8 "

PETRONELLA

PLAIN QUADRILLE

Music: **Quadrille, Land of Sweet Erin,** and **Adam's Favorite.**
From the manuscript of Elizabeth Foster Reed.
Dance changes called by Edson H. Cole, Freedom, New Hampshire. Recorded.

The quadrille is a very old dance, dating from the eleventh century, and is said to have been introduced into England by William of Normandy. A great variety of figures may be used in this dance to satisfy the ingenuity of fiddler or caller. From the simplest forms, the quadrille developed intricate patterns and special rhythms; the waltz, the polka, the medley all signifying particular dance figures in the quadrille parts. "The Lanciers" is an elaborate quadrille, and one set is given elsewhere in this section.

When plain-quadrille music is used, the first eight bars of the air are merely introductory; when popular tunes are played, the dance begins at once with four hands around and reverse. The old quadrille music was stately, but present usage inclines to faster rhythm. Of the tunes given here, the first and last, from an old manuscript, are probably of New England origin; the melody, "Land of Sweet Erin," used for the second part, is an Irish tune of unknown date.

THE DANCE

SQUARE FORMATION — FOUR COUPLES IN A SET

Figure One (Side couples repeat calls)

Wait	8 bars
All address partners, then address corners	8 "
First four right and left	8 "

Ladies chain	8 bars
Half right and left	8 "
Half promenade	8 "
Promenade all	8 "

Figure Two (Second, third, and fourth couples repeat calls)

First couple lead to the right	8 "
Four hands around	8 "
Right and left with the next couple	8 "
Ladies chain to next couple	8 "
Promenade all	8 "

Figure Three

First four lead to the right	8 "
Change partners (turn half around)	
Chasse out	8 "
Ladies chain	8 "
Half promenade	8 "
Half right and left	8 "
All forward and back	8 "
Turn partner in place	8 "
Ladies grand chain	8 "
Promenade all	8 "

QUADRILLE

Figure I

LAND OF SWEET ERIN

Figure II

ADAM'S FAVORITE

Figure III

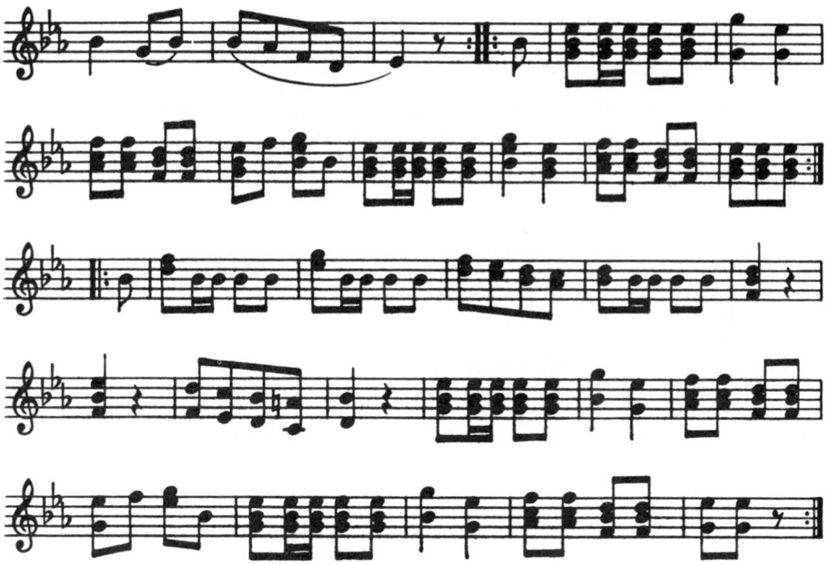

POP! GOES THE WEASEL

Music: **Pop! Goes the Weasel.**
Played by Willie Woodward of Bristol, New Hampshire. Recorded.
Dance changes called by Willie Woodward. Recorded.

This dance was once an old English singing game and was popular with the children as far back as the early seventeenth century. The origin is unknown. It was introduced in New England as a contra dance and remains a great favorite.

THE DANCE

CONTRA DANCE FORMATION	SIX COUPLES IN A SET
First couple down the outside and back	8 bars
Down the center and back	8 "
Circle three hand around	8 "

First couple join hands with the next lady and circle three hands once and a half around; the second lady stops opposite and faces her original place.

At the word "Pop" in the music, the first couple release the hands of the other lady, at the same time raising their own joined hands. This forms an arch under which the second lady passes as she returns to her own place. Now, "Pop the lady."

Circle three hands around with gentleman 8 bars

Repeat same as above with that gentleman. Now, "Pop the gentleman."

Repeat from beginning and go below one couple each time.

Third and fifth couples may begin the dance and continue until the end of the set is reached, when each couple rests one repetition of the dance. To the end the dance, call, "All balance partners" (4 bars) and promenade to seats.

POP! GOES THE WEASEL

PORTLAND FANCY

Music: **Portland Fancy.**
Played by Edson H. Cole of Freedom, New Hampshire. Recorded.
Dance changes called by Harry E. Brigham of Marlboro, Massachusetts.

How the name of this dance originated is not known, but it seems apparent that the center of the "Down East" section gave it its name. The melody is derived from an Irish reel and is written here as recorded from the playing of Edson Cole, who has used it for more than forty years. It is one of the favorites found on every country dance program.

THE DANCE

Form as for "Sicilian Circle," except that two couples are abreast in sets of four around the circle, as in quardrille formation.

Eight hands around	8 bars
Right and left	8 "
Ladies chain	8 "
Forward and back and pass through	8 "
Eight hands around, etc.	

PORTLAND FANCY

SOLDIER'S JOY

Music: **Soldier's Joy.**
Played by Willie Woodward, Bristol, New Hampshire. Recorded.
Dance changes called by Willie Woodward. Recorded.

"Soldier's Joy" is the name of one of the earliest dances recorded in England, but no date of origin has been established. It is still done in Girton Village as part of a festival dance. The tune is also well known in Ireland.

As the dance is enjoyed today, it is a matter of orchestral skill to keep playing for the huge circle in its reel till the dancers are exhausted. It is very popular and lively and is sure to be found on nearly every country dance program.

THE DANCE

FORM AS FOR "SICILIAN CIRCLE"

Swing four hands around	4 bars
Swing the opposite (take waltz position with the opposite lady and turn)	4 "
Swing partners	4 "
Ladies chain	8 "
Forward and back (join nearer hand with partner; walk forward, drop hands, pass through to the next couple)	4 "
All balance partners	4 "

In some towns the last figure is called as follows:

Form circle around the hall and—
Reel your partner once and one-half around
Reel the next, once and one-half around (the reel progresses as a grand right and left)
Keep a-goin'!
All balance and swing partners.

SOLDIER'S JOY

SPEED THE PLOUGH

Music: **Speed the Plough.**
Played by Willie Woodward, Bristol, New Hampshire. Recorded.
Dance changes called by Willie Woodward. Recorded.

The name of this dance clearly indicates that it comes from the ancient rituals connected with "Plough Monday" in Great Britain. This festival, celebrated in January, was part of the worship of agriculture which the early villagers practiced. The prayers for a good harvest were presented to the house gods with great ceremony; bread and cheese were set into the plough, and a like offering scattered to the fields for the crows. The first offering was to seek the blessing for the harvest; the second, to appease the adverse elements.

No source for the tune can be found. It is always the one played for this dance, however. The dance itself is very gay and frolicsome, and with a skillful caller is very popular.

THE DANCE

CONTRA DANCE FORMATION SIX TO EIGHT COUPLES IN A SET

Form right on now for "Speed the Plough"
First and every other couple cross over

Head lady balances to the first and second gentleman and swings three hands around	8 bars
Head gentleman balances to the first and second lady and swings three hands around	8 "
Turn your partner in the center, in the center (the couples that have crossed over turn in center while other couples on side remain in place)	4 "

Down the center and back with your partner (all couples that have crossed over go down center of the set and back) 8 bars
And cast off (go below the next couple)
Right and left to place—everyone back to place 8 "

Repeat from the beginning.

SPEED THE PLOUGH

STEAMBOAT QUICKSTEP

Music: **Steamboat Quickstep** (from the copybook of Elizabeth Foster Reed).

This melody was a great favorite in the 1800's and gave its name to a contra dance and waltz as well as to the march in double time which is given here.

As early as 1787 a steamboat was tried out on the Delaware River by John Fitch. Robert Fulton, in 1807, made his famous trip from New York to Albany, and such news of the day was immediately taken into the lives of the people to become a part of work and play.

STEAMBOAT QUICKSTEP

THE TEMPEST

Music: **The Tempest.**
Played by Edson H. Cole, Freedom, New Hampshire. Recorded.
Dance changes called by Edson H. Cole. Recorded.

This is an old country dance of English origin. The name probably was chosen arbitrarily, although the boisterous effect of the number of couples dancing at one time is comparable to a storm. The origin of this tune has not been verified.

THE DANCE

CONTRA DANCE FORMATION	SIX TO EIGHT COUPLES IN A SET
Form in two lines. Partners stand beside each other. The two head couples stand across the head of the set facing down the hall.	
First two couples down the center and back (four abreast,	8 bars
the first two couples go down the center, part at the foot, and return up the center four abreast)	8 "
First two couples right and left (with the couples next below, the ladies of the first and second couple pass between the opposite couple, gentlemen on the outside; ladies return, alternating with ladies and gentlemen of opposite couples)	8 "
Ladies chain (ladies give right hands across to opposite ladies and walk half around; give left hands to	

opposite gentlemen and turn; give right hands back to same ladies, walk four steps to place, give left hands to partners, and turn to place	8 bars
First two couples forward	8 "
First two couples right and left	8 "
First two couples ladies chain	8 "

THE TEMPEST

TWIN SISTERS

Music: **Twin Sisters.**
Played by Harry E. Brigham, Marlboro, Massachusetts.
Dance changes called by Harry E. Brigham.

It is possible that this dance comes from "The Twins," an English country dance found in Playford's *The Dancing Master*, published in 1707. The melody is probably derived from Neil Gow's old Irish tune, "Farewell to Whiskey." The dance probably takes its name from the method of execution.

THE DANCE

CONTRA DANCE FORMATION SIX TO EIGHT COUPLES IN A SET

First two ladies join hands, chasse between the opposite gentlemen and back	8 bars
First two gentlemen join hands, chasse between the opposite ladies and back	8 "
First couple down the center, back and cast off	8 "
Right and left	8 "

Fourth and fifth couples may start dancing at the same time as the first two couples.

TWIN SISTERS

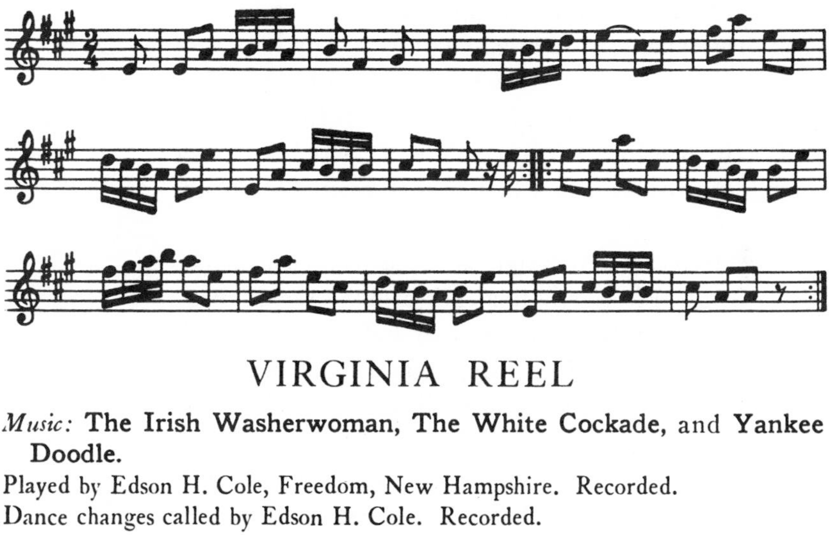

VIRGINIA REEL

Music: **The Irish Washerwoman, The White Cockade,** and **Yankee Doodle.**

Played by Edson H. Cole, Freedom, New Hampshire. Recorded.
Dance changes called by Edson H. Cole. Recorded.

The Virginia Reel is a survival of a dance of the crafts. It is an imitation of weaving, one figure representing the shuttle that moves through the warp and woof of thread. In the time of George III, it was known as the "Hemp-Dressers' Dance" and was important at court gatherings. King George III himself took part in this dance. It has always been popular as a concluding dance for assemblies. Under the title of "Sir Roger de Coverley," it had its own music, which was discarded in colonial New England for the three favorites given here.

"The Irish Washerwoman" is an old Irish reel, and as an English country dance tune it was published in 1688 and was known as "The Country Courtship." "The White Cockade" was published by Herd in 1776 and took its name from the cockade of the house of Stuart. "Yankee Doodle," which is played for the march, is generally supposed to have been introduced in America from the Continent in 1775.

THE DANCE

CONTRA DANCE FORMATION	SIX TO EIGHT COUPLES IN A SET
First lady and foot gentleman meet in center and balance	4 bars
First gentleman and foot lady meet in center and balance	4 "
First lady turn foot gentleman in center with right hand	4 "
First gentleman turn foot lady with right hand	4 "
First lady turn foot gentleman in center with left hand	4 "
First gentleman turn foot lady in center with left hand	4 "
First lady turn foot gentleman in center with both hands	4 "
First gentleman turn foot lady in center with both hands	4 "
Right hand to partner and reel down the set	32 "

Head couple link right arms, turn once and a half around. Head lady links left arm with gentleman next in line, while her partner links left arm with the lady next in line. Head couple then turn each other in center, right arms linked. Head couple turns next couple with the left, then turn each other in center with right, and so on down the set. There the head couple join hands and chasse up the center of the set to the head, where they separate, and each leads his own line in a march down the outside of the set.

When the head couple reach the foot, they join hands and chasse to the head of the set, the other couples following suit to their original places, where they raise their joined hands to form an arch, under which the head couple chasse to the foot. Thus the head couple become the foot couple, and the dance continues until all have danced back to their original positions. 16 bars

IRISH WASHERWOMAN

THE WHITE COCKADE

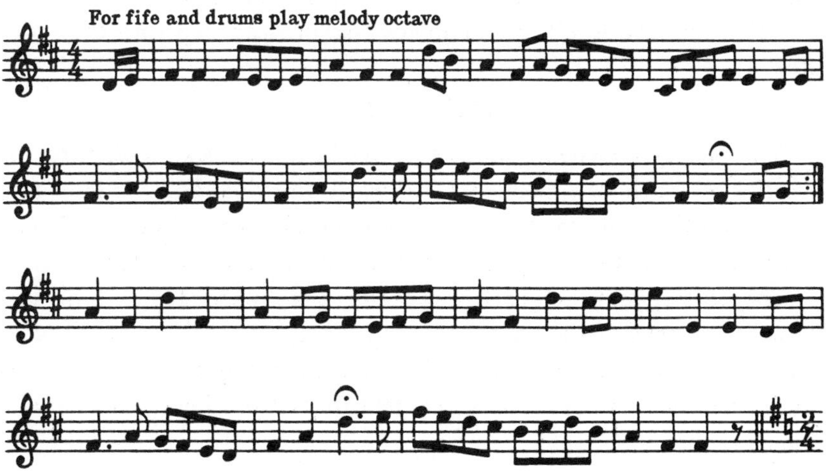

YANKEE DOODLE

THE WALTZ

Music: **Copenhagen Waltz** and **Swiss Waltz.**

Dance-step directions from "Good Morning," by Mr. and Mrs. Henry Ford.*

The Waltz as now danced comes from Germany, although it is a development of the "Volte," one of the most ancient dances of France, known in the fourteenth century. The Waltz is one of the first dances in which the steps were done by single couples as separate units, rather than as parts of groups. "Copenhagen Waltz" and "Swiss Waltz" are two melodies characteristic of the eighteenth century. A later development was the "Rye Waltz," which takes its name from the music "Coming Through the Rye" and combines a schottische step with the waltz step.

THE DANCE

The waltz movement consists of six beats and six steps, three of which the gentleman takes in a backward direction, and the lady forward, and three of which the lady moves backward and the gentleman forward. The waltz begins with the lady placing the right foot in a forward step and the gentleman taking a backward step with his left foot. The steps of the waltz are: step, slide, close. The accent comes on the first and fourth counts. The waltz is composed of three beats to the measure, and there are three steps to the bar. There is no definite

*Used by permission.

number of turns in any one direction. The gentleman usually guides by turning to the left or right for variation.

COPENHAGEN WALTZ

SWISS WALTZ

THE WHITE COCKADE

Music: **The White Cockade.**
Played by Dennis McClure, Willimantic, Connecticut.
Dance changes called by Dennis McClure.

This dance takes its name from the rosette or knot worn on the hat by servants of officers in the army or navy or diplomatic corps. The cockade of the house of Stuart was white. Military tunes played a prominent part in the hours of fun and relaxation. The melody was published by Herd in 1776.

THE DANCE

CONTRA DANCE FORMATION SIX TO EIGHT COUPLES IN A SET

First lady down the center, first gentleman down the outside and back	8 bars
First gentleman down the center, first lady down the outside and back	8 "
First couple down the center, back and cast off	8 "
Right and left	8 "

THE WHITE COCKADE

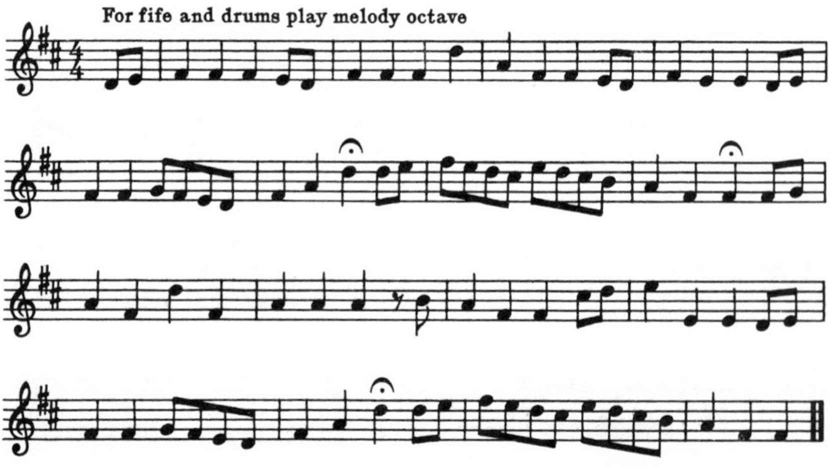

SEA CHANTEYS AND FO'CASTLE SONGS

It was the merchant ship that developed the chantey and the chanteyman, and long before the colonists separated from British rule, Yankee sailors served in ships laden with spice, tea, whale oil, and slaves—rich cargoes for far ports. From these English ships the Yankee sailor learned most of his chanteys, although as American commerce progressed the American seaman developed a few songs of his own.

As early as the sixteenth century, the cod fisheries of the Grand Banks of Newfoundland drew boats that set sail every spring from England to return in the fall. By provision of the first charter of Virginia, a fishing colony was established on the coast of Maine. Here, at the mouth of the Kennebec in May, 1607, was laid the keel of the *Virginia,* a thirty-ton seagoing pinnace, the first vessel built in America for commercial use. Corn was traded for beaver skins in Kennebec, cod was shipped to England.

Then shipbuilding began in earnest, the first American shipyard being established on the Mystic River in 1629. Two years later, July 4, 1631, the first seagoing vessel was launched. She was called *Blessing of the Bay* and was owned by Governor John Winthrop. As the vessels increased in size, the colonists began to take an interest in the West Indian trade. The New England settler was beginning to realize that he knew no want for which his own diligence could not provide.

The Revolution of 1776 further encouraged the New Englanders to use their own resources. The most famous ship of the following period was the *Constitution,* familiarly called "Old Ironsides," built by Colonel George Claghorn and launched at Hartt's Naval Yard in Boston, 1797.

Progress was slow until the beginning of the 1800's; from then to the Civil War, however, the great energy of the Yankee seaman developed to its utmost. It was a time of great achievement and the supreme era of the sailing vessel. In this period, the discovery of gold helped push the merchant marine to its greatest height.

The holystoned decks that rolled beneath the Thomaston and Searsport captains' boots were hewn from the trees of New England. When the Yankee square-riggers built of home-grown timber went down the ways, they carried at their mastheads the flag of a new race—a race which had learned that its natural resources were valuable in trade. Out of Bath, Bangor, and Boston, out of Portsmouth and New London, out of Salem, Chelsea, and Kennebunk, Yankee ships under Yankee command threatened the supremacy of Great Britain in commerce. Many Maine towns divided their wealth between lumber and shares in a vessel. Castine, the great salt depot of northern New England, had its part in trade. From New Bedford, the center of the whaling industry, Nantucket, and many other points, sailed the great square-sterned whalers to be gone two or three years or longer on a single voyage, in search of the precious oil that was fast changing the life in the home ports.

The launching, on the Merrimac, of the *Joshua Bates*, designed by Donald McKay, was a red-letter day in American shipping. This packet ship, the pioneer of Train's famous Boston and Liverpool line, brought together two great figures of American commerce, Enoch Train and Donald McKay. McKay established his great shipyard at East Boston and built for Train the famous packets that carried passengers, mail, and goods. With McKay's peerless designs began the day of the fast clipper ships, American-owned, many Boston-built, and under American command. These clippers, with their long, slim hulls and great spread of canvas, made record voyages that have never been broken by sail.

However, the shrewd Yankee builders down East knew that clipper ships were costly; so in the shipyards in Maine at Bath and Thomaston, in New Hampshire at Portsmouth, and in Connecticut at Stonington and Mystic, were built the "Down Easters," full-rigged wooden ships, generally of medium size, that required only half the crew that a clipper needed and provided much more space for cargoes of grain and lumber that were traded for rum, sugar, and molasses. The Down Easter was a magnificent ship. She pushed her Maine hackmatack and pine hull staunchly into heavy seas while the fiddlehead watched the bone in her teeth, as creaking under full sail she ploughed around the Horn.

The Yankee skipper, master of the spick-and-span Yankee sailing vessel, was born of rugged pioneer stock and was by training a man of stern discipline. He ruled his men with few words, helped by a bucko mate. Known to be kind-hearted ashore, he was often "hell afloat." By sheer force of character, his own indomitable will, and persistent industry, he often rose to command a vessel at a surprisingly early age. He was proud of his ship, proud of his discipline, and proud of his job. He is remembered today for an iron will, shrewd trading, and masterly seamanship. The Yankee skipper of the Cape Horner was said to be "such a superb navigator that he could take his ship to sea without a real sailor in the fo'castle."

Under a hard-boiled skipper cruelty to the crews made some vessels veritable hell-ships; but the captain, as well as the mate, had served his own hard time before the mast, and he knew the worth of a good seaman. He and his officers suffered neither fools, slackers, nor incompetents.

On these American sailing ships the crew were not all American, and they were, on the whole, a miscellaneous hard-bitten lot. Sailors came from farm and city, landlubber and seafaring stock, and from the general run of the merchant service of the times. With the captain's shore neighbor's son, who went to sea as cabin boy and aspired to command his own vessel, was the lowest type of adventurer. Crews on the packets, whalers, clippers, and Down Easters signed by choice or, more often, were shanghaied; but, once at sea, they were all soon knocked into shape. They were away from their home ports months and years at a time, and at best their life was hard.

The food was chiefly salt beef, salt fish, slumgullion, a ration of lime juice, a ration of grog, sometimes plum duff—and always hardtack.

The sailors' work was tedious, swabbing down decks, mending tackle, looking over gear, manning the pumps, heaving the lead, and always adjusting canvas to catch a favoring wind. Hard, long hours at monotonous tasks were interspersed with standing watch and brief leisure. Just before making the home port, a deep-water ship was ratted down, tarred, scrubbed, and painted.

Working the ship at any time called for teamwork; handling the ship in heavy weather meant that concerted action of the crew was absolutely essential. Everything in a sailing ship was done by hand. Thus the labor of working the ship developed the song that lightened the seaman's task. The sea chantey was sung aboard a sailing vessel to bring speed and efficiency to the performance of work.

Among the crew was certain to be one seaman who possessed more than the average ability in vocalizing and extemporaneous creation. By tacit understanding he became chanteyman, and though others contributed their efforts he held his place by sheer ability. A good chanteyman was respected by both officers and crew; he had his own favorite tunes with a great stock of entertaining lines, which he sang in his own particular way.

Certain chanteys were used for certain tasks only. The *short-drag chantey*, like "Johnny Boker," was suited to the single heave necessary in sheeting home or boarding the main tack, or bunting a foresail or mainsail; the *capstan* or *windlass chantey*, longer in form, was adapted to the tediousness and monotony of the work at the capstan (or windlass); the *halyard chantey* was used for hoisting the yards, the men hauling on deck. In this task, to make the work effective, the combined strength and weight of the men had to be thrown on the rope at the same instant. Of a rambling style and often of an amusing theme was the chantey used for pumping ship.

The fo'castle song was sung by the crew off duty for entertainment. In the repertory of the seamen were popular songs picked up on shore leave or learned from former associates. Here was a fine chance for any sailor to give way to his imagination and his memory. His sea songs were of the courage of such magnificent seamen as John Paul Jones, of bloody battles on the high seas, of gallant ships like the *Flying Cloud*, and of love and home.

But with the ascendancy of steam as power, sail slowly dropped below the horizon. One of the last of the wooden square-riggers, the *Paul Revere*, "swung her skysails well into the twentieth century," and in 1905 made her last port. Square-rigged shipping enjoyed a brief revival during the World War, since which the old ships have been becalmed.

With them disappeared the work that made the chantey and the chanteyman necessary. These sea songs are found today only in the memories of old-time skippers or chanteymen—memories of the glorious days of sail. Occasionally songs of the chanteyman may be heard along the modern trade routes, but they are only fragments sung for entertainment.

The days of the gallant square-riggers are over, and the men who manned them in a whipping salt sea wind are in snug harbor. With the last sail furled went the last full note of sea music that could send a great ship scudding.

AMSTERDAM

This old favorite capstan chantey is recalled by Captain Charlton L. Smith, yacht master and master mariner of Marblehead, Massachusetts, who sailed in steam and sailing ships more than sixty years ago.

There are several verses to this song but only the first verse, says Captain Smith, is fit to print; in fact, it is the only one he feels is fit to sing even when he acts as chanteyman for the dog watch dinners of the Boston Yacht Club.

The song, probably of 'longshore origin, tells the story of a sailor, released from the tiresome diet and relentless duties under sail, who, with a pocket full of pay, is looking for a companion with whom to share it and his shore leave.

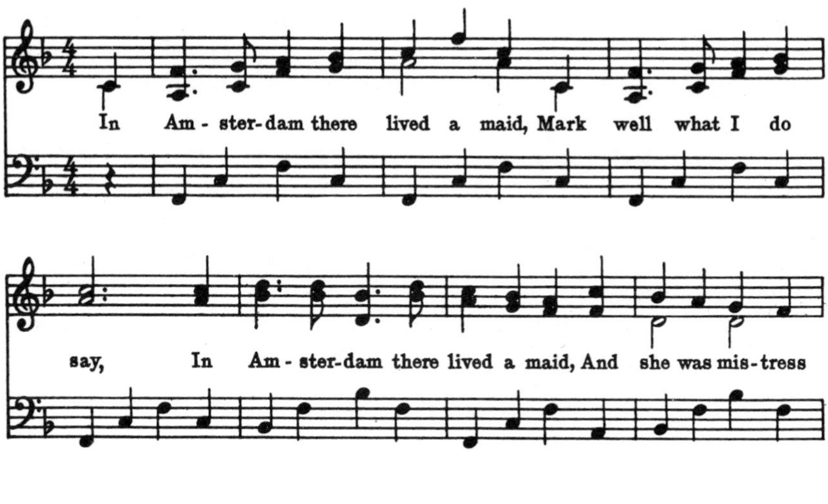

BLOW, BOYS, BLOW!

This halyard chantey, sung by James M. Linscott of Marblehead, Massachusetts, is remembered by him as one of the chanteys sung in the merchant marine when he sailed in the steamships *West Imboden* (which, translated from the American Indian, means Western Ocean) the *Capillo* of the American Republic Line, carrying cargo from Pacific ports to the eastern coast of South America, and the *Magmeric*, or, as the sailors dubbed her, *Maggie Marue*, of the South Atlantic Mail Line. Notwithstanding its traditional use, the singer recalls that the fragment presented here was sung on the *Magmeric* while rowing the longboat ashore.

Since the earliest known versions contain verses about the Congo River, this halyard chantey probably came from the West African coast trade.

Like all chanteys which were created for labor aboard a sailing vessel, it has ceased to be sung as a work song and has become one of entertainment.

2

Her masts and yards they shine like silver.
Blow, boys, blow, boys, blow!
Her masts and yards they shine like silver,—
And who do you think was the captain of her?
Blow, boys, blow, boys, blow!

3

What do you think we had for supper?
Blow, boys, blow, boys, blow!
What do you think we had for supper?
The starboard side of an old sou'wester!
Blow, boys, blow, boys, blow!

4

Oh, blow today and blow tomorrow,
Blow, boys, blow, boys, blow!
Oh, blow today and blow tomorrow,
And blow away all grief and sorrow.
Blow, boys, blow, boys, blow!

BLOW THE MAN DOWN

Sung by James M. Linscott of Marblehead, Massachusetts, who heard this chantey during his six years in the United States merchant marine.

Sailors the world over carry their music with their sea chests, and so from the port of Liverpool, England, we have this most famous halyard chantey of the Atlantic packet ships. The earliest version of this song concerns the Black Ball Line, which began its maritime service in 1818. The scorn with which chanteymen looked upon these Western Ocean packets and the crews that manned them is vividly expressed here:

> And when those old packets were ready for sea,
> You'd split your sides laughing, such sights you would see;
> There were tinkers and tailors and soldiers as well,
> All shipped as sailors on board the *Blue Bell.*

The melody has remained practically the same through the years of transition. "Blow," as used here by the sailor, means "knock." The street named in the song varies: the Winchester Street of some versions was the section where persons of rank lived; Paradise Street is said to have been a disreputable section along the waterfront.

The last stanza, which definitely lacks the full-bodied flavor of the rough seamen of sailing days, is certainly a modern addition, but this is the way it is sung today in the Pacific trade. Today, the chantey is sometimes sung in hauling the gangway prior to sailing.

3

As I was a-walking down Paradise Street,
Make a-weigh, heigh, blow the man down,
A handsome young damsel I happened to meet,
Give me some time to blow the man down.

4

I hailed her in English and hailed her all 'round,
Make a-weigh, heigh, blow the man down!
Ship ahoy! Ship ahoy! Oh, where are you bound?
Give me some time to blow the man down.

5

We've a very good mate and our Captain's a b—
Make a-weigh, heigh, blow the man down!
Come, bo'sun and mates, sing the chantey with me,
Give me some time to blow the man down!

6

Then we'll sail over the ocean blue,
With our hearts as light as the foam,
And we'll drop our anchor when day is done,
In the harbor of home, sweet home,
Oh, blow the man down, sailor, blow the man down!
Make a-weigh, heigh, blow the man down!
Then blow the man down, sailor, blow the man down!
Give me some time to blow the man down!

CAPTAIN KIDD

Nearly all of the text of this fo'castle song, Mrs. Lucy Palmer Johnson of Somerville, Massachusetts, remembers from the singing of her mother, in whose family it has been traditional.

No figure has ever been more picturesque than the pirate William Kidd, who lived in the seventeenth century and was active in American waters. He began his nautical career by holding a commission in the British navy. The Christian name has been changed to Robert in the ballad, which was first printed in broadside form at the time of Kidd's execution in 1701. An account of Kidd's career in detail may be found in Knapp and Baldwin's *Newgate Calendar,* one of the earliest tracts written to show that crime does not pay. From the early part of the eighteenth century until today, a favorite means of attempting to get rich quickly has been digging for Captain Kidd's treasure chests, believed to have been buried in many places on the New England coast.

This is a condensed version.

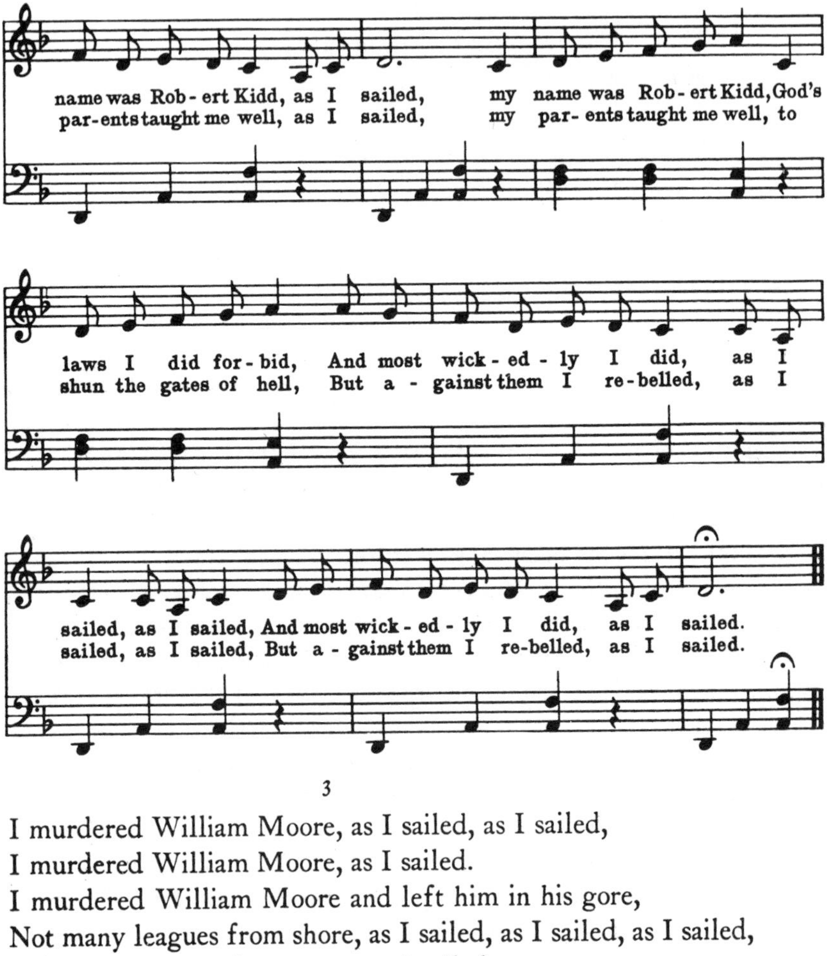

3

I murdered William Moore, as I sailed, as I sailed,
I murdered William Moore, as I sailed.
I murdered William Moore and left him in his gore,
Not many leagues from shore, as I sailed, as I sailed, as I sailed,
Not many leagues from shore, as I sailed.

4

And being cruel still, as I sailed, as I sailed,
And being cruel still, as I sailed,
And being cruel still, my gunner I did kill,
And his precious blood did spill, as I sailed, as I sailed, as I sailed,
And his precious blood did spill, as I sailed.

5

My mate was sick and died, as I sailed, as I sailed,
My mate was sick and died, as I sailed,
My mate was sick and died, which me much terrified.
He called me to his bedside, as I sailed, as I sailed, as I sailed,
He called me to his bedside, as I sailed.

6

And unto me did say, "See me die, see me die,"
And unto me did say, "See me die."
And unto me did say, "Take warning now by me,
There comes a reckoning day, you must die, you must die, you must die,
There comes a reckoning day, you must die."

7

I steered from sound to sound, as I sailed, as I sailed,
I steered from sound to sound, as I sailed,
I steered from sound to sound, and many ships I found,
And most of them I burned, as I sailed, as I sailed, as I sailed,
And most of them I burned, as I sailed.

8

I spied three ships from France, as I sailed, as I sailed,
I spied three ships from France, as I sailed,
I spied three ships from France, to them I did advance,
And took them all by chance, as I sailed, as I sailed, as I sailed,
And took them all by chance, as I sailed.

9

I spied three ships from Spain, as I sailed, as I sailed,
I spied three ships from Spain, as I sailed,
I spied three ships from Spain, I fired on them amain,
Till most of them were slain, as I sailed, as I sailed, as I sailed,
Till most of them were slain, as I sailed.

10

I'd ninety bars of gold, as I sailed, as I sailed,
I'd ninety bars of gold, as I sailed,
I'd ninety bars of gold, and dollars manifold,
With riches uncontrolled, as I sailed, as I sailed, as I sailed,
With riches uncontrolled, as I sailed.

11

Then fourteen ships I saw, as I sailed, as I sailed,
Then fourteen ships I saw, as I sailed,
Then fourteen ships I saw, and brave men they were,
Ah! they were too much for me, as I sailed, as I sailed, as I sailed,
Ah! they were too much for me, as I sailed.

12

To Newgate I am cast, and must die, and must die,
To Newgate I am cast, and must die,
To Newgate I am cast, with a sad and heavy heart,
To receive my just desert, I must die, I must die, I must die,
To receive my just desert, I must die.

13

Take warning now by me, for I must die,
Take warning now by me, for I must die,
Take warning now by me, and shun bad company,
Lest you come to hell with me, for I must die, I must die, I must die,
Lest you come to hell with me, for I must die.

THE DEAD HORSE

Sung by Stanton King of Cambridge, Massachusetts, who recalls this halyard chantey from twelve years in sailing ships.

This chantey was sung both as a work song and for the ceremony that attended "working up the first month's advance."

In olden days, the sailor was paid one month in advance and as these wages were usually spent by the time he put to sea, he felt that he was working for nothing. Therefore, the day that the seaman began to draw wages once more in return for his labor was marked with celebration. A figure, stuffed with straw and clothed in discarded attire, was dragged or marched about the deck. Then with shouting and singing the effigy was hauled to the yardarm and in one final burst of feeling it was cut and dropped to rest with Davy Jones. To cap the ceremony, all hands adjourned to the galley to "splice the main-brace."

(*Solo*)	It's up aloft the horse must go,
(*Chorus*)	And I say so, and I hope so;
(*Solo*)	We'll hoist him up, then bury him low,
(*Chorus*)	Oh, poor old man!

THE GALLANT VICTORY
or
LOWLANDS LOW

Sung by Mrs. Lucy Palmer Johnson of Somerville, Massachusetts. Both text and tune of this old sea ballad are traditional in the Palmer family.

The oldest surviving version of this ballad of the sea, printed in 1682 from a copy formerly the property of Mr. Samuel Pepys, makes Sir Walter Raleigh the owner of the ship attacked by the pirate and saved by the cunning and daring of the cabin boy, who swam underneath the pirate vessel and sank it by boring holes in the hull. This sea song, known to be widely current in the United States, was first recorded in Vermont by Mr. Phillips Barry in 1904.

The windlass chantey, "Lowlands Low," bears no relation to this ballad, which is known by several titles, of which the most common are "The Golden Vanity" and "The Sweet Trinity."

3

Then Jack he took his auger and overboard went he,
And swam along the side of the *Gallant Victory,*
He put out her* lights and he let the water in,
And he sank her in the Lowlands, Lowlands, Lowlands,
And he sank her in the Lowlands low.

4

The boy he bent his breast, swam around the ship's side,
"Oh, messmates, take me in, I am going with the tide."
His captain took him in, and on the deck he died,
And they sank him in the Lowlands, Lowlands, Lowlands,
And they sank him in the Lowlands low.

*Refers to the enemy.

HAUL AWAY, JOE!

Sung by Captain Charlton L. Smith, master mariner and yacht master since 1889, who remembers the chantey as it was sung in deepwater ships, aboard which he sailed as "chips," or ship's carpenter. During his last eight years at sea he served as officer.

This is a short-drag chantey and was used exclusively for tightening the sheet. The last word "Joe," was the moment for all hands to haul together.

Additional verses were added by the chanteyman until the duty was done to the mate's satisfaction. This chantey is thought to have appeared on Yankee ships sometime between 1812 and the Civil War, although it was known much earlier among British sailors.

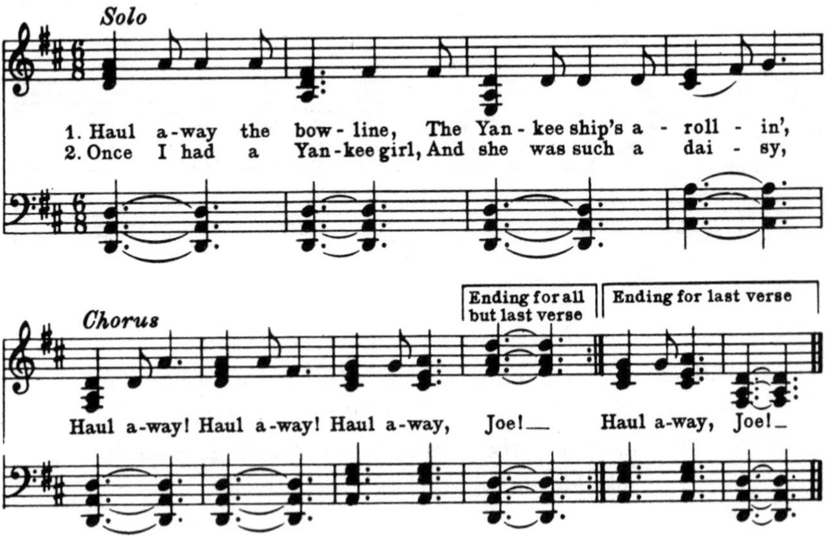

3

Once I had a Scotch girl,
And she was fat and lazy,
Haul away! Haul away!
Haul away, Joe!

4

Then I had an English girl,
And she was tall and crazy,
Haul away! Haul away!
Haul away, Joe!

HAUL THE BOWLINE

Sung by Captain Charlton L. Smith of Marblehead, Massachusetts, who remembers it from his many years in sailing and steam ships.

This is one of the oldest chanteys known and is said to have been a favorite in the time of Henry VIII.

The bowline is a small rope on the leech of a squaresail for steadying it. It was a different rope but an important one in the rigging of the sailing ships of the fifteenth century. This chantey, once used for the bowline, passed into use for such work as hauling aft the fore and main sheet and sweating up halyards. As the chanteyman sings the verse, all hands prepare for the final word, "HAUL!" At this signal all give a tremendous heave till the sail is sheeted home.

From the pages of records one finds that the naming of ships has been a matter of following the fashion of the moment, which might be to placate or ingratiate the spirits of the deep, to inspire a favorable voyage, commemorate valiant deeds, or honor the hero of the hour.

In this chantey is mentioned the packet ship, *Daniel Webster*, built by Donald McKay at his shipyard at East Boston, Massachusetts, for Train's Liverpool Line, and launched in 1850.

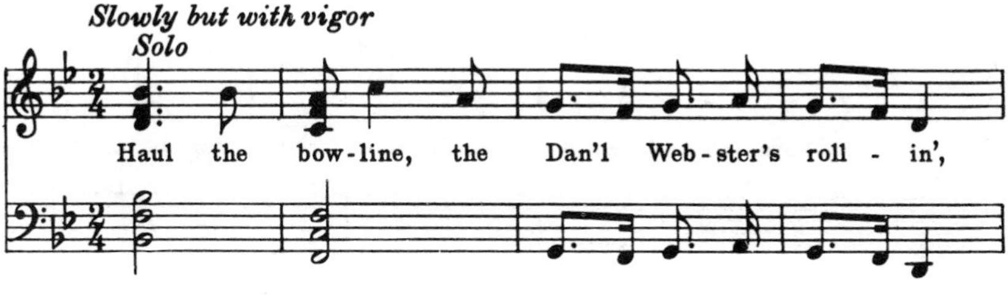

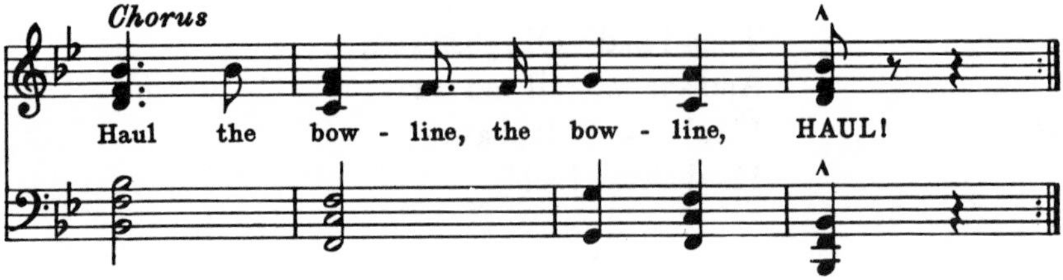

HOMEWARD BOUND

The old capstan chantey of which this is a fragment was a favorite in sailing days and was sung the world over. As Captain Charlton L. Smith of Marblehead, Massachusetts, recalls it, the name of the home port never varied. He recalls that the chanteymen on the ships he sailed in would always sing of Liverpool.

In the latter part of the nineteenth century and the early twentieth, when great numbers of tramp steamers were found all over the seas, the old square-rigger sometimes had to remain in port months for cargo. She could not clear the port for home till the seasonable harvest was reaped or conditions favored a profitable voyage.

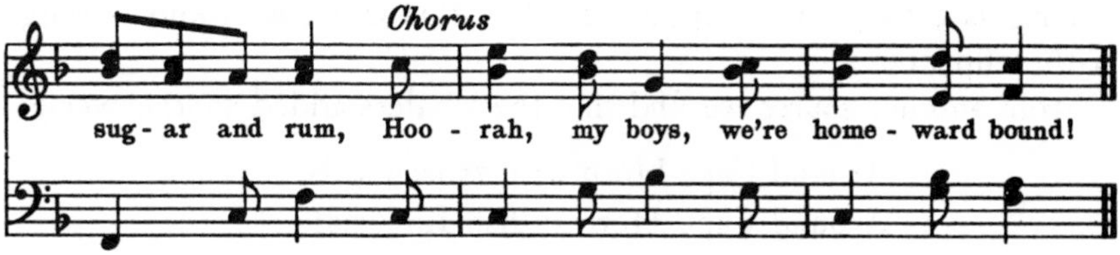

JOHNNY BOKER

James M. Linscott of Marblehead, Massachusetts, heard the sailors of the steamships *West Imboden* and *Capillo* sing this short-drag chantey, which is one of the oldest ones known. Probably of American origin, it was used for sheeting home, boarding the main tack, or sweating up a taut rope. At these tasks of reefing or furling sail, or for that one last heave on the taut sheet, the men sway back and forth till the chanteyman reaches the final "do"; then all hands roar, "Do!" and fall back together on the rope with all their might.

A LONG TIME AGO

Sung by Captain Charlton L. Smith, yacht master and master mariner of Marblehead, Massachusetts, who went to sea when he was fifteen years old and recalls this chantey from his years in deep-water sailing ships.

Sung as a halyard or capstan chantey, this was a well-known song on the clippers.

From another source we find that the whalers added another verse:

Around Cape Horn with frozen sails,
Around Cape Horn to fish for whales.

OLD HORSE

While serving in the United States merchant marine James M. Linscott of Marblehead, Massachusetts, heard the sailors sing this rhyme, known as "the sailor's grace." It probably comes from the Maine sailors. "Saccarap" is Saccarappa, now Westbrook, Maine. Formerly an important industry of the section was the cutting of paving-blocks, which were hauled by horses to Portland for shipment by vessel.

In the days of sailing ships, food for the sailor was both scant in quantity and poor in quality. Salt beef and salt fish alternately were chosen for the pièce de résistance. Kept in brine barrels, this food was neither savory nor palatable. A particularly bad piece of beef was apt to start this derisive ditty.

Occasions arise today when the crew roar these words at some especially unpalatable rations handed out by a steward too anxious to pocket personal gain at the expense of the crew.

The tune seems to be an offshoot of "Mulb'ry Bush."

REUBEN RENZO

Captain Charlton L. Smith of Marblehead, Massachusetts, recalls this chantey from his many years at sea in the sailing ships of the mahogany trade. These ships went out of Liverpool to South America, in the middle of the nineteenth century.

It is a halyard chantey that was popular about fifty years ago and is thought originally to have been one of the songs of the whaling fleet. Whether the name of the hero is a corruption of the Portuguese "Lorenzo" is not definitely established, though it is generally known that the Yankee whalers carried a large number of "Portygee" sailors on their long and dangerous but profitable voyages.

It is probable too that Lorenzo may be a mythical hero, for his rise to the captaincy gave chance for sly digs at officers. No amount of book learning was ever known to make a sailor.

The "limejuice whaler" refers to the custom of rationing lime juice to prevent scurvy on the whaling ships that were so long out of port.

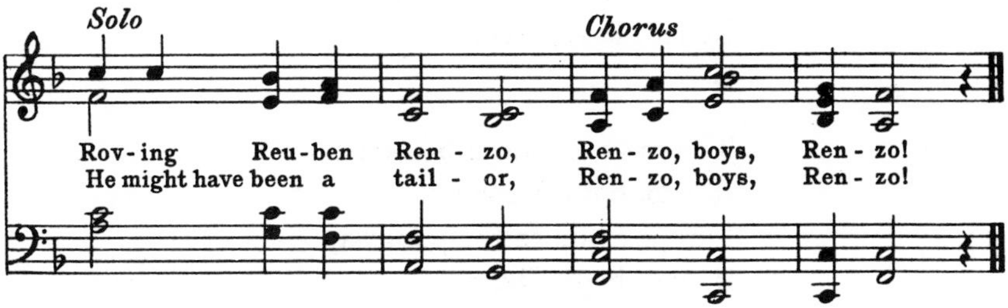

3

Renzo took a notion,
Renzo, boys, Renzo,
That he would plough the ocean,
Renzo, boys, Renzo!

4

So he sold his plough and harrow,
Renzo, boys, Renzo,
And likewise sold his barrow,
Renzo, boys, Renzo!

5

And Renzo had a pony,
Renzo, boys, Renzo,
And sold him to a loidy,
Renzo, boys, Renzo!

6

He went to London city,
Renzo, boys, Renzo,
Where the barmaids are so pretty
Renzo, boys, Renzo!

7

He joined a limejuice whaler,
Renzo, boys, Renzo,

And tried to be a sailor,
Renzo, boys, Renzo!

8

The mate he was a bad man,
Renzo, boys, Renzo;
He took him to the gangway,
Renzo, boys, Renzo!

9

He gave him five and twenty,*
Renzo, boys, Renzo;
And that was a plenty!
Renzo, boys, Renzo!

10

But the skipper he was a fine old man,
Renzo, boys, Renzo;
He took him to his cabin,
Renzo, boys, Renzo!

11

And taught him navigation,
Renzo, boys, Renzo;
And now he ploughs the ocean,
Renzo, boys, Renzo!

RIO GRANDE

Captain Charlton L. Smith of Marblehead, Massachusetts, recalls this chantey as part of "the sailorizing learned on merchant ships."

This is a fragment of a windlass or capstan chantey and dates from the time of the Mexican War, when Yankee ships sailed every sea, many of them gambling with the adventure of carrying contraband.

* Refers to the number of lashes of the cat-o'-nine-tails, an instrument commonly used for punishing the refractory.

Captain Smith has sung this chantey at the dogwatch dinners of the Boston Yacht Club. According to Stanton King, the dogwatch is so called because it was shortened or "cur-tailed" so that sailors would stand different watches on successive days. Watches aboard ship were divided into four-hour periods, and the watch from four to eight P.M. was halved. It was customary at sea for the captain to take the starboard, and the mate the port watch. Each man with the exception of the cook stood watch.

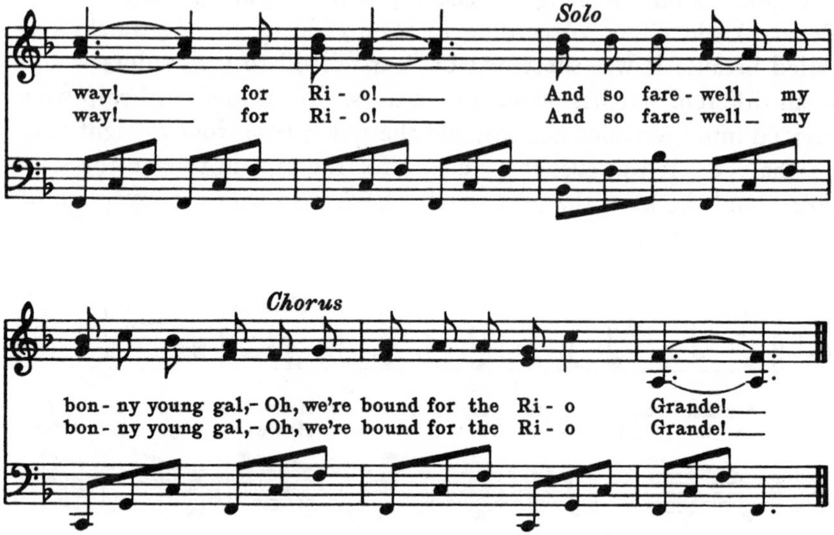

SHENANDOAH
or
THE WIDE MISSOURI

On voyages of the steamships *Capillo, West Imboden,* and *Magmeric* of the United States merchant marine, James M. Linscott of Marblehead, Massachusetts, heard this chantey sung.

The exact origin of this capstan chantey is still questioned among authorities on sea songs. Captain Whall states that it was probably derived from a song of the American or Canadian boatmen who plied the rivers and canals along the chief trade routes. His version, from which the one shown here has very evidently come, connects Shenandoah, the famous Indian chief, with the theme of the chantey.

Possibly it came from the time when the Yankee ships sailed out of New England to the Gulf ports.

Certainly it is agreed that "Shenandoah" is of American origin. There are many versions of this slow, melodious chantey, and all of them are most pleasing in verse and tune. The chantey was used for weighing anchor and was sung to no set time. This version is but a fragment.

Oh, Shenandoah! I'll take your daughter,
Away my rolling river goes.
Oh! far across the wide blue water,

Where my rolling river flows.
Oh, we're bound away, away for the wide Missouri.

TOMMY'S GONE TO HILO

Sung by James M. Linscott of Marblehead, Massachusetts, who recalls hearing it sung by the older sailors in the steamship *Capillo* of the American Republic Line, carrying cargo from Pacific ports to the eastern coast of South America.

This is a fragment of a halyard chantey the origin of which is doubtful. It seems probable that the Hilo named is the Peruvian port where nitrates were loaded.

Other versions of this halyard chantey, found in standard collections of sailors' songs, contain more verses than are given here. Names of different ports around the world were used as suited the fancy of the singer and nearly every final stanza mourned the loss of Tommy. This version, however, is the one sung today in the United States merchant marine, not as a song of labor, but as one for entertainment.

WHISKY JOHNNIE

From his thirty years at sea in square-riggers and steam Captain Charlton L. Smith of Marblehead, Massachusetts, recalls this chantey. It is one of the oldest chanteys and probably came originally from English ships.

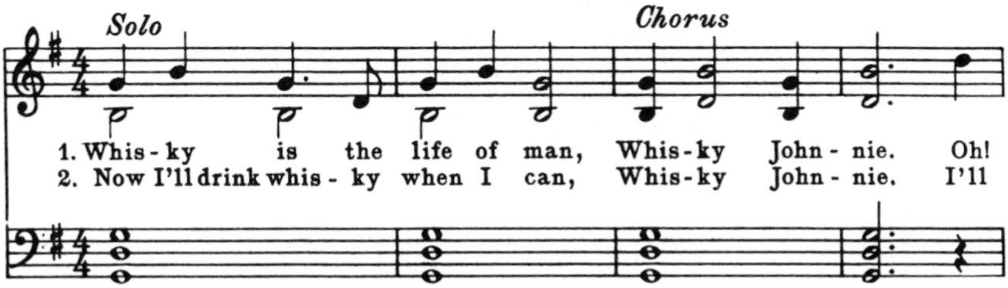

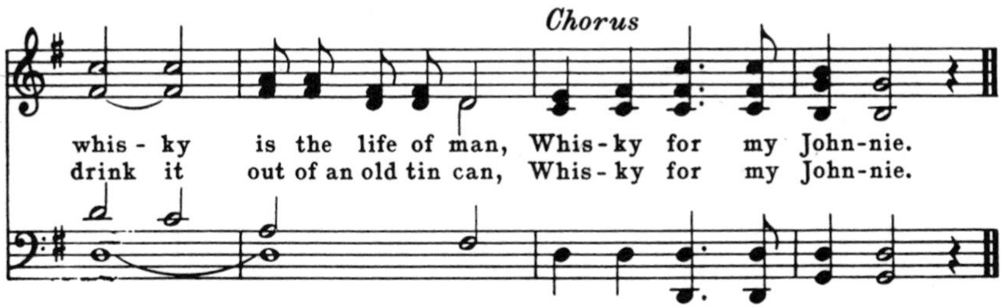

3

Whisky gave me a broken nose,
Whisky Johnnie.
Whisky made me pawn my clothes,
Whisky for my Johnnie.

4

Whisky drove me around Cape Horn,
Whisky Johnnie,
It was many a month when I was gone,
Whisky for my Johnnie.

5

I thought I heard the old man say,
Whisky Johnnie,
"I'll treat my crew in a decent way,"
Whisky for my Johnnie.

6

A glass of grog for every man,
Whisky Johnnie,
And a bottleful for the chanteyman,
Whisky for my Johnnie.

BALLADS, FOLK SONGS, AND DITTIES

From generation to generation the descendants of the New England colonists have handed down for three hundred years much of the music that was an outlet of emotion for the first settlers.

In the family circle, at neighborhood gatherings, or whenever occasion arose, the ballads and songs with which they already were familiar were sung. So much was at hand to be done that—with no time nor inclination for using native material, though it may have been there—it was almost a hundred years before the first native American ballad appeared in print.

The ballad itself was probably first sung as an accompaniment for a dance, but today the ballad is known as a song that tells a story, with a simple rhythmic melody to set the tonal background for the narrative.

In the notes that follow, the phrases "broadside ballad" and "black-letter broadside" are used. The broadside ballad was printed in plain type, and the black-letter broadside was printed in Gothic or Old English type. Both were printed on one side of the paper only. These ballads usually appeared upon small sheets not so very different in appearance from the handbills found today on every householder's doorstep. The melody was not usually printed.

The folk song is generally accepted as a song of undetermined authorship, although some scholars feel that oral transition may create changes in songs of determined origin, thus giving them a folk interpretation. The folk song and the ballad as a part of the manner of living of a people picture the customs and manners of the times. Such folk music has been preserved in the structure of living of the intelligent and educated groups.

The little ditties are those songs (probably of extemporaneous composition) of such nonsense as would catch the passing fancy with a tuneful inclination.

The folk song and folk ballad cannot be set to rule. This music is free and unconfined, and the personality of the singer influences the melody, which he bends to the words. Words and tune must not get in the way of each other, and the singer may not always sing alike the same lines of a song with several verses, as in "Peter Emily."

In some of the ballads is found the quarter-tone value, which though not uncommon in ballad singing is extremely rare except in folk music. One authority has briefly stated that he who sings these songs "must keep the melody clearly in mind, juggling the words to fit the music."

To one particular place, the nursery, the oldest songs found their way, and there they remained unspoiled much longer than if they had been exposed to the changing conditions of the outside world. Though the gruesome subjects seem more appropriate for an adult audience in a state quite thoroughly awake, many of these ballads were sung as lullabies. It was commonly believed that the monotony of the tune would be soporific and the children wouldn't understand the words anyway. And youngsters were much more fascinated by a bloody subject than one of tender sentiment. What a field for the modern psychologist!

It is important in recording this music of old New England to realize that British ballads cannot always be separated from the songs indigenous to New England, for the Yankee versions of British songs took on the flavor of life for three hundred years in the New England settlements. It has been said that the "stamping ground of American balladry is in the state of Maine." Here, richly preserved, is the music of the deep woods, the sea, and the home.

With very few exceptions these songs are traditional in the families that came from the British Isles to settle in New England. Many are known in other parts of the United States, but the New England versions have persisted so strongly that today the children of the old families are learning the tunes and verses that have come down through three hundred years and across three thousand miles of sea.

It must be observed that certain songs and the desire and ability to sing them run in strains through a family. Abiah Ashley, great-great-grandmother of the present generation, so tradition tells, was a "singer with a lovely voice"; so the old songs were bound to be carried on by at least one child in her family of twelve, though in this particular instance all the youngsters could sing their mother's songs.

The ballad singer may have a little better voice than those of the assembled company, but there are always those happy souls who sing with what voice they possess. And that is the essence of folk music—created, sung, and passed along by the ordinary person with the ordinary voice and always with the rich flavor of the singer's personality.

These are the songs of the Yankee settlers—sung and recorded for you by their descendants in old New England.

ALL BOUND 'ROUND WITH A WOOLEN STRING

With a concertina accompaniment, Dr. Frank Allen Hubbard of Taunton, Massachusetts, used to sing this song to his children. They remember it as one of their father's favorites of the concert that frequently ended the Sunday evening Bible stories.

Very little is known about the origin of the text, although the words seemed to be related to the swing waltz, "All Around My Hat," which was a Ferry dance tune. The air of this ditty is evidently derived from "Old Rose Tree," an Irish air.

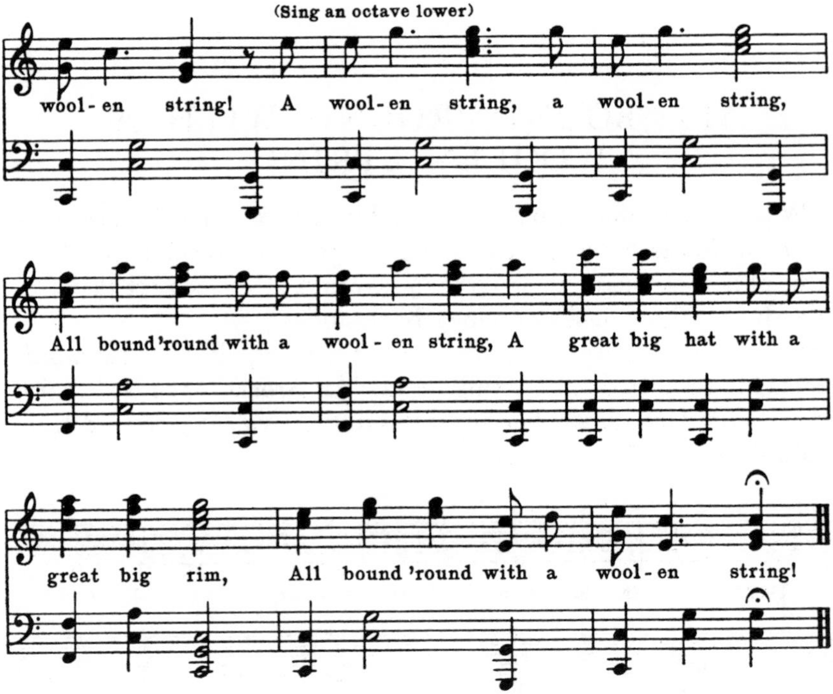

AWAY DOWN EAST

Mrs. Jennie Hardy Linscott remembers hearing her mother and her grandmother sing this song, which has been handed down in the family for many years. It was a favorite of the Hutchinsons, a singing family that traveled through New England, giving local concerts, but the melody and words recorded here are those known to our singer through oral tradition.

"The pyramid of slabs" refers to the monstrous piles of waste boards near the sawmills which, with the advent of steam, replaced water as power for the vast lumber operations.

In this song, too, one gets a picture of the dress of the early nineteenth century. "Drabs" was the colloquial word for the clothes, made of yellowish brown homespun, that were worn in that period.

1. There's a fa-mous fa-bled coun-try nev-er seen by mor-tal eyes,
2. It is called a land of no-tions, of ___ ap-ple sauce and greens,
Where the pun-kins are a-grow-in', and the sun is said to rise,
A ___ par-a-dise of pun-kin pies, a land of pork and beans.
Which man doth not in-hab-it, Nei-ther rep-tile, bird, nor beast.
But where it is who know-eth? Nei-ther mor-tal, man, nor beast.
But _ one thing we're as-sured of, it's A - WAY DOWN EAST!
But _ one thing we're as-sured of, it's A - WAY DOWN EAST!

3

Once a man in Indiana took his bundle in his hand,
And he went to New York City for to find this famous land.
But how he stares on learning this curious fact at least:
He'd nowhere near begun to get AWAY DOWN EAST!

4

So he traveled on to Bangor, whereby he soiled his drabs,
And the first that greets his vision is a pyramid of slabs.
Oh, sure this must be Egypt, 'tis a pyramid, at least.
And he thought that with a vengeance, he had found DOWN EAST.

THE BAILIFF'S DAUGHTER OF ISLINGTON

Sung by Mrs. Asenath Buckley Slade of Fall River, Massachusetts, who learned it from her aunt, a descendant of Mary Ann (Buckley) Tetlow, who emigrated from Heywood, England, in 1842, to Providence, Rhode Island.

The earliest text of this ballad was printed before 1695, and an air to it, unlike ours, was sung in a ballad opera, "The Jovial Crew," in 1731. The air given here is of later date; it was printed in 1850 by E. F. Rimbault, in music illustration to Bishop Percy's *Reliques of Ancient English Poetry*. The ballad is believed to have come from the north of England but several versions of the song found in Ulster are thought to be older. One theory of the origin of the ballad is that men quartered in English garrisons in Ireland brought the song back to Devonshire. It seems likely, however, that its root was in England and that other versions in Great Britain sprang from this source.

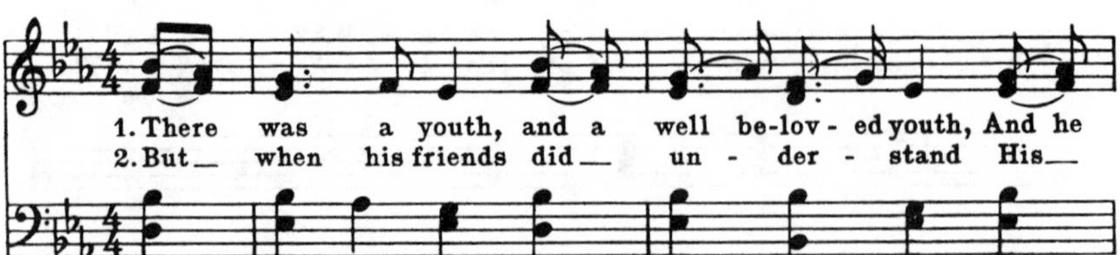

was a squire's son He loved the bai - liff's
fond and fool - ish mind, They sent him up to fair
daugh - ter, dear, That lived in Is - ling - ton.
Lon - don town, An ap - pren - tice for to bind.
Yet she was coy and would not be-lieve That
And when he had been seven long years a - grow - ing, and
he did love her so; No, nor at an - y
nev - er his love could see. Man-y a tear have I shed for
time would she An - y coun - te-nance to him show.
her sake, When she lit - tle thought of me.

3

Then all the maids of Islington
Went forth to sport and play,
All but the Bailiff's daughter dear.
She secretly stole away,
And as she went along the highroad,
The weather being hot and dry,
She sat down upon a green bank,
And her true love came riding by.

4

She started up with a color so red,
Catching hold of his bridle rein,
"One penny, one penny, kind sir," she said,
"Will ease me of much pain."
"Before I give you a penny, sweetheart,
Pray tell me where you were born?"
"At Islington, kind sir," she said,
"Where I have had many a scorn."

5

"I prithee, sweetheart, tell to me,
Oh, tell me whether you know
The Bailiff's daughter of Islington?"
"She is dead, sir, long ago."
"If she be dead, then take my horse,
My saddle and bridle also,
For I will to some far country,
Where no man shall me know."

6

"Oh, stay, oh, stay, thou goodly youth,
She standeth by thy side.
She is here alive, she is not dead,
And ready to be thy bride."

"Oh, farewell, grief, and welcome, joy,
Ten thousand times therefore,
For now I have found mine own true love,
Whom I thought I should never see more."

BARB'RY ELLEN
or
BARBARA ALLEN

Sung by Mary Elwood Harmon of Cambridge, Massachusetts, who remembers it from her father's singing. He was a descendant of Ralph Ellwood (Ellingwood), who came from England on the ship *Truelove* in September, 1635, to Salem. This text and tune are traditional in the singer's family.

The original background of this ballad is Scottish. Pepys in his *Diary*, January 2, 1666, tells of hearing his friend, Mrs. Mary Knipp, the actress, sing her "little Scotch song of Barbary Allen." "Barb'ry" or "Barbary" is a corruption of Barbara. The Scottish text was first printed by Allan Ramsay in 1740 and reprinted by Francis J. Child. In 1765 Oliver Goldsmith heard the ballad sung in the Irish midlands. Versions derived from Scotland, Ireland, and England are widely current in the United States. The song as given here is an especially simple and primitive version.

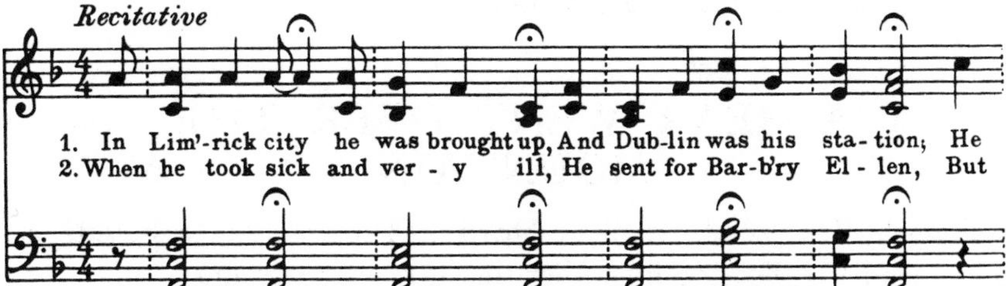

3

"Dying. Oh, no! That ne'er can be—
One kiss from you would cure me."
"One kiss from me you ne'er shall get
If your very heart was breaking!"

4

He died and was buried in the churchyard near,
And she was buried in the choir.
And out of his grave grew a red, red rose,
And out of hers grew a brier.

5

They grew and grew to the steeple top—
They could not grow any higher.
And then they twined in a truelove's knot
The red rose and the brier.

A BEAR WENT OVER THE MOUNTAIN

Sung by Dr. Frank Allen Hubbard of Taunton, Massachusetts, as he remembered hearing his father sing it many years ago.

This comical nonsense has been sung for generations, with varying words. The tune is one of the oldest melodies known and is said to have been sung by the Crusaders under Godefroy de Bouillon during the latter part of the eleventh century. It is familiar as a march and dance tune, and is one of the most widely sung.

3 and 4. Same as verses 1 and 2.

BILLY BOY

Mrs. Elizabeth Wheeler Hubbard of Taunton, Massachusetts, heard this from her father, Dr. Edward Reed Wheeler of Spencer, Massachusetts, and later sang it to her own children as a nursery song.

No other song has been more popular throughout the years than "Billy Boy." Many variants are found all over Great Britain, and from these diversified sources the American settlers brought several forms of the same ballad to New England. It is suggestive of the ancient ballad "Lord Randall"; but it is doubtful if it is derived from "Lord Randall," which will be found elsewhere in this collection in the New England version "Dirante, My Son." The question-and-answer type of text is common to both songs.

3

Did she set for you a chair, Billy Boy, Billy Boy,
Did she set for you a chair, charming Billy?
She did set for me a chair,
She had ringlets in her hair,
She's a young thing and cannot leave her mother.

4

Can she make a cherry pie, Billy Boy, Billy Boy,
Can she make a cherry pie, charming Billy?
She can make a cherry pie,
Quick's a cat can wink her eye,
She's a young thing and cannot leave her mother.

5

Can she make a feather bed, Billy Boy, Billy Boy,
Can she make a feather bed, charming Billy?
She can make a feather bed,
Put the pillows at the head,
She's a young thing and cannot leave her mother.

6

How old is she, Billy Boy, Billy Boy,
How old is she, charming Billy?
Three times six, four times seven,
Twice twenty and eleven,
She's a young thing and cannot leave her mother.

BINGO

Contributed by Miss Lucy Allen of West Newton, Massachusetts, who remembers the song as it was sung at the family gatherings, which until recently have been held in the same Allen homestead in Medfield, Massachusetts, for three hundred years. This song was one of the favorites of the small children, among whom was our singer, a descendant of James Allen.

The song has a Scotch background and was first published in 1780. There is a difference of opinion as to the derivation of the word "Bingo." One theory is that "Bingo" is derived from "Bango" which is the term found in the Sussex harvest-supper song, and is thought to have come from "ban-dog" as the mastiff watchdogs were called. In this instance it probably is the shortened form of banning-dog—meaning a dog that keeps away or guards. Thomas Moore and Shakespeare refer to "banning-dog." The second theory is that "ban-dog" is a contraction of band-dog—a chained or bound mastiff watchdog. The ancient story of this song was one concerning the miller's dog, but as "Bingo" the Allens have cherished and sung it.

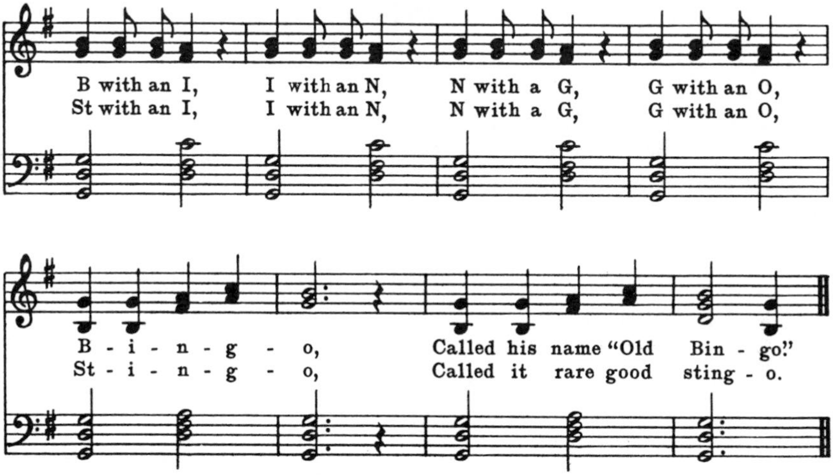

3

Now don't you think this a pretty song?
Yes, I do, by Gingo! G-i-n-g-o,
Yes, I do, by Gingo! G with an I,
I with an N, N with a G, G with an O,
G-i-n-g-o-. Yes, I do, by Gingo!

BLOW, YE WINDS, BLOW
or
THE ELFIN KNIGHT

Sung by Lucy Allen of West Newton, Massachusetts, who remembers as a child hearing it from her uncle, Joseph Allen, in the 1870's. At the words of the refrain, "Blow, Ye Winds, Blow," her uncle would blow a mighty puff through his bushy white beard. The song has been a favorite in this singing family for many generations.

The oldest form of the ballad, known as "The Elfin Knight," was printed as a black-letter broadside in 1670 and makes the suitor a supernatural being. The action turns on a person's skill in solving riddles or performing impossible tasks. It is thought that this was once a dancing song.

An interesting contribution from Miss Mary Burt, of the *Boston Evening Transcript*, recalls a portion from *Dr. Le Baron and His Daughters*, by Jane Austin, as follows:

"Captain Simeon Samson, of Plymouth, a descendant of Myles Standish and brave defender of the colonies during the Revolution, has just received, by the new post rider service in Plymouth, a letter from a young kinswoman, ardent to take a man's part in the country's struggle for freedom. He takes the letter home to his energetic wife, Deborah, whom he finds spinning and singing a version of this ballad. At the end of this song, Samson applauds the song and asks his wife, 'Where did you learn that ballad?' To which Dame Deborah replies, 'Learn it. Sim? Why, I always knew it.' "

3 (*He*)

You must dry it on yonder thorn,
Blow, blow, blow, ye winds, blow,
Where the sun never yet shone on,
Blow, ye winds that arise, blow.

4 (*She*)

My father's got an acre of land,
Blow, blow, blow, ye winds, blow,
You must dig it with a goose quill,
Blow, ye winds that arise, blow.

5 (*She*)

You must sow it with one seed,
Blow, blow, blow, ye winds, blow,
You must reap it with your thumbnail,
Blow, ye winds that arise, blow.

6 (*She*)

You must thrash it on yonder sea,
Blow, blow, blow, ye winds, blow,
And not get it wet or let a kernel be,
Blow, ye winds that arise, blow.

7 (*She*)

You must grind it on yonder hill,
Blow, blow, blow, ye winds, blow,
Where there yet has ne'er stood a mill,
Blow, ye winds that arise, blow.

8 (*She*)

When you're done and finished your work,
Blow, blow, blow, ye winds, blow,
Bring it unto me and you shall have your shirt,
Blow, ye winds that arise, blow.

BOLD DICKIE

Sung by the Misses Mary P. and Serena J. Frye of Brookline, Massachusetts. They spent several summers when they were little girls at Plymouth, Massachusetts, and recall this song as sung by one of the Watson family of Clark's Island off Cape Cod.

Where or how this story of a pirate originated is not known, but all accounts of it create a very old background. It is known that the song was *not* sung by women. The text and tune are traditional.

3

"Oh, no, oh, no, Bold Dickie," said he.
"No, no, no, that never could be;
For forty men is full little enough
And I for to ride in their companie."

4

"Ten to hold the horses in,
Ten to guard the city about,
And ten for to stand at the prison door,
And ten to fetch poor Archer out."

5

They mounted their horses and so rode they,
Who but they so merrilie?
They rode till they came to a broad riverside
And there they alighted so manfullie.

6

They mounted their horses and so swam they,
Who but they so manfullie?
They swam till they came to the other side
And there they alighted so drippinglie.

7

They mounted their horses and so rode they,
Who but they so gallantlie?
They rode till they came to that prison door
And there they alighted so manfullie.

8

"Poor Archer, poor Archer," Bold Dickie says he.
"Oh, look you not so mournfullie,
For I've forty men in my companie
And I have come to set you free."

9

"Oh, no, no, no," poor Archer says he,
"Oh, no, oh, no, that never can be,
For I have forty weight of good Spanish iron
Betwixt my ankle and my knee."

10

Bold Dickie broke lock,
Bold Dickie broke everything he could see.
He took poor Archer under one arm
And he carried him out so manfullie.

11

They mounted their horses and so rode they,
Who but they so merrilie?
They rode till they came to that broad river,
And there they alighted so manfullie.

12

"Bold Dickie, Bold Dickie," poor Archer says he,
"Take my love home to my wife and children three,
For my horse grows lame, he cannot swim,
And here I see that I must dee."

13

They shifted horses and so swam they,
Who but they so daringlie?
They swam till they came to the other side,
And there they alighted so shiveringlie.

14

"Bold Dickie, Bold Dickie," poor Archer says he,
"Look you yonder there and see,
For the High Sheriff he is a-coming
With a hundred men in his companie."

15

"Bold Dickie, Bold Dickie," High Sheriff says he,
"You are the worst rascal that ever I see;
Go bring me back the iron you stole
And I will set the prisoner free."

16

"Oh, no, no, no," Bold Dickie says he,
"Oh, no, no, that never can be;
For the iron will do to shoe the horses
The blacksmith rides in our companie."

17

"Bold Dickie, Bold Dickie," High Sheriff says he,
"You are the worst scoundrel that I ever see."
"I thank you for nothing," Bold Dickie says he,
"And you are a big fool for following me."

THE BROOKFIELD MURDER

This song records a local New Hampshire tragedy. It was sung by Mrs. Winifred Allard Piper of Wolfeboro, New Hampshire, which adjoins Brookfield. The third verse was supplied by Dana Cate of Sanbornville, New Hampshire, who remembers hearing the song as a boy from Warren Stevens, an old man of ninety.

The crime was committed in 1847. According to the story, "Old Pike," a local character, urged Susan Hanson to sue Joseph Buzzell for heart balm when he jilted her. Buzzell was so angry that he hired the half-wit, Charles Cook, to kill his former sweetheart. While at work on the Henry Jones house in Wolfeboro, the wrath of Mr. Buzzell had cooled enough for him to be seized with a change of mind and he thereupon leaped on his horse and galloped for dear life to Miss Hanson's home in Brookfield. It was a matter of some ten miles over "the back road." He arrived too late; Miss Hanson had been done away with.

The case dragged on in the courts for five years before the law finally caught up with the murderer and his accomplice. Only a charge of arson on another case against Cook brought matters to an end. Buzzell was hanged and his accomplice, Cook, imprisoned for life.

2

She sued for damage which if he'd paid
Would have saved the time while in jail he laid.
But he with murder born in his heart
Soon caused young Susan to depart.

3

On Monday evening as we tell,
Miss Susan Hanson was known full well,

Sat at her table doing some work,
She little thought death so near did lurk.

4

The thief and murderer with gun in hand
Beside the house outside did stand.
Discharged his gun through windowpane,
And thus the promised bride was slain.

5

It was a dreadful shock to the aged mother,
The lamp was lit by the son and brother.
There lay the daughter once so fair
In death cold arms and bloodstained hair.

6

No farewell words to her friends could say,
But shot dead on the floor did lay.
So young and fair and in life's bloom,
To be hurried away so soon to the tomb.

7

Come, all young ladies, a warning take,
And shun such reptiles for Susan's sake.
For he who shot this lady gay,
Would burn your home while in bed you lay.

THE BUNNIT OF STRAW

Sung by Mrs. Mildred Miner Hadley of Fall River, Massachusetts, who remembers hearing it from her mother, Mrs. Ida R. Miner. The family were Nantucket Quakers and thought it wicked to sing; however, Mr. Clisby, who married Mrs. Miner's aunt, taught his niece the song.

The first straw bonnet braided in the United States was made by Miss Betsey Metcalf in Providence, Rhode Island, in 1798. Straw bonnets were worn long before straw hats; and although the art of plaiting straw is very ancient, it was not known in England until introduced there by James I.

The tune of this song is Irish and in the mixolydian mode, which is one of the four principal Greek arrangements of the eight tones of an octave. This melody, with the minor seventh, except in the last phrase, is very likely much older than the text.

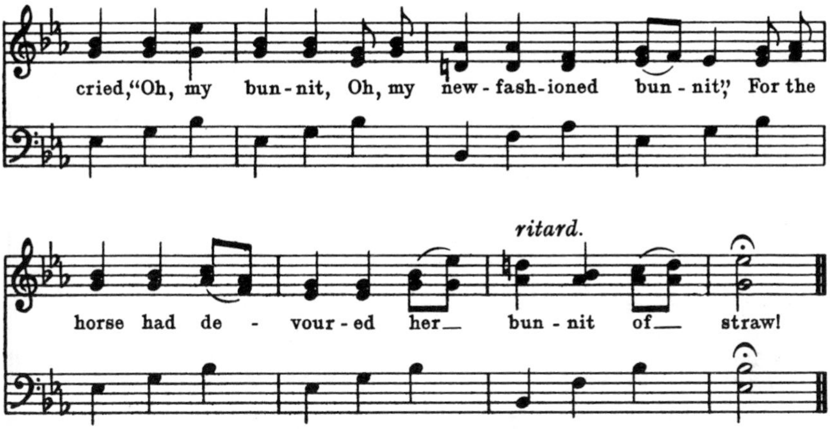

THE BUTCHER BOY

Ada F. Kelley of West Harwich, Massachusetts, learned this song from her uncle, a descendant of David O'Killy, who came from Ireland about the middle of the seventeenth century. It has been a great favorite in the Kelley family for many generations.

The song is widely current in many forms in the United States and Britain. It is said to have originated in Essex County, England. In its earlier form, it goes back to the seventeenth century, when the heartaches of milkmen and similar humble characters enjoyed more than a passing vogue. The original hero was probably a sailor instead of a butcher boy.

The song that we know as "There Is a Tavern in the Town" is derived from it, for although the melody only faintly resembles this English tune, the theme of the ballad has remained the same.

2

It's grief for me, I'll tell you why,
Because she has more gold than I.
But her gold will melt and her silver fly,
In time of need she'll be as poor as I.
I go upstairs to make my bed,
But nothing to my mother said.
My mother comes upstairs to me,
Saying, "What's the matter, my daughter dear?"

3

"O mother, mother, do you not know
What grief and pain and sorrow, woe?
Go get a chair to sit me down,
And a pen and ink to write it down."
On every line she dropped a tear,
While calling home her Willie dear,
And when her father he came home,
He said, "Where is my daughter gone?"

4

He went upstairs, the door he broke,
He found her hanging upon a rope.
He took his knife and he cut her down,
And in her breast these lines were found,
"Oh, what a silly maid am I,
To hang myself for a butcher boy!
Go dig my grave both long and deep,
Place a marble stone at my head and feet,
And on my breast a turtle dove,
To show the world I died for love."

CANADAY-I-O

Sam Young of North Anson, Maine, sang this song in Maine lumber camps fifty years ago.

It is said to have been composed by Ephraim Braley, a lumberman who lived in Hudson, Maine, near Oldtown, and was probably written about 1854. The song is based on an old English sea song—in turn derived from an older love song, "Caledonia," first printed in 1800 in the *Caledonian Garland.*

This song followed the timber west and was sung in the Lake states camps of the nineties—possibly of the eighties—and the refrain concerned "Michigan-I-O," instead of "Canaday-I-O."

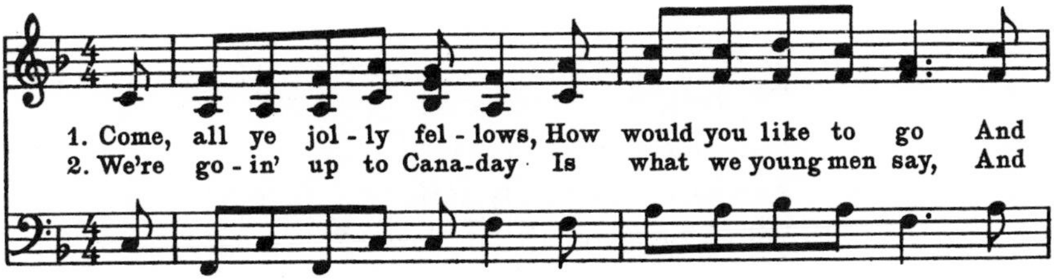

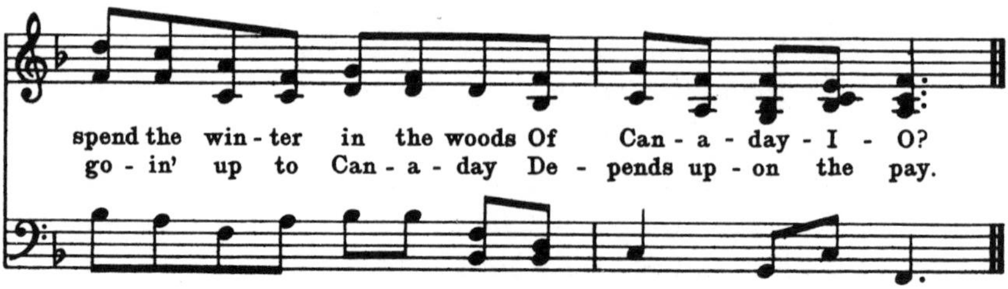

3

It's "Sure, we'll pay good wages,
We'll pay your passage out,
But you must sign the papers
That you will stay the route.

4

"But if you should get homesick
And say back home you'll go,
We will not pay your passage
From Canaday-I-O."

5

We had a pleasant journey
The route we had to go,
Then we landed in Three Rivers
In Canaday-I-O.

6

Oh, then the Norcross agent
He come a-prowlin' round
And said, "My jolly fellows,
Why don't you all lay down?"

7

Our food the dogs would bark at,
Our beds were on the snow;

We suffered worse than poison there
In Canaday-I-O.

CAROLINE OF EDINBORO TOWN

Sung by Mrs. Lucy Palmer Johnson of Somerville, Massachusetts, who remembers it from her mother's singing. The text and tune have been traditional in the Palmer family, descended from Nathaniel Palmer, who came from Wales to Scituate, Massachusetts, about 1748.

No printed records of this old Scotch ballad can be traced further than the early decades of the nineteenth century, but it is of ancient and unknown origin.

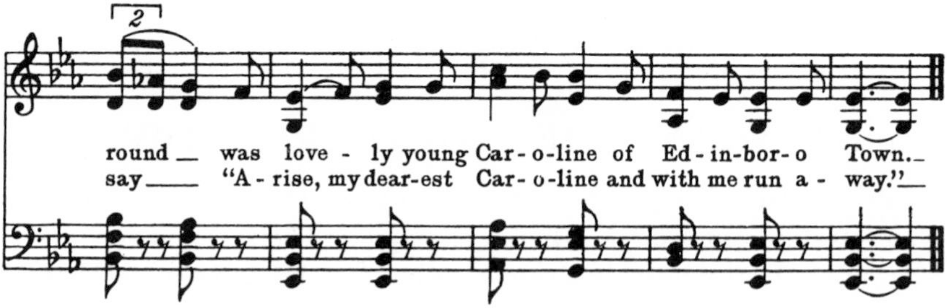

3

"We will both go to London, love, and there we'll wed with speed,
And then my lovely Caroline shall have happiness indeed."
Now persuaded by young Henry, she put on her other gown,
And away went young Caroline of Edinboro Town.

4

Over hill and lofty mountains together they did roam,
In time arrived in London, far from her happy home;
She said, "My dearest Henry, pray never on me frown,
Or you'll break the heart of Caroline of Edinboro Town."

5

They had not been in London for more than half a year
When hard-hearted Henry proved to her most severe;
Said Henry, "I will go to sea, your friends did on me frown,
So beg your way, without delay, to Edinboro Town."

6

"The fleet is fitting out, to Spithead dropping down,
And I am going to join that fleet, to fight for king and crown;
The gallant tars may feel the scars, or on the water drown,
Yet I never will return again to Edinboro Town."

7

Then many a day she passed away in sorrow and despair,
Her cheeks, though once like roses, were grown like lilies fair;

She cried, "Where is my Henry?" and often she did swound,
Crying, "Sad's the day I ran away from Edinboro Town."

8

Oppressed with grief, without relief, the damsel she did go
Into the wood, to eat such food as on the bushes grow;
Some strangers they did pity her, and some did on her frown,
And some did say, "What made you stray from Edinboro Town?"

9

Beneath a lofty spreading oak, this maid sat down to cry;
And watching of the gallant ships, as they were passing by,
She gave three shrieks for Henry, then plunged her body down,
And away floated Caroline to Edinboro Town.

10

A note, likewise her bonnet, she left upon the shore,
And in the note a lock of hair, with the words, "I am no more."
But fast asleep within the deep, the fishes watching found,
Once comely young Caroline, of Edinboro Town.

11

Come, all you tender parents, ne'er try to part true love,
You're sure to see, in some degree, the ruin it will prove;
Likewise young men and maidens, ne'er on your lovers frown,
Think of the fate of Caroline, of Edinboro Town.

THE CARRION CROW

Sung to the children of the Hubbard family by their nurse, "Nana" Howard, about 1900. This is a very popular old ballad of English origin and is supposed to have been recorded in another form about the time of Charles I. It was probably known as early as 1489.

3

The tailor shot and missed his mark,
Derry, derry, derry dekko;
And shot his old sow through the heart,
Sing heigh-o, the carrion crow,
Derry, derry, derry dekko!

4

The old sow died and the bells did toll,
Derry, derry, derry dekko;
And the little pigs prayed for the old sow's soul,
Sing heigh-o, the carrion crow,
Derry, derry, derry dekko!

COMMON BILL

Sung by Mrs. Jennie Hardy Linscott of Waldoboro, Maine, who learned it from her mother seventy-five years ago, and in whose family it was always sung.

This song comes from Leicestershire, England. It has been said to be a "woman's song," never sung by men. The air resembles that used for the ballad of the "Golden Vanity" in an ancient version.

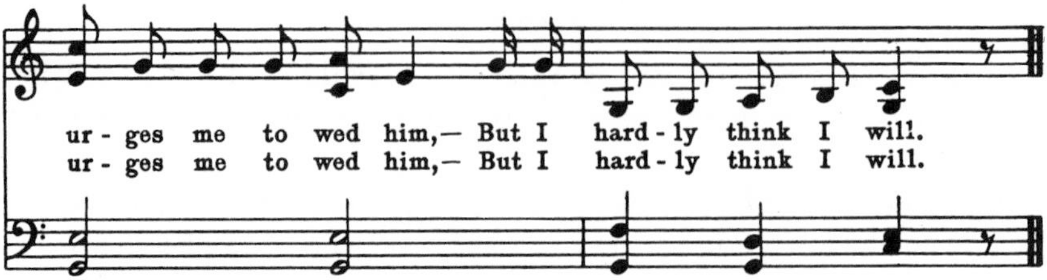

3

I should, I should not choose him,
But the very deuce is in it:
He says if I don't wed him,
He cannot live a minute;
And you know the blessed Bible
Plainly says thou shalt not kill.
So I've thought the matter over,
And I rather think I will.

THE DEVIL AND THE FARMER'S WIFE

Sung by Henry Prescott of Hyde Park, Massachusetts, who remembers hearing his father sing it. It was the traditional song in this family that was sung to bury the superfluous arrivals in the cat family and, as such, made the occasions hugely enjoyed.

The ballad is of ancient English origin, commonly sung to the air of "Lilliburlero." Very often the refrain is whistled, and as a country whistling song it is known in Sussex, England.

In this New England version, however, there was much depth of feeling that could be expressed only in the chorus.

3

"Oh, no," says the devil, "it's not your oldest son."
Fol-lol, fol-li-dee-i-lee,

"Oh, no," says the devil, "it's not your oldest son,
But that old scolding woman's the very one."
Scratch-a fol-lee,
Fol-lol, fol-li-dee-i-day.

4

The devil he got her right onto his back,
Fol-lol, fol-li-dee-i-lee,
The devil he got her right onto his back,
And down into hell he went snappety-crack,
Scratch-a fol-lee,
Fol-lol, fol-li-dee-i-day.

5

He set the young devils preparing some chains,
Fol-lol, fol-li-dee-i-lee,
He set the young devils preparing some chains,
She up with her foot and kicked out all their brains,
Scratch-a fol-lee,
Fol-lol, fol-li-dee-i-day.

6

"Oh, now," says the devil, "we'll h'ist her up higher."
Fol-lol, fol-li-dee-i-lee,
"Oh, now," says the devil, "we'll h'ist her up higher."
She up with her foot and kicked nine in the fire,
Scratch-a fol-lee,
Fol-lol, fol-li-dee-i-day.

7

The devil he got her right onto his back,
Fol-lol, fol-li-dee-i-lee,
The devil he got her right onto his back,
And back to the farmer went snappety-crack,
Scratch-a fol-lee,
Fol-lol, fol-li-dee-i-day.

8

And now it's no use for the women to tell
Fol-lol, fol-li-dee-i-lee,
And now it's no use for the women to tell,
For I know one old woman got sent back from hell,
Scratch-a fol-lee,
Fol-lol, fol-li-dee-i-day.

DIRANTE, MY SON
or
LORD RANDALL

Ada F. Kelley of West Harwich, Massachusetts, learned this song from her uncle, a descendant of David O'Killy of Ireland, who came to North Harwich about the middle of the seventeenth century.

This is a New England version of the traditional English ballad, "Lord Randall, My Son," and was sung in the Kelley family for generations as a lullaby.

The earliest text to be printed with the air, a fragment in James Johnson's *The Scots Musical Museum* (1787), was taken down by Robert Burns. Our version belongs to a tradition associated with the Soper family of London, represented in America by the descendants of Joseph Soper, who settled in Boston in 1656. The substitution of the grandmother for the false-true love of the older Scottish and English texts may have been influenced by a secondary form of the ballad known in Scotland as "Croodlin Doo."

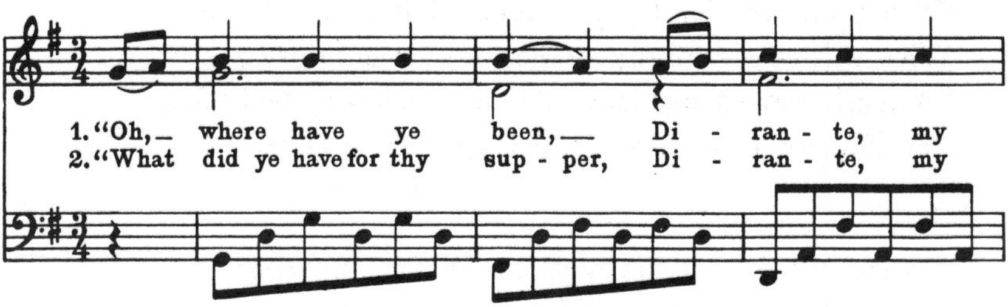

3

"What will ye give to thy mother, Dirante, my son?
What will ye give to thy mother, my sweet pretty one?"
"A coach and six maidens. Mother, make my bed soon,
For I'm sick at my heart, and I want to lie down."

4

"What will ye give to thy sister, Dirante, my son?
What will ye give to thy sister, my sweet pretty one?"

"Finger rings and fine jewels. Mother, make my bed soon,
For I'm sick at my heart, and I want to lie down."

5

"What will ye give to thy grandmother, Dirante, my son?
What will ye give to thy grandmother, my sweet pretty one?"
"A halter to hang her. Mother, make my bed soon,
For I'm sick at my heart, and I want to lie down."

6

"Where will I make thy bed, Dirante, my son?
Where will I make thy bed, my sweet pretty one?"
"In the northeast corner of the churchyard. Mother, make my
bed soon,
For I'm sick at my heart, and I want to lie down."

FAIR ROSAMOND
or
ROSAMOND'S DOWNFALL

Sung by Mrs. Edith I. Kidder and Miss Helen Irons of Assonet, Massachusetts, descendants of Abiah Ashley, in whose family the songs traditional to the Hatheway family have been preserved.

This is presumably the first time that this ballad has been recorded in this country.

It is one of the oldest of all known English ballads, dating from the twelfth century, when Henry II of England took for his mistress Rosamond Clifford. History records how his queen, Eleanor of Aquitaine, poisoned Rosamond. The story of this ballad, however, has come down as quite different in theme. The air is in the Dorian mode, one of the four principal Greek arrangements of the eight tones of the octave. It should be sung dramatically, with the rhythm of the melody dependent on the words rather than on a defined beat. In two other ballads, "Fair Rosamond," by Thomas Deloney, and "Queen Eleanor's Confession," will be found the theme of the poisoning. The only known relative of our ballad is a dull broadside entitled "Rosamond's Overthrow."

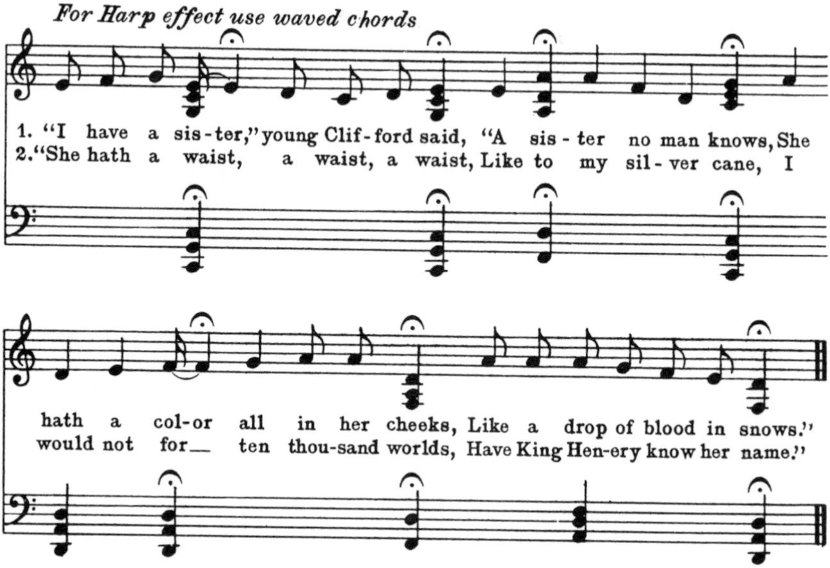

3

King Henery in his fair bower
Was hid so close and still,
That every word young Clifford said
He wrote down in a bill.

4

The first fair line she looked upon,
She did begin to smile;
The next fair line she looked upon,
The tears ran down in ile.

5

"Oh! 'cursèd be my brother Clifford,
Oh! 'cursèd may he be!

Can't he dote on his hawks and hounds?
But he must dote on me."

THE FARMINGTON CANAL SONG

Sent in by Henry A. Castle, Plainville, Connecticut.

This jovial song was entirely local to the town of Plainville, and "was sung about town during the time the canal was in use between New Haven, Connecticut, and Northampton, Massachusetts, from 1828 until 1848. It was very likely written by some forgotten local poet and was sung while Captain Dick Norton guided his boat from New Haven to Plainville during the years mentioned."

Mr. Castle says that there never was a set tune, but the words were sung noisily and not too harmoniously, with no two men on the same key. As "The Rout" was very popular about that time and is as near the meter as many folk tune and text combinations, we think the words and melody answer the purpose for the singer. "The Rout" is the English tune "Girls and Boys Come Out to Play."

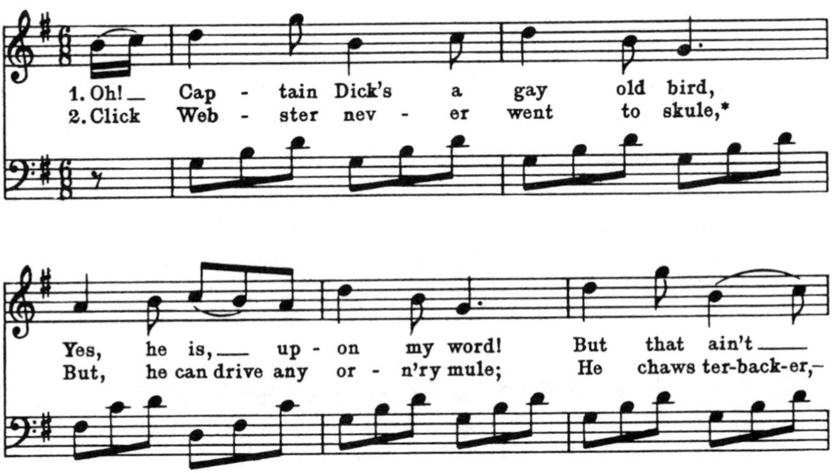

*School.

3

The boat ties up at Whitin's dock
Two, three times a week, 'bout four o'clock,
Out comes Adney and old Eb too,
Gub Homer, Bela, and the rest of the crew.

4

They pull and haul and cuss and swear,
Unload the cargo and then repair
To the store to licker up and smoke,
Tell tall stories, swap lies, and joke!

FIDDLE DEE DEE

Sung as a lullaby by Mrs. Elizabeth Wheeler Hubbard of Taunton, Massachusetts, to her children, about 1900. She learned it from her father, Dr. Edward Reed Wheeler, who knew and sang many songs traditional in the Reed family.

Ballads of this type that gave the animals human characteristics were great favorites in the sixteenth and seventeenth centuries, and they remain favorites with the children of today.

3

Fiddle dee dee, Fiddle dee dee,
The Fly has married the Bumblebee.
So when Parson Beetle had joined the pair,
They both went out to take the air.
Fiddle dee dee, Fiddle dee dee,
The Fly has married the Bumblebee.

4

Fiddle dee dee, Fiddle dee dee,
The Fly has married the Bumblebee.
And the flies did buzz and the bells did ring,
Did you ever hear so merry a thing?
Fiddle dee dee, Fiddle dee dee,
The Fly has married the Bumblebee.

5

Fiddle dee dee, Fiddle dee dee,
The Fly has married the Bumblebee.
And then to think that of all the flies,

The Bumblebee should carry the prize.
Fiddle dee dee, Fiddle dee dee,
The Fly has married the Bumblebee.

FIRST FAMILIES OF FALL RIVER

Sung by Miss Eliza M. Lindsay of Fall River, Massachusetts, who first heard it about forty years ago.

It is told in this old colonial settlement that an inebriated gentleman, feeling jovial in the wee small hours of the morning, would roar this song at the street corners, calling out with gusto the names of the first families. The phrasing and general rhythm suggest the old English ballad, "Widecombe Fair," known probably at the end of the eighteenth century.

A FROG HE WOULD A-WOOING GO

Sung by Mrs. Elizabeth Wheeler Hubbard, of Taunton, Massachusetts, who learned it as a child in Spencer, Massachusetts, from the singing of her father, Dr. Edward Reed Wheeler. With his grandchildren this song was a great favorite; for each youngster was allowed to choose one song for his particular lullaby, and this merry ballad had so many verses that it delayed the final good night by several precious minutes.

The text and tune recorded here are just as they have been handed down in the singer's family for many generations.

The tale of the "Frog He Would a-Wooing Go" has been popular for four centuries. The earliest record of the song appears in The Complaint of Scotland, a play first printed in 1549. The line "He strung his fiddle over his knee" may refer to the old bagpipes, which had a strap that had to be fastened across and around the right knee.

3

"Yes, kind Sir Frog, I sit to spin," m-m, m-m,
"Yes, kind Sir Frog, I sit to spin.
Pray, Mister Frog, won't you walk in?" M-m, m-m.

4

He said, "My dear, I've come to see," m-m, m-m,
He said, "My dear, I've come to see,
If you, Miss Mousie, will marry me." M-m, m-m.

5

"I don't know what to say to that," m-m, m-m,
"I don't know what to say to that,
Till I can see my Uncle Rat." M-m, m-m.

6

When Uncle Rat came riding home, m-m, m-m,
When Uncle Rat came riding home,
Said he, "Who's been here since I've been gone?" M-m, m-m.

7

"A fine young gentleman has been here," m-m, m-m,
"A fine young gentleman has been here,
Who wants to marry me, it is clear." M-m, m-m.

8

So Uncle Rat he rode to town, m-m, m-m,
So Uncle Rat he rode to town,
And bought his niece a wedding gown, m-m, m-m.

9

"Where shall our wedding supper be?" M-m, m-m.
"Where shall our wedding supper be?"
"Down in the trunk of some hollow tree." M-m, m-m.

10

The first to come was a Bumblebee, m-m, m-m,
The first to come was a Bumblebee,
He strung his fiddle over his knee, m-m, m-m.

11

The next to come was a Crawly Bug, m-m, m-m,
The next to come was a Crawly Bug,
He broke the bottle and smashed the jug, m-m, m-m.

12

The next to come was the Captain Flea, m-m, m-m,
The next to come was the Captain Flea,
He danced a jig with the Bumblebee, m-m, m-m.

13

The next to come was the big Black Snake, m-m, m-m,
The next to come was the big Black Snake,
And on his head was the wedding cake, m-m, m-m.

14

The Frog and Mouse they went to France, m-m, m-m,
The Frog and Mouse they went to France,
And this is the end of my romance, m-m, m-m.

A FOX WENT OUT ON A STARRY NIGHT

Sung by Mrs. Elizabeth Wheeler Hubbard of Taunton, Massachusetts, to her children as a nursery song under the name of "Old Mother Fiddle Faddle." She learned it from her father who enjoyed the family songs with many verses.

This old ballad has been traced back to 1492. The air, very popular in 1783, was introduced into John Keefe's "Poor Soldier" in the first part of the nineteenth century.

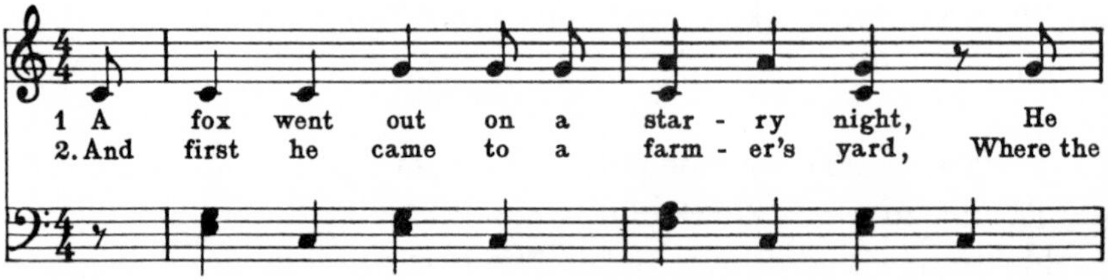

3

He took the gray goose by the sleeve,
Says he, "Madam Goose, and by your leave,
I'll take you away without reprieve,
 And carry you home to my den O!"

4

He seized the black duck by the neck,
And swung her all across his back,
The black duck cried out, "Quack! Quack! Quack!"
 With her legs hanging dangling down O!

5

Old mother Fiddle Faddle jumped out of bed,
And out of the window she popped her head.
"John, John, John, the gray goose is gone,
And the fox is off to his den O!"

6

Then John he went up to the hill,
And he blew a blast both loud and shrill,
Says the fox: "This is very pretty music. Still,
I'd rather be at my den O!"

7

At last the fox got home to his den,
To his dear little foxes, eight, nine, ten,
Says he, "You're in luck, here's a good fat duck,
With her legs hanging dangling down O!"

8

He then sat down with his hungry wife,
They did very well without fork or knife,
They never ate a better goose in all their life,
And the little ones picked the bones O!

FROG IN THE WELL

Sung by Mrs. Edith I. Kidder of Assonet, Massachusetts, who remembers it from the singing of her grandmother, Susan Hatheway, Assonet, Massachusetts.

This is another version of "The Frog He Would a-Wooing Go." The air is very old, and with the text has been handed down in the family for generations.

One melody of this ballad was printed in *An Antidote for Melancholy* in 1719.

Slowly and sadly
1. There was a frog lived in the well. Fol, lol, de, ly, de, o. There
2. Oh, Unc-le Rat when he came home, Fol, lol, de, ly, de, o. Oh,
was a frog lived in the well. Fol, lol, lay! There
Unc-le Rat when he came home, Fol, lol, lay! Oh
was a frog lived in the well, Mis - tress Mouse she kept the mill,
Unc-le Rat when he came home, Cried, "Who's been here since I've been gone?"
Kit-ty a - lone, Kit-ty a - lone, Kit-ty a - lone and I.
Kit-ty a - lone, Kit-ty a - lone, Kit-ty a - lone and I.

3

There has been here a nice young man.
Fol, lol, de, ly, de, o,
There has been here a nice young man.
Fol, lol, lay!
There has been here a nice young man,
And I shall catch him if I can,
Kitty alone, Kitty alone, Kitty alone and I.

4

Where shall the wedding breakfast be?
Fol, lol, de, ly, de, o,
Where shall the wedding breakfast be?
Fol, lol, lay!
Where shall the wedding breakfast be?
Down in yonder hollow tree,
Kitty alone, Kitty alone, Kitty alone and I.

5

First there came the little sea-tick,
Fol, lol, de, ly, de, o,
First there came the little sea-tick,
Fol, lol, lay!
First there came the little sea-tick,
Walking with his hickory stick,
Kitty alone, Kitty alone, Kitty alone and I.

6

Cat took rat and kit took mouse,
Fol, lol, de, ly, de, o,
Cat took rat and kit took mouse,
Fol, lol, lay!
Cat took rat and kit took mouse,
And away they scampered through the house,
Kitty alone, Kitty alone, Kitty alone and I.

GO TELL AUNT RHODY

The melody of this little ditty, recalled by Mrs. Jennie Hardy Linscott of Waldoboro, Maine, is a variation of the "Good Shepherd" tune. It was sung in the Hardy family as a nursery song and its nonsense suggests the consternation of the New England housewife at the loss of one of the flock that she had depended upon to provide winter comfort by contributing to the light feather mattress she intended to make.

3

He died this morning,
He died this morning,
He died this morning,
Swimming across the pond.

GYPSY DAISY

Sung by Mrs. Asenath B. Slade, Fall River, Massachusetts, who remembers it from the singing of her mother more than fifty years ago.

This ballad belongs to the English tradition, founded on the original Scottish ballad, "The Gypsy Laddie." The earliest version, printed in

1740, calls the gypsy chief Johnny Faw—an Anglicization of his Gaelic name, Seanin an Faith, "Johnny the Seer"—who according to an unfounded tradition eloped with Lady Cassilis. The origin of the tradition may be ascribed to some disgruntled minstrel who took revenge in slander and set his lampoon to the tune known as "Lady Cassilis's Lilt." Johnny Faw was said to have been recognized by James V of Scotland in 1540 as Lord and Earl of Little Egypt. The gypsies were expelled from Scotland in the following year, and again in 1609 by Parliament. Gypsy chiefs named Johnny Faw were sentenced to be hanged for contempt of this decree in 1611 and 1624.

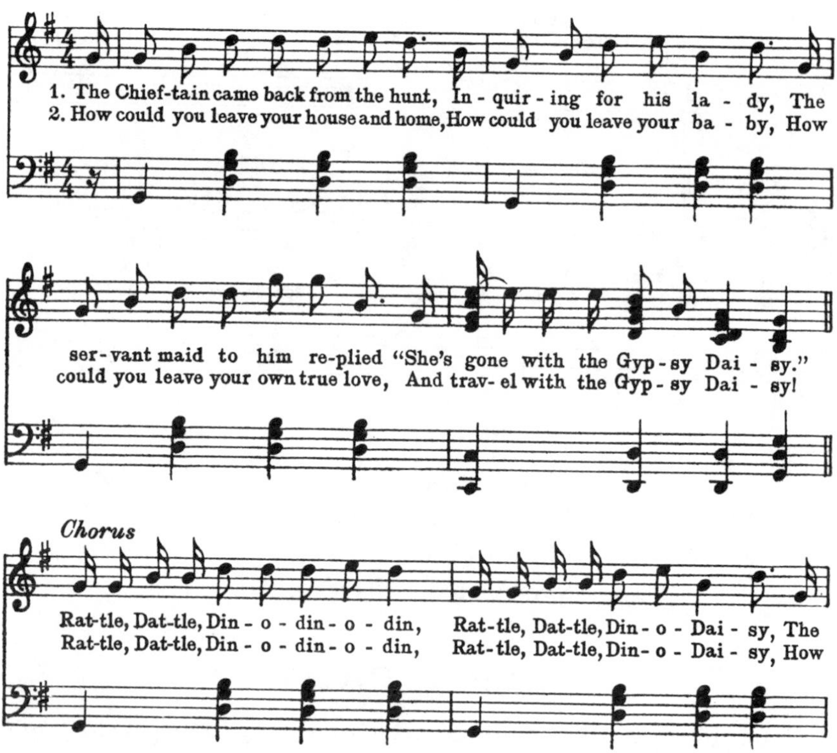

3

"I never loved you in my life,
I never loved your baby,
I married you against my will,
And I'm going with the Gypsy Daisy."

HERE WE GO UP

Sung to her children as a lullaby by Mrs. Jennie Hardy Linscott of Waldoboro, Maine, who learned it from her mother more than fifty years ago.

From County Donegal comes this Irish dance tune. There is a possibility that this tune is more nearly related to one very popular in 1641, called "Hey, Boys, Up Go We," which appeared in Thomas D'Urfey's *Pills to Purge Melancholy*. It is possible that the first stanza contains dance directions.

I HAD A LITTLE NUT TREE

Sung by Mrs. Elizabeth Wheeler Hubbard, who learned it from her father, Dr. Edward Reed Wheeler of Spencer, Massachusetts.

This old song, whose story is founded on the visit of Joanne Castile to the court of Henry VII in 1506, has always been a great favorite with children.

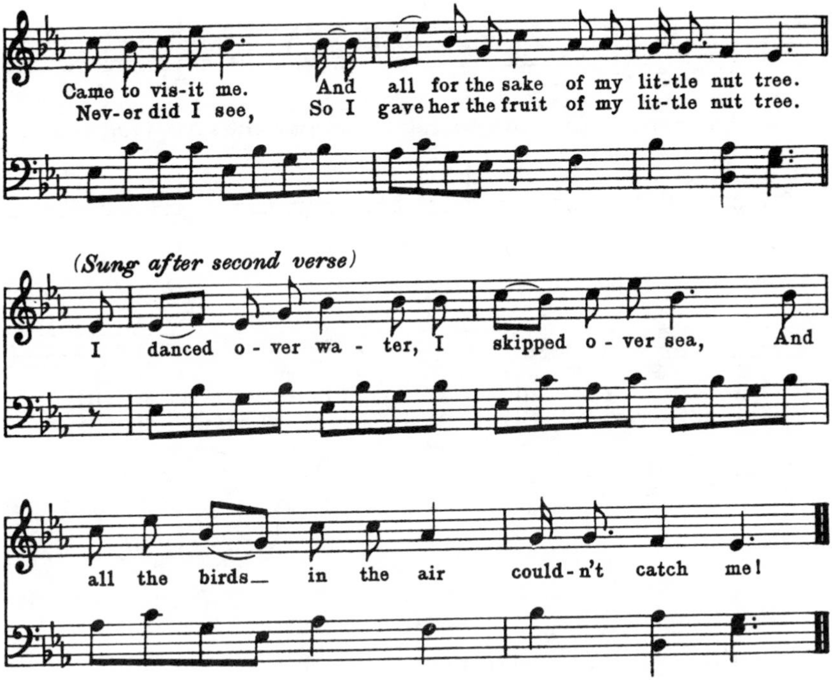

I'LL NOT MARRY AT ALL

This song, so tradition goes, was brought from Ireland by the O'Killy family, ancestors of the present Kelley family, to North Harwich, Massachusetts, and is recalled by Miss Ada F. Kelley of West Harwich, Massachusetts.

Gibes at the married state are frequent in popular tradition. Usually it is the man who complains most, as in two of the ballads in Child's collection, "The Wife Wrapped in Weather's Skin" and "The Farmer's Curst Wife." In "The Ladle Song," presented elsewhere in this chapter, "Sweet Sixteen" breaks a heavy ladle over the head of the aged and wealthy skinflint she had married, with what effect on a skull of threescore and ten the song does not say. A companion piece to the present song is supposed to be sung by the man who would not marry a thin woman since her neck would be long and she would never die.

3

I'll not marry a man that's poor,
He'll go beg from door to door.
I'll not marry at all, at all,
I'll not marry at all!

4

I'll not marry a man that's rich,
He'll get drunk and fall in the ditch.
I'll not marry at all, at all,
I'll not marry at all!

5

He loves me a little, not much, none at all,
He will marry me if he could but he can't,
This year, next year, next year, next year,
This year, next year, year after—NEVER (spoken).

IN GOOD OLD COLONY TIMES

From her grandmother and her mother, Mrs. Jennie Hardy Linscott of Waldoboro, Maine, learned this song, which is a favorite of her grandchildren today.

The three rogues in this ballad are the super-knaves of popular tradition. It took nine tailors to make a man, but one was enough to make a thief. Every schoolboy knows from *Silas Marner* that weavers were unsociable persons, believed to be on better terms with the devil than with their neighbors. As for the miller, in folk tradition he has generally been credited with every crime from petty larceny to murder. The song is of English origin, perhaps from Somersetshire, in which tradition the time given is that of King Arthur.

The Yankee, of course, has made the song fit colonial times.

3

The miller he stole corn,
The weaver he stole yarn,
The little tailor he stole broadcloth,
For to keep these three chaps warm.

4

But the miller got drowned in his pond,
And the weaver got hanged in his yarn,
And the little tailor got caught by His* claw,
With the broadcloth under his arm.

JACK HAGGERTY
or
THE FLAT RIVER GIRL

Sung by Charles Young of Moultonboro, New Hampshire, who learned this popular song of the lumberjacks while in camp. True to the traditions of the song, the singer himself did not know Haggerty but insisted that he knew some one who did. Haggerty, a river driver, was regarded as a king among men, and the story of the song is held to be true. The singer knew that Haggerty's name is chiseled on a rock along the Flat River.

The song is said to have come from Larry Gorman, and of the several known versions the one presented here is related to the older forms. It seems entirely possible that when the lumberman moved from Maine to the Middle West in the first migration, along with his peavey and his calked boots he took his songs and planted them in the new territory, where they absorbed the local place names. The Flat River is near Greenville, Maine, at the foot of Moosehead Lake; West Hegan† may be a corruption of Miss Hegan's, which was a famous rendezvous in Bangor for the blow-in of the lumberjack.

The peavey, a short pole with an adjustable hook used in driving logs, was invented in 1858 by Joseph Peavey, a blacksmith of Stillwater Village, Maine.

*The devil's.

†Pronounced Haygan.

3

My occupation—I'm a river driver
Where the white waters roar;
My name it is engraved on

The rocks on the sand' shore.
I'm a lad that stands happy
Where the white waters roll;
I'm a-thinking of Hannah,
She's a-hauntin' my soul.

4

One day on Flat River
A letter I received,
Saying, "Johnny, of all your promises,
You now are relieved;
For to be wed to another,
My heart's long delayed,
And the next time you see me
I'll not be a maid."

5

Now to her mother, Jane Tucker,
I lay all the blame,
She has turned her against me,
She's gone back on my name;
She has uncast the rigging
That God would have tied,
She has made me a wand'rer
From that day till I die.

6

Here's adieu to Flat River,
And the girl I love best,
I'll shoulder my peavey,
And I'll strike for the West;
I'll go back to West Hegan
Some pleasures to find,
And I'll leave my old sweetheart
And Flat River behind.

7

Now come, all you jolly rivermen,
With your hearts fond and true.
Don't depend on the women—
You'll get left if you do;
But if you should chance to meet
With one with dark chestnut curls,
Pray think of Jack Haggerty
And his Flat River girl.

THE JAM ON GERRY'S ROCKS

Over the origin of this wood ballad there has been great controversy; but Samuel Young of North Anson, Maine, who sang it in lumber camps for more than thirty years, has never questioned its Maine parentage. He says that Gerry's Rocks (Gerrish) are up above The Forks, Maine, and that the tragedy is marked on a rock and tree on the Kennebec River.

The "Sagmor Town" may be a corruption of "Saginaw" and this may in turn be a corruption of "Saguenay," a famous river and location of an Indian settlement. It is well known that migrations from both sides of the border were frequent, and the intermingling of dialects and colloquialisms would be sufficient for the singer to impart the distinctive flavor of his own diction. All through northern New England can be found just such corruptions of pronunciation. For example, a certain street is called "Sewiggin" Street, but the name on the signpost reads "Souhegan" and really means South Hegan.

This ballad, one of the best known of the lumberjack songs, is given here in its older form. It may be noted that the foreman is simply Munroe; and Craigin's Point, our singer says, may be some small point of land that thrusts into the river. Stewart Holbrook, author of "Holy Old Mackinaw" says that "this song and 'Little Red Bulls' appear to be the only two lumberjack ballads to reach Pacific Coast camps."

1. Come all ye jo-vial shant-y boys, Wher-ev-er you may be, I
2. 'Twas on one Sun-day morn-ing In the spring-time of the year, Our
hope you'll pay at-ten-tion And lis-ten un-to me; Con-
logs were pil-ing moun-tain high, We could not keep them clear; When our
cern-ing six brave shant-y boys With cour-age strong and brave, Who
boss, he cried: "Brave boys, turn out, Set your hearts a-void all fear— We'll
broke the jam on Gerr-y's rocks And met with a wa-t'ry grave.
break the jam on Gerr-y's rocks And for Crai-gin's Point we'll steer."

3

Now some of them were willing,
While others did hang back,
For to go to work on Sunday
They did not think it right.
When six Canadian shanty boys
Did volunteer to go,
To break the jam on Gerry's Rocks
With the foreman young Munroe.

4

Now they had not rolled off many logs
When the boss to them did say,
"I'd have you be on your guard—
This jam will soon give way."
He had no more than spoke those words
When the jam did heave and go
And carried away those six brave youths
And their foreman, young Munroe.

5

Now when their comrades at the camp
The sad news came to hear,
In search of their dead bodies
Down the river they did steer.
When to their sad misfortune,
To their sad grief and woe,
All bruised and mangled on the beach,
Lies the head of young Munroe.

6

We picked it up most carefully,
Smoothed down his raven hair.
There was one fair form among them
Whose cries would rend the air.

There was one fair form among them,
A girl from Sag'mor town,
Whose screams and cries would rend the skies,
For her true love was drowned.

7

His mother was a widow,
Nearby the riverside,
Miss Clark she was a very nice girl
And his intended bride.
The money that was due to him
The boss to her did pay,
She received a large subscription
From the shanty boys next day.

8

We buried him quite decently,
Being on the sixth of May.
Come all you jovial shanty boys,
And for your comrades pray,
For engraved upon a hemlock tree,
Which on the beach did grow,
The day, the date, and the drowning fate
Of our comrade, young Munroe.

THE JOLLY MILLER

Sung by Mrs. Jennie Hardy Linscott, Waldoboro, Maine, who learned it from her mother and grandmother nearly seventy-five years ago.

The tune of this song was introduced in "The Devil to Pay" as a cant song in 1730. In this place it sets forth the fine art of "budgeoning," which consisted of stealing into houses to rob the occupants of their clothing and apparel. When it was sung in Covent Garden, two stanzas were added. As the song is sung now, it is far removed from its original version.

JOLLY OLD ROGER

Contributed by Mrs. Harriet Moore Deming, Winsted, Connecticut, who recalls it from the singing of her mother.

Every New England housewife looked forward to the coming of the tin peddler, for with his infinite variety of household wares and his skill with the soldering iron he brought the news of the countryside. His visits were as true as the seasons—sure to appear but of indefinite date. The rattle of his cart to the farm or cottage door brought the housewife to the back porch and children too small for school tumbling from swing, haymow, and apple trees. Dangling from the tailboard, the new pans caught the morning sun and banged deliciously as old Nell plodded over the rutted roads. In the fascinating hodgepodge of his wares the peddler was sure to find some small gift for the youngster of the customer.

maid - ens and ma - trons, of him I would sing.
stumped round his shop on a stiff tim - ber toe.
Refrain
There nev - er was yet a boy or a man, Who bet - ter could mend tin
ket - tle or pan or buck - et or skim - mer or dip - per or can, Than
jol - ly old Rog - er, the tin - mak - er man. Chee - whang! Chee - whang! Chee -
whang! Chee - whang! Te - rat - tle, te - rat - tle, te - rat - tle te - BANG!

3

Jolly old Roger had two pairs of eyes,
His glasses, called "specs" were uncommon in size;
His nose, like a strawberry, racy and red,
Was a "snuffer" by day and a trumpet in bed.

4

But jolly old Roger could not live alway;
The "nippers" of death cut his life thread one day;
And down in the churchyard they tramped him in,
Poor jolly old Roger, the mender of tin.

5

If down to New Amsterdam's churchyard you go,
Be sure that you stop, it's a great place for woe;
You'll find by the tombstone the step and the mall,
Where jolly old Roger lies under the wall.

JULIA GROVER

Sung by Mrs. Jennie Hardy Linscott, who learned it as a small child in Waldoboro, Maine.

A merrier tune for a minstrel to play at a frolic would be hard to find. From such a song one learns the customs and manners of the people of the time. This "Down East" song that smacks of the earth was not considered proper for young girls to sing, but nevertheless was very popular.

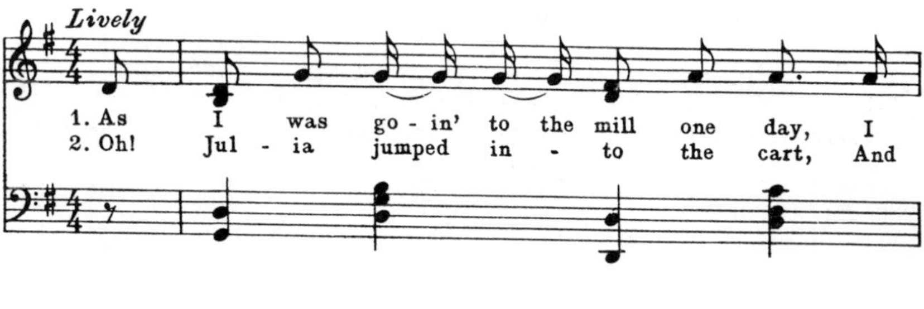

3

Julia, the chick of the old blue hen,
Flew at me like fury then,
Scratched my face and tore my hair
And that is all that made me swear. (*Chorus.*)

KATY CRUEL

Miss Lucy Allen of West Newton, Massachusetts, recalls this song from the singing of her uncle at the last gathering of the Allen family in Medfield, Massachusetts. The homestead, which once was a station of the underground railroad for fleeing negroes in the Civil War, was filled to overflowing. As evening came the youngest children were put to bed upstairs, and around the great fireplace in the wide-beamed living room the men sang the haunting song with deep emotion.

Two years ago a small parchment was found on which were the names of all those present at one of these reunions and, set apart in a small space: "Upstairs: Mary, Hannah, Alice, John, Lucy,* . . ."

Where this song came from is unknown. A second version, the only other known, is a marching song used by the American troops in the Revolutionary War.

*These are not the true names on record.

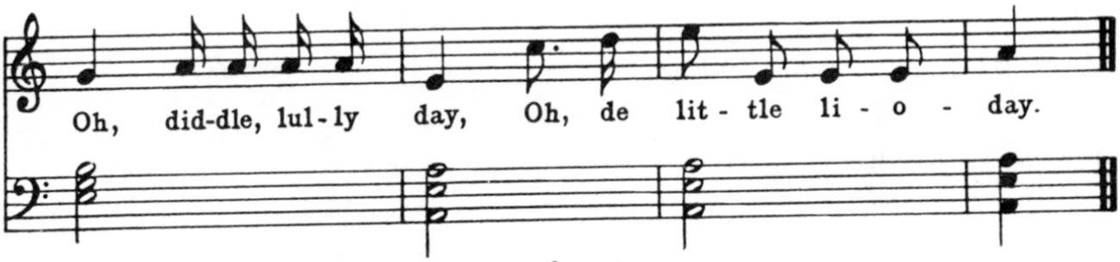

3

I know whom I love,
I know who does love me,
I know where I'll go,
And I know who'll go with me.
Oh, diddle, lully day,
Oh, de little li-o-day. (*Refrain.*)

4

Through the woods I'll go,
Through the boggy mire,
Straightway on the road,
Till I come to my heart's desire.
Oh, diddle, lully day,
Oh, de little li-o-day. (*Refrain.*)

5

Eyes as bright as coal,
Lips as red as a cherry,
And 'tis her delight,
To make the young folks merry.
Oh, diddle, lully day,
Oh, de little li-o-day. (*Refrain.*)

THE LADLE SONG

From her father, Lyman A. Smith, a fine singer of Weston, Massachusetts, Mrs. Ella May Wright learned this merry song, which suggests the horrors of marrying an old man and a satisfactory method of revenge. It is a traditional song in the Smith family, but is found with variations elsewhere and is derived from an old Irish melody.

3

Early the next morning I arose,
And after putting on my clothes,
While he lay sleeping on his bed,
Oh! I did my ladle break over his head.

4

Then he began to scold about,
I being courageous, bold and stout,
I told him such works* I never would have,
And then another blow I gave.

*Colloquial.

5

Now all young women who intend to marry,
Now mind what housing stuff you carry,
And wherever you go, or whatever you do,
Be sure and carry a ladle or two.

6

Come all young women who have cross men,
And don't know how to govern them,
'Twas with my ladle I brought him to,
And that is the way you all must do.

LAVENDER'S BLUE

Sung by Mrs. Elizabeth Wheeler Hubbard, Taunton, Massachusetts, who remembers hearing it from her aunt, Hannah L. Bishop, with whom it was a favorite.

This song, of English origin, is connected with the amusements of Twelfth Night and refers to the choosing of the king and queen of the festivities. It is significant for the place it holds in showing the diversions and customs of the early days. In New England it has lost its place as a singing game and is sung only as a tuneful ditty.

3

Some to the wheel, diddle, diddle,
Some to hoe corn,
While you and I, diddle, diddle,
Keep ourselves warm.

4

If you should die, diddle, diddle,
As it may hap,
You shall be buried, diddle, diddle,
Under the tap.

5

Who told you so, diddle, diddle,
Pray tell me why?
That you might drink, diddle, diddle,
When you are dry.

LET'S GO TO THE WOODS
or
THE HUNTING OF THE WREN

Sung by Mrs. Elizabeth Wheeler Hubbard of Taunton, Massachusetts, to her children as a nursery song.

The story is based on a very ancient fable of a contest of the birds. It was resolved that whoever could fly the highest should be king of the birds. By perching on the head of the eagle, the wren won the contest.

The Hunting of the Wren is a folk drama in commemoration of the birds' desire to kill the cheat. In Ireland, Wales, and elsewhere, it was the custom on St. Stephen's Day for mummers to catch a wren, hang it, and parade the village with the dead bird, while they sang the Wren Song. When they came to a manor house, and the lord of the estate passed out cakes and ale, he was hilariously acclaimed by the company. If, however, the visitors were driven off, they vented their wrath by working mischief and playing pranks on the householder. An interesting account of the Wren ceremony is in *The Half-Sir,* a novel of Irish country life, by Gerald Griffin.

The present generation, in similar manner, greets the householder who answers the bell on Hallowe'en with "feast or forfeit."

3

"We'll shoot us a wren," says Robbin to Bobbin,
"We'll shoot us a wren," says Bobbin to Robbin,
"We'll shoot us a wren," says John-all-alone,
"We'll shoot us a wren," says every one!

4

"How'll we get it home?" says Robbin to Bobbin,
"How'll we get it home?" says Bobbin to Robbin,
"How'll we get it home?" says John-all-alone,
"How'll we get it home?" says every one!

5

"With a cart and six horses," says Robbin to Bobbin,
"With a cart and six horses," says Bobbin to Robbin,
"With a cart and six horses," says John-all-alone,
"With a cart and six horses," says every one!

6

"Who will cook it?" says Robbin to Bobbin,
"Who will cook it?" says Bobbin to Robbin,
"Who will cook it?" says John-all-alone,
"Who will cook it?" says every one!

7

"I will cook it," says Robbin to Bobbin,
"I will cook it," says Bobbin to Robbin,
"I will cook it," says John-all-alone,
"I will cook it," says every one!

8

"Who will eat it?" says Robbin to Bobbin,
"Who will eat it?" says Bobbin to Robbin,
"Who will eat it?" says John-all-alone,
"Who will eat it?" says every one!

9

"We'll all of us eat it," says Robbin to Bobbin,
"We'll all of us eat it," says Bobbin to Robbin,
"We'll all of us eat it," says John-all-alone,
"We'll all of us eat it," says every one!

10

"What'll we do with the bones?" says Robbin to Bobbin,
"What'll we do with the bones?" says Bobbin to Robbin,
"What'll we do with the bones?" says John-all-alone,
"What'll we do with the bones?" says every one!

11

"Leave the bones for the crows," says Robbin to Bobbin,
"Leave the bones for the crows," says Bobbin to Robbin,
"Leave the bones for the crows," says John-all-alone,
"Leave the bones for the crows," says every one!

LORD LOVELL

This was one of the songs, traditional in her mother's family, that Mrs. Jennie Hardy Linscott, of Waldoboro, Maine, remembers hearing her grandmother sing.

In the county of Northumberland, England, the name of Lovell is ancient and well known. The ballad itself is connected with border history and is said to commemorate an incident concerning one of this family.

3

He had only been gone twelve months and a day,
Foreign countries for to see,
When languishing thoughts came into his head,
Lady Nancy he'd go to see,
Lady Nancy he'd go to see.

4

So he rode and he rode on his milk-white steed,
Till he came to London Town,
And there he heard St. Pancridge's* bells,
And the people a-mourning around,
And the people a-mourning around.

5

Lady Nancy she died, as it might be today,
Lord Lovell he died as tomorrow,
Lady Nancy she died, out of pure grief,
And Lord Lovell he died out of sorrow,
And Lord Lovell he died out of sorrow.

*St. Pancras.

6

Lady Nancy was laid in St. Pancridge's church,
Lord Lovell was laid in the choir,
And out of her bosom there grew a red rose,
And out of her lover's a brier-ier,
And out of her lover's a brier.

7

So they grew and they grew, to the church steeple top,
And they couldn't grow no higher,
So they twined themselves in a true lover's knot,
For all lovers true to admire-ire,
For all lovers true to admire.

THE LUMBERMAN'S ALPHABET

While Charles Young of Moultonboro, New Hampshire, was river-driving on the Penobscot River, he learned this song in the lumber camp. In that region he was guide and woodsman for over ten years.

It is said that nearly all the really good tunes and woodsmen's songs were made up by Larry Gorman, one of the most famous fighting lumberjacks of Maine. He was supposed to have come from Prince Edward Island and to have lived near the headwaters of the Penobscot. Many of the men from the provinces were attracted by the good wages paid in the New England woods and crossed and recrossed the border.

There are several variations of this song, the most popular ones unprintable; the earliest known printed version appeared in the *Maine Sportsman*, in February, 1904.

As Charles Young sang the song, the chorus was used after the first, second, third, and last stanzas only; but he remarked that in the woods he'd probably sing the chorus after every verse, to pass the time.

1. A is for Ax, as you ver - y well know;
2. E is for the Ech - oes that through the woods ring;
B is for the Boys that use them just so. C is for the Chop-ping that
F is for the fore-man, the head of the gang, G is for the Grind-stone that
soon will be - gin, And D is for the Dan-ger we al-ways stand in.
swift-ly goes round, And H is for the Han-dle so smooth and so round.
Chorus
Sing Hi, der - ry- o, so mer - ry are we, There's
no one one-half as hap - py as we. With a Hi, der - ry- o, Hi,

3

I is for Iron, with which we mark pine, and
J is for Jolly Boys, all in a line.
K is for the Keen edge our axes we keep, and
L is for the Lice that over us creep. (*Chorus.*)

4

M is for the Moss that we chink into our camps,
N is for the Needle which mendeth our pants,
O is for Owls that hoot in the night, and
P is for the Pines that we always fall right. (*Chorus.*)

5

Q is for Quarrels, which we don't have round,
R is for River, where we drive our logs down;
S is for Sled, so stout and so strong, and
T is for the Team to draw it along. (*Chorus.*)

6

U is for Use, which we put our teams to, and
V is the Valley which we draw our sleds through, and
W is for Woods that we leave in the spring,
And now I have sung all I'm going to sing.
That's all.

MAPLE SWEET

In the Jackson family of Vermont this song of the early nineteenth century has been sung for five generations. It was contributed by Mrs. Addie Jackson Morse of Underhill, Vermont.

When the first warm days of spring appear, usually in March, the maple trees are tapped and hung with buckets to catch the thin colorless sap that flows so freely after the cool nights. From three to four weeks, usually, the men in the sugar bush are busy tapping, gathering, and boiling down the sap. "Sugaring off" is candy-making time at the sugar camp, when the thick hot syrup is dropped from a great iron spoon on pans of snow to harden and make "frogs on snow." Sometimes it is poured into saucers to be stirred quickly to a creamy, firm sugar.

ma - ple puls - es play, Till con - gest - ed with its sweet-ness, it de -
o - pen kitch-en door, How the ea - ger chil - dren ral - ly, ev - er
Chorus
lights to bleed a - way.
loud - ly call - ing, "More!"
Oh! Bub-ble, bub-ble, bub-ble, bub-ble,
bub - ble goes the pan,
Fur - nish sweet - er mu - sic for the
sea - son if you can,
See the gold - en bil - lows,
watch their ebb and flow,
Sweet-est joys in-deed, we sug-ar mak-ers know.

3

Do you say you don't believe it? Take a saucer and a spoon,
Though you're sourer than a lemon, you'll be sweeter very soon.
Why, the greenest leaves you see,
On the spreading maple tree,
Though they sip and sip all summer, will the autumn beauties be.

(*Chorus.*)

4

And for home or love, or any kind of sickness, 'tis the thing,
Take in allopathic doses, and repeat it every spring;
Until every one you meet,
If at home or on the street,
Will be half a mind to bite you, for you look so very sweet. (*Chorus.*)

THE MILL

Sung by Mrs. Jennie Hardy Linscott of Waldoboro, Maine, who learned it more than seventy-five years ago from her mother, Elizabeth Arnold Hardy.

This song in transition has lost its music-box characteristics, which are so apparent in the German form. It does retain the thudding motion of the water wheel as it turns, and is most effective as a lullaby for the younger generation.

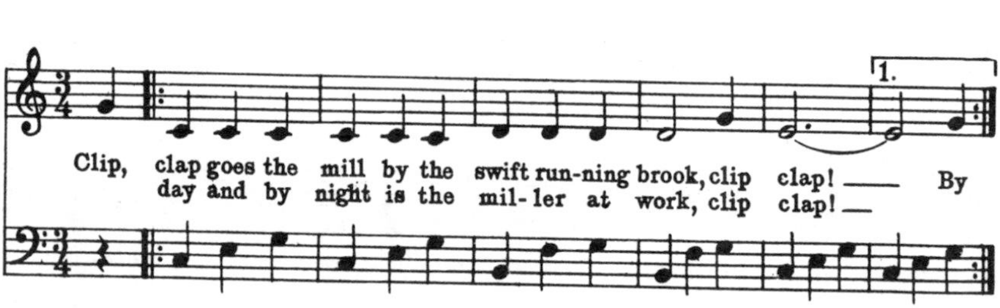

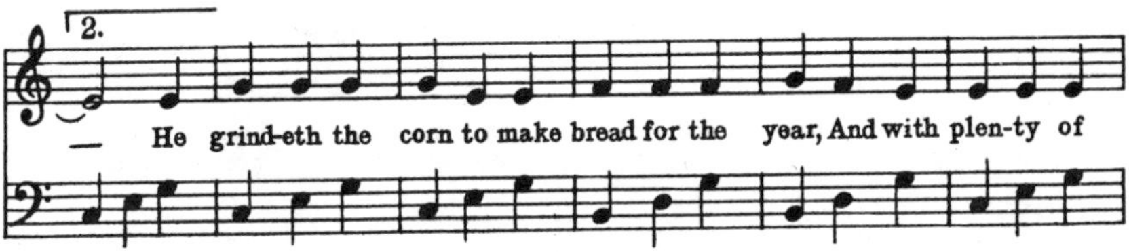

THE MONKEY'S WEDDING

Sung by Mrs. Jennie Hardy Linscott of Waldoboro, Maine, who remembers it as traditional in her family.

This tune that has survived through generations is known as "The Drunken Sailor," and as such was sung with verses by seamen and land dwellers alike. The words were:

What shall we do with the drunken sailor?
Put him in a boat and let him bail her!
What shall we do with the drunken sailor?
Put him out to sea!

It has also been popular as a fiddle tune and is widely known.

Smacked his lips and — then — he — kissed her,
White gauze veil and a green- glass- breast pin,
Kissed so — hard — he — raised a — blis - ter, She set up a
Red kid- slip-pers she was ver-y in-ter-est - ing, She was quite a
yell; The brides-maid put — on a stick - in' — plas - ter, —
belle; The bride-groom swelled with a new shirt col - lar, —
Stuck so — hard — could - n't stick an - y fast - er. —
Black silk — stock — that — cost a — dol - lar, —
Was - n't — that a — sad — dis - as - ter? But it soon got — well.
Large false whis-kers the fash - ion to fol - low, He cut a mon-strous swell.

3

What do you think they had for supper?
Black-eyed peas and bread and butter,
Ducks in a pan all aflutter,
Pickled oysters too.
What do you think they had for a fiddle?
An old banjo with a hole in the middle,
A tambourine made out of a riddle,
And that's the end of my song.

MY GRANDMOTHER LIVED ON YONDER LITTLE GREEN

Sung by Mrs. Ethel Kidder Fuller, who learned it from her mother, Mrs. Edith Irons Kidder, of Assonet, Massachusetts, descendant of Abiah Ashley, who sang to her family of twelve children the songs that she learned from her grandmother, handed down by family traditions.

The tune of this ballad is "The Old Rose Tree, or The Rose Tree in Full Bearing," of Irish origin. It has always been a great favorite and has many variants, the commonest being the familiar "Turkey in the Straw" and "Old Zip Coon."

It will be heard more than once during an evening. Sometimes the words long familiar in the Hardy family are sung to the melody:

OH!—There was an old soldier
And he had a wooden leg,
No terbaccy did he have,
No terbaccy could he beg:
T'other old soldier, a sly old fox,
Always had terbaccy in his old terbaccy box.

2

SAID!—One old soldier,
"Will ye give me a chew?"
Said t'other old soldier:

"I'll be danged if I do!
Quit yer loafin' 'round
And git ter crackin' rocks
And ye'll allers have terbaccy
In yer own terbaccy box!"

3

The first who came courting was honest young Green,
As fine a young gentleman as ever was seen;
But the words of Grandma so rang in my head,
I could not attend to one word that he said.

4

The next who came courting was honest young Grover,
With him I engaged in a joyful love,
Such a joyful love you need never be afraid,
For 'tis better to be married than to die an old maid.

5

Oh, dear, what a fuss these old ladies make!
Thinks I to myself there must be some mistake,
For if all the old ladies of young men had been afraid,
Why, Grandma herself would have died an old maid!

THE OCEAN BURIAL

Sent in by Phillips Barry, Cambridge, Massachusetts, who learned it from a Civil War veteran in Boston, in 1904.

"The Ocean Burial" was written by the Reverend Edwin H. Chapin (1814–1880), a famous Universalist clergyman, and published in the *Southern Literary Messenger* in 1839. It was set to music in 1850 by George N. Allen, and was sung in public at the concerts of Ossian N. Dodge and in innumerable homes. It was carried westward by some

New England or Canadian youth, who went from punching logs to punching cattle, and was re-created as "The Lone Prairie," sung to the old ballad air, "Hind Horn."

3

"Oh bury me not in the deep, deep sea,
Where the billowy shroud will roll o'er me,
Where no light will break through the dark, cold wave,
And no sunbeam rest upon my grave.

4

"It matters not, I have oft been told,
Where the body may lie, when the heart grows cold;
But grant, oh, grant this boon to me,
Oh, bury me not in the deep, deep sea!

5

"For in fancy I've listened to the well known words,
The free, wild winds, and the song of the birds;
I have thought of home, of cot and bower,
And of scenes loved in childhood's hour.

6

"I have always hoped to be laid, when I died,
In the old churchyard, on the green hillside.
By the bones of my father, oh, there let me be!
Oh, bury me not in the deep, deep sea!

7

"Let my death slumbers be where a mother's prayer
And a sister's tears can be mingled there.
Oh, 'twill be sweet, sweet, ere this heart's throb is o'er,
To know when its fountains shall gush no more,

8

"That those it so fondly longed for will come
To plant the first wild flower of spring on my tomb!
Let me lie where those loved ones can weep o'er me.
Oh, bury me not in the deep, deep sea!

9

"And there is another, whose tears will shed
For the one who sleeps far in a cold ocean bed;
In hours that it pains me to think of now,
She has twined these locks and kissed this brow.

10

"In the hair she has wreathed, shall the sea snake hiss?
This brow she has pressed, shall a cold wave kiss?
For the sake of my loved one that weeps o'er me,
Oh, bury me not in deep, deep sea!

11

"Oh, bury me not—" And his voice failed there;
But they gave no heed to his dying prayer;
They have lowered him slow o'er the vessel's side,
And above him has closed the dark, cold tide.

12

Where to dip her light wings, the sea bird rests,
Where the blue waves dance with their foaming crests,
Where the billows bound, and the wind blows free,
They have buried him there in the deep, deep sea!

THE OLD MAN WHO LIVED IN THE WOOD

Contributed by Phillips Barry, Cambridge, Massachusetts.

This ballad is of Scotch origin and is based on a well-known theme in folklore. The oldest version of the story in English goes back to the late fifteenth century. It appeared in James Johnson's *Scots Musical Museum* in 1787.

The song is widely known throughout New England.

3

The old woman took the staff in her hand,
And went to drive the plough;
The old man took the pail in his hand,
And went to milk the cow;

But Tiny hinched and Tiny flinched,
  And Tiny cocked her nose;
And Tiny hit the old man such a kick
  That the blood ran down to his hose.

4

'Twas, "Hey, my good cow," and, "Ho, my good cow,"
  And, "Now, my good cow, stand still.
If ever I milk this cow again,
  'Twill be against my will."
And when he'd milked the Tiny cow,
  For fear she should go dry,
Why, then he fed the little pigs,
  That were within the sty.

5

And then he watched the bracket hen
  Lest she should lay astray;
But he forgot the reel of yarn
  His wife spun yesterday;
He swore by all the leaves on the tree,
  And all the stars in heaven,
That his wife could do more work in a day
  Than he could do in seven!

OLD POD-AUGER TIMES

From the book of *Comical Brown's Songs.*

This very popular ballad of the last century was composed by Comical Brown, an itinerant entertainer who traveled through the East giving a one-man show. The pod-auger was a bit used to bore wooden piping.

3

Young gals didn't hug nor kiss their fellers,
Whenever they came to court,
Nor paddle around upon roller skates,
Nor pound the pianoforte;

But they kept the men at a good arm's length,
And made 'em know their place,
And they played upon washboards and kettles and brooms
With amazin' skill and grace;
They didn't lie abed till eleven A.M.
But got up in the morning betimes,
And they didn't elope with the old man's coachman,
In old pod-auger times.

4

The old men didn't drive fast hosses,
Nor gamble with keerds and dice,
Nor they didn't run church lotteries,
For it wasn't considered nice;
But now they'll gamble and drink mean rum,
And lead hypocritical lives,
And wives run away with each other's husbands,
And husbands with other men's wives;
And folks didn't have delirious trimmin's,
Nor perpetuate horrible crimes,
For the cider was good and the rum was pure,
In old pod-auger times.

THE OLD SOW SONG

Sung by Henry A. Castle of Plainville, Connecticut, who remembers the song from his grandfather's singing.

The text and tune are traditional, although the theme may be very definitely traced to the British traditional song, "Red Herring." The melody first appeared in print in *Story Parade* and the words were published in *Phebe Fairchild Her Book* by Lois Lenski.

3

What did we do with the old sow's hair?
Made good enough satin for anyone to wear;

Satin or broadcloth—any such thing!
The old sow took the measles
And she died in the spring.

4

What did we do with the old sow's feet?
Made good souse for any one to eat;
Souse or pickled—any such thing!
The old sow took the measles
And she died in the spring.

5

What did we do with the old sow's insides?
Made a good mess of sassage hides;
Good for sassage—any such thing!
The old sow took the measles
And she died in the spring.

6

What did we do with the old sow's squeal?
That we couldn't either see or feel;
We couldn't use that for one single thing
When the old sow took the measles
And died in the spring!

THE OLD WOMAN IN DOVER

Sam Young of North Anson, Maine, sang this ballad in logging camps thirty years ago. It resembles "Johnny Sands," which is based on "The Old Woman of Slapsadam," known also as "Old Woman of London," and in Scottish folklore as "The Wily Auld Carle." Our ballad and "Johnny Sands" are said to be founded on a folk tale.

3

"Go and get three marrowbones
And make him suck them all;
Then," says he, "my gay old lady,
He can't see you at all." (*Chorus.*)

4

She went and got three marrowbones
And made him suck them all,
And says he, "My gay old lady,
I can't see you at all." (*Chorus.*)

5

"And now here I must suffer
And alone here I must die;
I'd surely drown myself
If I could find a way." (*Chorus.*)

6

She says, "My gay old husband,
You need not go astray
I'll take you by your lily-white hand
And I'll show you the way." (*Chorus.*)

7

She took him by his lily-white hand
And led him down to the brim
'Twas nimberly he whisked about
And then he pushed her in. (*Chorus.*)

8

And as she was a-strugglin'
For mercy she did call.
Says he, "My gay old lady,
I can't see you at all!" (*Chorus.*)

9

But as she was a-stranglin'
And swimmin' up to the brim
He was so mighty fond of it
He kicked her further in. (*Chorus.*)

10

But now my song is ended
And I'll not sing no more
She must have been a damned old fool
Or she'd swum for the other shore. (*Chorus.*)

THE OLD WOMAN WHO WENT TO MARKET

Sung by Mrs. Elizabeth Wheeler Hubbard, Taunton, Massachusetts, who learned it as a child in Spencer, Massachusetts, from her father, Dr. Edward Reed Wheeler, a country physician who measured pills and music with wisdom and humor.

This rollicking old favorite comes originally from Ulster, in the north of Ireland. It is related to the "Wee Wifie Kee."

OUR GOODMAN

When he thought no one could overhear him, a certain young man of North Irish extraction sang this naughty song to his little sister. Since this little sister is today too much of a gentlewoman, she could not sing the last verse; but she finally consented to write it.

This ballad was first printed by David Herd in 1776. It is the kind of ballad which permits the singer to make up new verses as he goes along, until he runs out of ideas. This text is traditional in the singer's family, and the tune, which is theirs also, is that of "Sweet Rosy Nell." To this tune are sung "The Baffled Knight," "The Derby Ram," "The Wonderful Hunter," "Swinging in the Lane," etc. The last-named song was published as early as 1710.

Rollicking
1. Oh, the old man he came home one night, As drunk as he could be, He saw a hat up-on the rack, Where his hat ought to be. "Oh, my good wife, my dear wife, My wife so dear to me, Whose hat is that up-on the rack, Where my hat ought to be?" "Oh you
2. Oh, the old man he came home one night, As drunk as he could be, He saw a horse with-in the stall, Where his horse ought to be. "Oh, my good wife, my dear wife, My wife so dear to me, Whose horse is that with-in the stall, Where my horse ought to be?" "Oh you

3

Oh, the old man he came home one night,
As drunk as he could be,
He saw a face between the sheets,
Where no face ought to be.

"Oh, my good wife, my dear wife,
  My wife so dear to me,
Whose face is that between the sheets,
  Where no face ought to be?"
"Oh, you old fool, you darn fool,
  You doddering fool," says she,
"It's nothing but a little kid
  My uncle sent to me."

Chorus:

"I've traveled the whole world over,
  Ten thousand times or more,
But a little kid between the sheets,
  I never saw before!"

OVER THE WATER TO CHARLIE

Sung by Mrs. Jennie Hardy Linscott of Waldoboro, Maine, who learned it from her grandmother, Mary Sullivan Hardy, sister of Major-General John Sullivan of Revolutionary times.

In transition both the children's game and the Scottish reel that were once associated with this tune have been lost. The Yankee version too has supplanted the roast beef of Old England with the corn meal of New England.

When Prince Charles attempted to wrest the crown of Britain in 1745, many of his followers wrote innumerable songs to gain his favor. He was a great traveler, a rather democratic soul, and very gay. He was extremely popular with the people.

This is one of the best surviving songs and was sung long before Jacobite songs were fashionable.

3

I'll have none of your Indian meal,
I'll have none of your barley,
I'll have only the best of white flour,
To make a cake for Charlie.

THE OXEN SONG

Sung by Samuel Young of North Anson, Maine, who learned it when as a lumberjack he "drove the river" for twenty-two years, on the Connecticut, Androscoggin, Penobscot, and Kennebec rivers. Sam Young started driving logs when he was thirteen years old and lived in Penobscot. He is known far and wide as the lumberjack who can sing all night and never repeat himself.

As he was singing the song in camp one night, the boss approached and asked him not to continue, as Jack Carpenter, whom Young did not know, was present in the crew.

This song, like many others, is said to have been composed by the famous lumberjack and fighter, Larry Gorman. As far as is known, this is the first record of the song. One of the legendary figures of lumberjack tradition is that of John Ross, who was undoubtedly nearly as big as the tales about him. Another figure, well known in the lumber country, is that of Sebat, who was supposed to have lived about the sixties or seventies of the last century, and who probably came originally from New Brunswick.

Logging operations were begun in South Berwick Township, Maine, in 1631. Either oxen or horses were used for hauling. The bunk chains mentioned in the song are used to bind the logs onto the sled or, as the lumberjack says, the "bunk." Ox teamsters were also known as bullwhackers and were said to have the prize vocabulary of strong language. The tally board was the record kept in camp to count the logs; to "run another turn" was to make another trip. "Hovel" is the lumberman's term for the lumber-camp barn.

This is a fine example to show the mixture of Irish, French, Canadians, and Yankees who made up the logging crews.

3

'Twas early in the season,
In the fall of Twenty-five,
John Ross he sent four oxen up
For Carpenter to drive.

4

John Ross he sent four oxen up,
And I must pen this down,
He had some spruce and pine to haul
Off of the Scottbrook town.

5

Now the first load we brought from the farm,
It was two bales of hay
With lots of other knickknacks
That he had stored away.

6

He took with him six bags of meal
And his bunk chains also,
All for to bind his spruce and pine
While hauling through the snow.

7

As I strolled out one morning,
Just at the break of day,
I heard two men a-talking.
These words I heard them say:

8

Says Carpenter unto Flemmons,
"I'll show them to haul spruce,
For my oxen in the snow, you see,
Are equal to bull moose!"

9

Now the first day we was hauling
We landed forty-nine,
And in a short time after that
We began to fall behind.

10

They kept a-failing every day,
The tally board tells it all;
Now to do our best it's ten a day
Is all that he can haul.

11

Sebat he went to Carpenter,
These words to him did say:
"We've got to run another turn
For this will never pay.

12

"We've got to run another turn,
And we'll all work together;
I've found a wonderful bunch of pine
'Way up at the head of the medder."

13

Now the crew that 'tend those oxen,
Their names to you I'll tell;
The jobber's name was Crowley—
The boys all knew him well.

14

There was Flemmons, Reddy, and Griffin,
Three boys that know no fear,
There was Gillis and Long Archie,
Sebat brought up the rear.

15

Old Duke and Swan all on the pole,
So vigorous they do lug,
While Swan's the head with a collar and hames,
And a pair of leather tugs.

16

Old Brighty in the hovel lay,
They say his feet are sore
But it was a strain that caused his pain,
And now he'll haul no more.

17

Now his oxen they have got so poor,
To haul they are not fit,
His sled looks like a butcher block,
All smeared with blood and grit.

18

He tried to keep his oxen fat,
But found it was no use;
For all that's left is skin and bones,
And all the horns are loose.

19

Now to conclude and finish
I'm going to end my song.
I hope I haven't offended you
If I've said anything wrong.

PERRIE, MERRIE, DIXI, DOMINI

When the eldest daughter of Mrs. Elizabeth Wheeler Hubbard of Taunton, Massachusetts, was ten years old, she was given the evening duty of singing her small brother to sleep, and no other song that she knew would induce so prompt a drowsiness as the monotonous rhythm of this old ballad.

About the fifteenth century, riddles were a favorite form of balladry, and this tuneful survivor is a very fine example of that particular type of ballad. In the refrain, the Latin invocation may be the last trace of the Roman conquest in Great Britain, or a remnant of the mixture of English and Latin so common in the old English carols.

3

The third sent a blanket without any thread,
Perrie, merrie, dixi, Domini;
The fourth sent a book that no man had read,
Petrum, partrum, Paradisi, tempore,
Perrie, merrie, dixi, Domini.

4

When the cherry's in blossom, there is no stone,
Perrie, merrie, dixi, Domini;

When the chicken's in the egg, there is no bone,
Petrum, partrum, Paradisi, tempore,
Perrie, merrie, dixi, Domini.

5

When the blanket's on the sheep's back there is no thread,
Perrie, merrie, dixi, Domini;
When the book is in the press, then no man hath read,
Petrum, partrum, Paradisi, tempore,
Perrie, merrie, dixi, Domini.

PETER EMILY

Sam Young of North Anson, Maine, learned and sang this ballad during the thirty years he worked in the woods of Maine as driver and logger.

The song, also known as "Peter Emery" or "Amberley," is one of the lumberjacks' great favorites and one of the oldest. The melody seems to be derived from a fine old Irish tune, and the song is a good example of the tragedy that always stalked the logger but appealed to him as a gambler.

Peter is thought to have come into Maine about 1882 from Nova Scotia, and the tradition goes that the dying logger composed the whole song in his last moments.

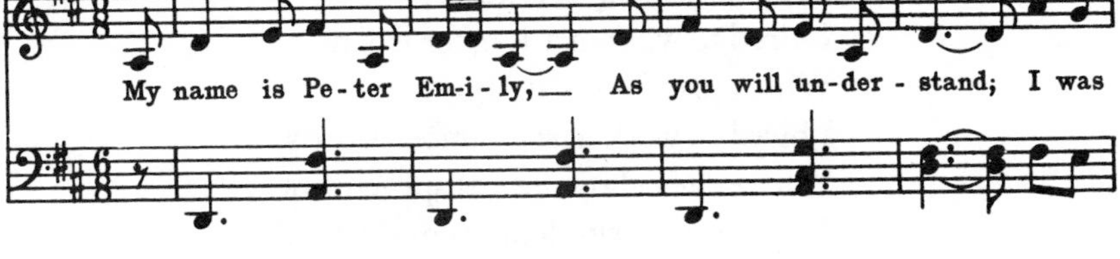

2

I landed in New Brunswick,
That lumbering counteree,
I hired to work in a lumber woods,
Which proved my destiny;
I hired to work in the lumber woods,
Where they chop the tall spruce down,
And loading two sleds from the yard,
I received my fatal wound.†

*Pursue.
†Old pronunciation.

3

Now there's danger on the ocean,
When the waves roll mountain-high,
There's danger on the battlefield,
Where the angry bullets fly,
There's danger in the lumber woods,
And death seems solemn there,
And I befell a victim
Unto its monstrous snare.

4

Here's adieu unto my father;
'Twas you that drove me here,
For I could not agree with you,
Your treatment was severe.
A man should never drive a boy,
Or try to keep him down,
For it often sends him from his home
When he is far too young.

5

Here's adieu unto my mother,
She was my friend so dear.
How could I think I'd fall a victim
When I left her tender care?
It's little did my mother know
When she sang sweet lullabies
In what foreign parts I'd end my days
Or the death that I should die.

6

Here's adieu to Prince Edward Island,
That garden of the seas;
No more I'll roam its flowery banks
And enjoy a summer breeze;

No more I'll watch those gallant ships
As they go sailing by,
With colors flying brightly
Above the canvas high.

7

Here's adieu unto those other friends
Those Island girls so true,
Long may they live upon the isle
Where my first breath I drew;
The world will go on just the same
As before I passed away—
What use to him the life of man
When his body is but clay?

8

There is a land beyond the tomb
And there I'm nearing on,
Where man is more than mortal
And death will never come.
A deathly glaze has closed my eyes—
I am no longer here,
My spirit it has taken flight
To that other heavenly sphere.

9

Now when I'm dead and passed away
There's just one thing I crave,
That some good holy father
Will bless my silent grave;
Near by the site of Boiestown
My moldering bones must lay
To wait the awful coming
Of that great Judgment Day.

POLLY OLIVER

Sung by Mrs. Lucy Palmer Johnson, Somerville, Massachusetts, who remembers hearing her mother sing it more than fifty years ago.

After the suppression of the Insurrection of 1798, many Irish airs were carried back to England, and this soldiers' song was one of them. It is still as modern as the last edition of the Girl Scouts' songbook! It was first printed as a broadside ballad.

3

She rode till she came to fair London Town,
She dismounted her horse at the Sign of the Crown.
The first that came to her was a man from above,
The next that came down was Polly Oliver's true love.

4

"Good evening, good evening, kind Captain," said she,
"Here's a letter from your true love, Polly Oliver," said she.
He opened the letter and a guinea was found,
"For you and your companions to drink her health round."

POLLY VAN

Miss Lucy Allen of West Newton, Massachusetts, contributed this old ballad, which has been handed down in the traditions of the Allen family.

The ballad is known also as "Molly Bawn" or "The Shooting of His Dear," and in the text may occur a swan, hind, or other magic symbol.

The white apron of Polly in this version is the symbol of enchantment. In Irish lore, the bewitched maiden is mistaken for a doe.

It is an ancient Irish belief that ducks or other birds flying at night are human souls in bird form.

ware of a shoot - ing at the set - ting of the
joints they grew weak, — his — eyes scarce could —
sun, For her true love went a - hunt - ing and he shot in the
see, He em - braced her in his arms when he — found she was
dark, But — oh, and a - las! — Pol - ly Van was his — mark.
dead, And a foun - tain of tears for his true love he — shed.
Chorus
For she'd her a - pron a - bout her, and he took her for a
swan; But oh, and a - las! — it was she, Pol - ly — Van.

3

He took her in his arms, and home quickly ran,
Crying: "Father! Dear father! I've shot Polly Van!
I've shot that fair female in the bloom of her life,
And I always intended to make her my wife." (*Chorus.*)

4

At midnight, in his chamber, Polly Van did appear,
Crying: "Jimmy, dear Jimmy, you have nothing to fear,
But stay in your country till the trial comes on,
You shall not be convicted for what you have done." (*Chorus.*)

5

In the midst of his trial, Polly Van did appear,
Crying: "Uncle! Dear Uncle! Jimmy Randall must be clear!"
The judges and lawyers stood round in a row,
Polly Van in the middle like a fountain of snow. (*Chorus.*)

THE QUAKER'S WOOING

The twelve children of Abiah Ashley could not help learning the songs that were handed down to her by family traditions. Abiah had an unusual voice, and her descendants consider her songs a precious heritage. Although the game of "The Quaker's Wooing" was never played by this family, it has been preserved in other families of New England.

The game is a variation of "The Keys to Heaven," from which the old singing game, "I'll Give to You a Paper of Pins," is derived. The background of this song is explained in Singing Games, page 20. The ballad is a dramatic representation and probably was a mummers' dance.

Slowly and pompously
1. "Mad - am, I have come a court-in' Oh— dear— me!
2. "I've a ring that's worth a shil-lin', Oh— dear— me!
I'm for pleas-ure, not for sport-in', Oh— dear— me!"
Thou may'st wear it if thou'rt will - in', Oh— dear— me!"
Reply—Gay, vivaciously, double time
"I want none— of your Quak-er— ac-tion, Fol lol lol lol lay,
"I don't want your ring— or your mon-ey, Fol lol lol lol lay,
You're e - nough to— breed dis-trac-tion, Fol lol lol lol, fol lol lay."
I want a man that will call me hon- ey, Fol lol lol lol, fol lol lay."

3

"Love, I'll be a Presbyterian,
  Oh-dear-me!
Then we'll be of one persuasion,
  Oh-dear-me!"
"I want none of your turncoat religion,
  Fol lol lol lol lay!
I want a man that's a real good Christian,
  Fol lol lol lol, fol lol lay."

4

"Must I go without one token?
  Oh-dear-me!
Then I'll die with my heart broken,
  Oh-dear-me!"
"Take thy cheer, my loving brother,
  Fol lol lol lol lay!
Since you can't catch me—go catch another,
  Fol lol lol lol, fol lol lay."

THE ROLLING OF THE STONES
or
THE TWA BROTHERS

Sung by Mrs. Mary E. Harmon of Cambridge, Massachusetts. She remembers hearing it from her father, who enjoyed singing many songs traditional in his family.

This is a very ancient ballad, probably of Scottish origin. The version presented here is a corruption of the second version found in Francis J. Child's collection, *English and Scottish Popular Ballads*, and like that version makes the wound accidental. The event from which the ballad gets its theme happened near Edinburgh in 1589, when one of the Somervilles was killed by the accidental discharge of his brother's pistol. It seems also to be related to the German ballad, "Graf Friedrich," in which the bridegroom's sword slips and inflicts the fatal wound.

This fragment, as sung in the Ellingwood family, is known as "The Rolling of the Stones," and is related to the Maine version, in which Susie is the sweetheart and no longer the sister. It would seem that the ballad, with Lizie Wan and Edward, all came from the same root.

3

They had not danced but one single dance
More than once or twice around
Before the sword that hung by Bell's side
Gave him his fatal wound.

4

They took him up and they carried him out,
For he was in distress,
They carried him and buried him all in the green woods,
Where he was content to rest.

5

Pretty Susie she came mourning by,
With a tablet on her arm.
(The next two lines are missing)

6

She charmed the fish all out of the sea,
And the birds all out of the nests,
Until she came where her true love lay,
Where he was content to rest.

THE SAWMILL SONG

Sung by Dana Cate of Sanbornville, New Hampshire, who says, "I made it up when I worked in the sawmill thirty years ago. They were so slow it used to make me mad; I knew the ice would cave in before they got that lumber across Lake Marion. Never did though!"

The text notes all the operations of Clark's sawmill, for which the monotonous droning of the tune is sufficient background.

The first sawmill was set up and operated by colonists in South Berwick, Maine, on the Salmon Falls River in 1631, and water power was not entirely replaced by the steam-driven circular saw until two hundred years later, when in 1821, the Bath Steam Mill Company began burning slabs.

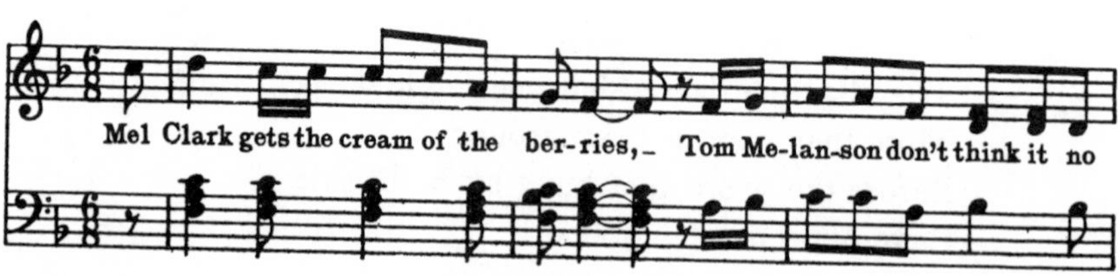

fun; Lit-tle Joe Dy-er, in the pit a-hol-ler-in', Won-ders
why the damn' thing don't run; The fire-man gets her a-
turn-ing, The saw-yer rolls up his sleeve; When he
4
pulls back the lev-er, The mark-er don't have time to breathe; The
mark-er cuts slabs for the fire-man, While the roll-er thinks of his

past,— Wish-ing that the team-sters Would-n't pull logs in so
fast;— Next in line comes the chop-pers,— They
sit a-round and don't care a - bit,— They got hell from Me-lan-son this
morn-ing,— They grow fat on the hell they git.— Last of
all comes the board job, When the ice it will be so thin;— The

SCOTLAND'S BURNING and THREE BLIND MICE

Traditional in the Hubbard family. Sung by Mrs. Elizabeth Wheeler Hubbard, Taunton, Massachusetts.

These two rounds are among the oldest favorites that have been passed from generation to generation. The round as a song form was known as early as 1611 and appeared in "Melismata."

The historical significance of the first round is possibly based on the struggles and battles that have marked the rugged country's history.

Where and when the second round first appeared is not known.

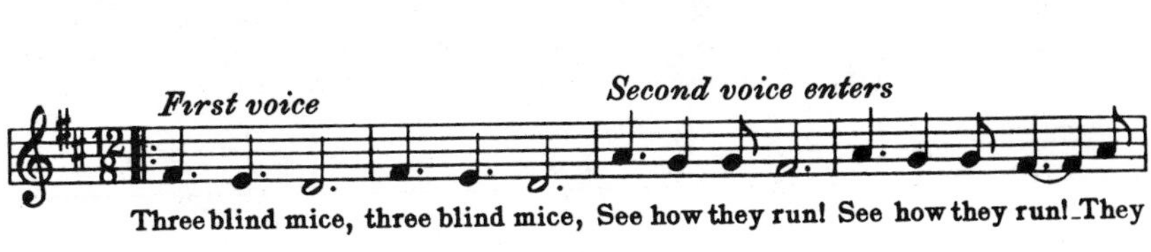

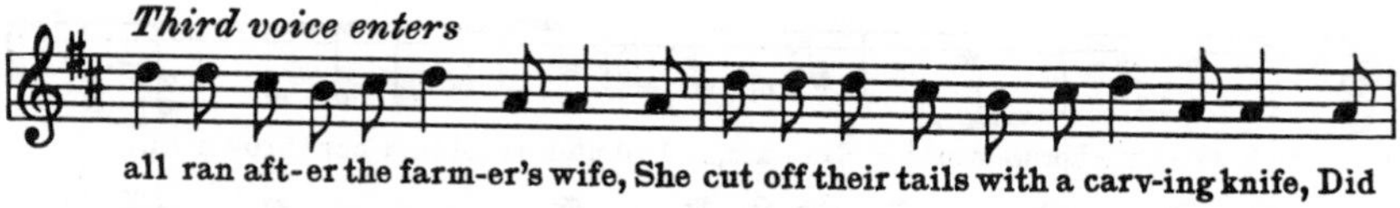

A SHIP A-SAILING

Sung by Mrs. Elizabeth Wheeler Hubbard of Taunton, Massachusetts, who learned it about fifty years ago as a small child in Spencer, Massachusetts, from her aunt, Hannah Louise Bishop, who possessed a very lovely singing voice. The song has been handed down in the Foster family as a lullaby.

It was once a game song known in England as the "Duck Dance"; but the game has been lost for many years, and only the delightful story remains.

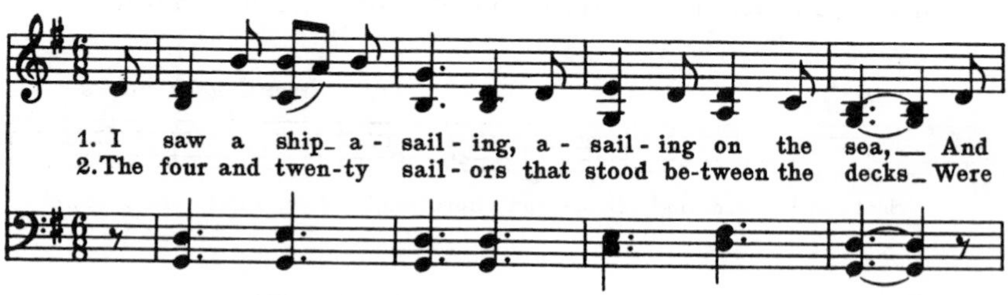

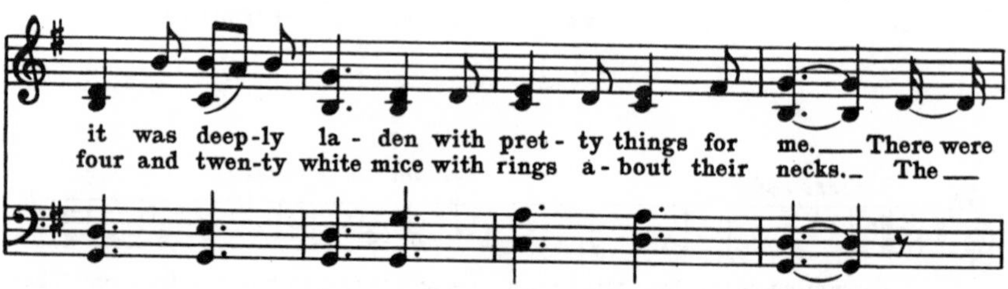

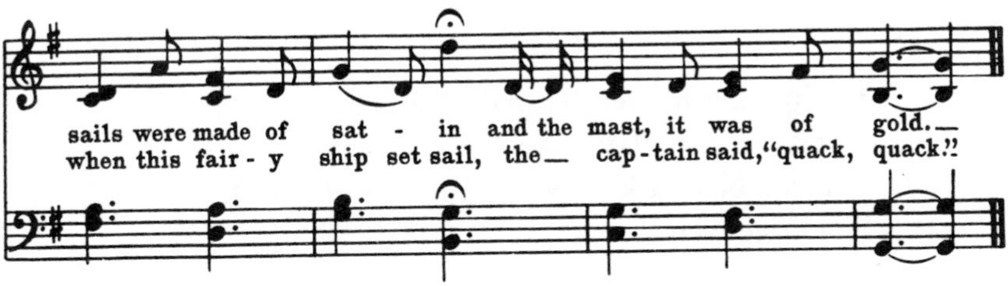

SPRINGFIELD MOUNTAIN
or
THE BLACK SARPENT

Traditional in the Ellingwood family, and sung by Mrs. Mary E. Harmon of Cambridge, Massachusetts, as remembered from the singing of her mother.

This is the first known native American ballad. It is founded on fact, and the date of the event was 1761. In an earlier version, the story tells how Tommy Blake came back to the home of his sweetheart, Molly Bland, and how she tried to save him. The grave of Tommy Blake, victim of the "pesky sarpent" may be seen today in Vermont. The tune and text given here are traditional in the Ellingwood family.

3

He had not mowed but half the field,
Tur-i-lee, tur-i-lay, tur-i-lee, tur-i-lay,
When a big black sarpent bit him in the heel,
Tur-i-lee-i-lay.

4

Then he took sick, lay down, and died,
Tur-i-lee, tur-i-lay, tur-i-lee, tur-i-lay,
From the bite of the sarpent on the mountain-side,
Tur-i-lee-i-lay.

5

Now all young men, my warning take,
Tur-i-lee, tur-i-lay, tur-i-lee, tur-i-lay,
Beware of the bite of the big black snake,
Tur-i-lee-i-lay.

SWEET KITTY CLOVER

Sung by Mrs. Elizabeth A. Hubbard of Taunton, Massachusetts, who learned it from her father, Dr. Edward Reed Wheeler of Spencer, Massachusetts, a singer with a fine voice and a fund of humor and song.

The history of this merry song has been lost. The text and tune are traditional in the Hubbard family; a copy of the song is to be found in the copybook of Elizabeth Foster Reed (1796–1823), Dr. Wheeler's grandmother.

Sweet Kit-ty Clo-ver, she both-ered me so, Oh, oh, oh, oh, oh! Oh,
oh oh, oh, oh! Sweet Kit-ty Clo-ver, she both-ered me so, Oh,
oh, oh, oh, oh, oh, oh! Her face was round and red and fat, Like a
pul-pit cush-ion or red-der than that. Sweet Kit-ty Clo-ver, she
both-ered me so, Oh, oh, oh, oh, oh, oh, oh, oh, oh, oh!

THREE CHILDREN SLIDING ON THE ICE

Traditional in the Hatheway family. Sung by Mrs. Edith I. Kidder and Miss Helen Irons of Assonet, Massachusetts, who learned it as one of the songs handed down from Abiah Ashley, their grandmother.

The tune to this song is that of "Chevy Chase," first sung about 1450. The story was taken from a poetical tale in *Choyce Poems,* published in London in 1662.

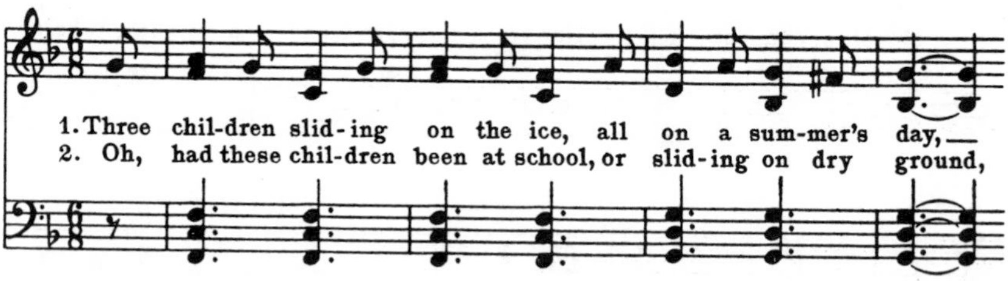

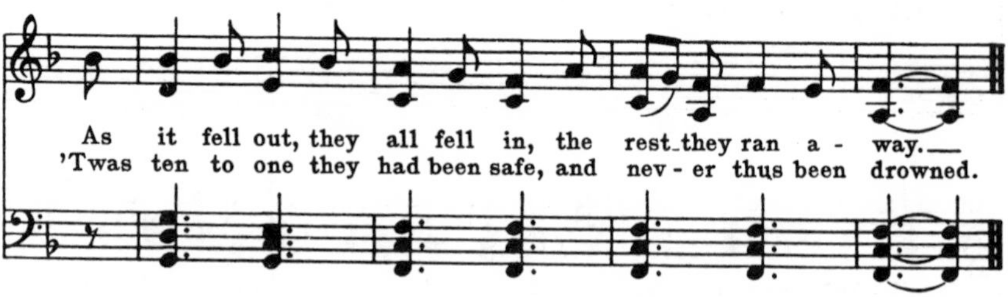

3

You parents that have children dear,
Also you that have none,

If you would have them safe abroad,
Pray keep them safe at home.

THREE CROWS

The text and tune are traditional in the Stuart family. Sung by Mrs. Sara Stuart Wilkins, Manchester, New Hampshire, who remembers hearing her mother sing it.

The air is part of the Scotch melody, "Bonnie Doon." The ballad was first printed in 1611 and is known in Scotland as "The Twa Corbies." A dirge with another tune is found in "Melismata" and is one of a collection made by Ravenscroft. The ballad itself is of unknown antiquity. As published in *Scots Musical Museum,* it pictures a knight lying dead beneath his shield, with his hounds around him and his leman to care for his remains and mourn for him. The scene is said to be laid in Dumfriesshire.

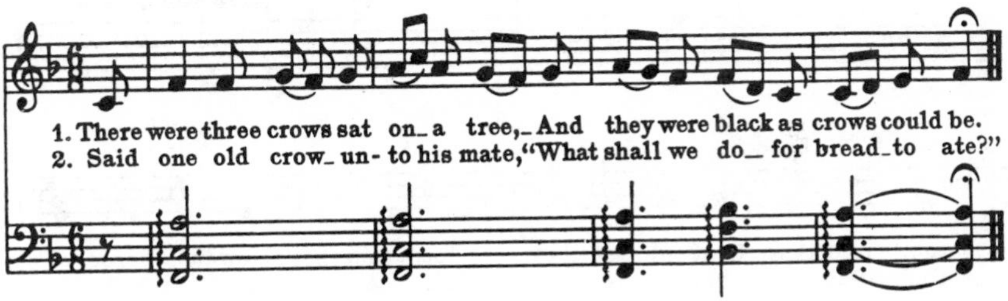

3

"An old dead horse in the meadow lies,
We'll go and peck at both his eyes.

4

"We'll perch ourselves on his backbone,
And pick his eyes out one by one."

THREE JOVIAL HUNTSMEN

Sung as a nursery song to her children by Mrs. Elizabeth Wheeler Hubbard and recalled by them as a choice that all five youngsters could agree on for bedtime music. The singer learned this ballad of many verses from her father, who enjoyed the old family songs, especially the ones with many verses.

This is a favorite old English ballad; and although the New England version varies from that printed by Randolph Caldecott it is nevertheless the same ballad. The Hutchinson family, who went about the country singing old songs, found this a most popular one.

3

The first he said it was a barn,
The second he said, "Nay."
The third said 'twas a meetin'house,
With the steeple blown away.
Look ye there now, look ye there now.

4

They hunted and they halloed,
And nothing could they find,
But a stone in a wall,
And this they left behind.

5

The first he said it was a stone,
The second he said, "Nay."
The third said 'twas an egg
That the bracket hen did lay.
Look ye there now, look ye there now.

6

They hunted and they halloed,
And nothing could they find,
But a frog in a pool,
And this they left behind.

7

The first said it was a frog,
The second he said, "Nay."
The third said 'twas a canary bird
With the feathers blown away.
Look ye there now, look ye there now.

8

They hunted and they halloed,
And nothing could they find,
But an owl in an olive bush,
And this they left behind.

9

The first he said it was an owl,
The second he said, "Nay."
The third said 'twas the Evil One!
And they all three rode away.
Look ye there now, look ye there now.

TITTERY NAN

Sent in by Professor Henry V. Hubbard, Milton, Massachusetts, who learned it from an old man in Maine several years ago.

This is a popular and widely known ballad in Maine. It is probably founded on fact. The tradition of the ballad is local, and several versions are known.

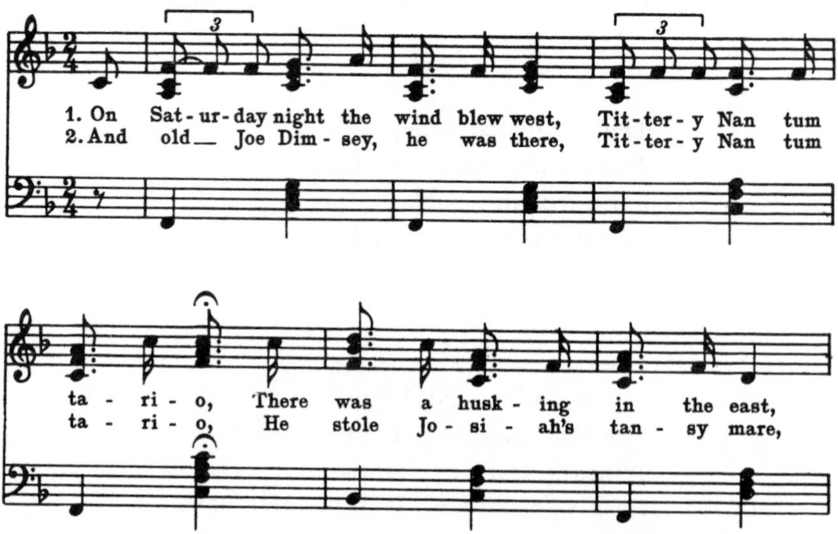

3

And old Josiah after him took,
Tittery Nan tum ta-ri-o,
And caught him by the sounding brook,
Fairy-nay, Tory-no,
Tittery Nan tum ta-ri-o.

4

And old Josiah to him said,
Tittery Nan tum ta-ri-o,
"How came you for to steal my jade?"
Fairy-nay, Tory-no,
Tittery Nan tum ta-ri-o.

5

"Oh rumty toodle, 'twasn't I,"
Tittery Nan tum ta-ri-o,
"You damned old rascal, how you lie!"
Fairy-nay, Tory-no,
Tittery Nan tum ta-ri-o.

6

So old Josiah threw him down,
Tittery Nan tum ta-ri-o,
And scrubbed his nose upon the ground,
Fairy-nay, Tory-no,
Tittery Nan tum ta-ri-o.

TOO-RIL-TE-TOO

Sung to the children of Dr. and Mrs. Frank Allen Hubbard, who remember it vividly. Surely Tip-oo-tib, one of the pet kittens, would never have been guilty of such cruelty, but as the youngsters could not be quite certain, this particular gray cat was forced to lead a more circumspect life under the watchful eyes of his small mistresses.

The melody of this tragic little tale comes from Samuel Lover's interpretation of "Rory O'More," whose roistering story is sweet to the Irish patriot. Variations of the verses are found in different parts of New England.

TYBURN HILL

As remembered from the singing of Dr. Frank Allen Hubbard, who learned it from his father, Dr. Simeon Pease Hubbard, more than eighty-five years ago. This song is recalled as being very effective when sung to the accompaniment of a concertina.

The melody of this song is very old; both tune and text are traditional in the Hubbard family.

The last execution on Tyburn gallows took place in 1783. From that time, Newgate was the scene of capital punishment for Middlesex. The beggar's staff is known for its greasy sleekness.

3

They stole his wallet and they stole his staff,
Rumsty-O, Rumsty-O,
They stole his wallet and they stole his staff,
And then they broke out in a great hoarse laff,
Rumsty-O, Rumsty-O.

4

As I was going down Newgate stairs,
Rumsty-O, Rumsty-O,
As I was going down Newgate stairs,
I saw those two thieves saying their prayers,
Rumsty-O, Rumsty-O.

5

As I was going up Tyburn Hill,
Rumsty-O, Rumsty-O,
As I was going up Tyburn Hill,
I saw those two thieves hanging there still,
Rumsty-O, Rumsty-O.

WASHING DAY

As sung to the children of Mrs. Elizabeth Wheeler Hubbard of Taunton, Massachusetts, who learned it from her father, Dr. Edward Reed Wheeler, more than sixty years ago. It has been traditional in the Reed family.

This is a Scotch-reel tune, and the words were printed in a broadside ballad in the early part of the nineteenth century. The tune is known as "There's Nae Luck Aboot the Hoos" and was signed "Jean Adams."

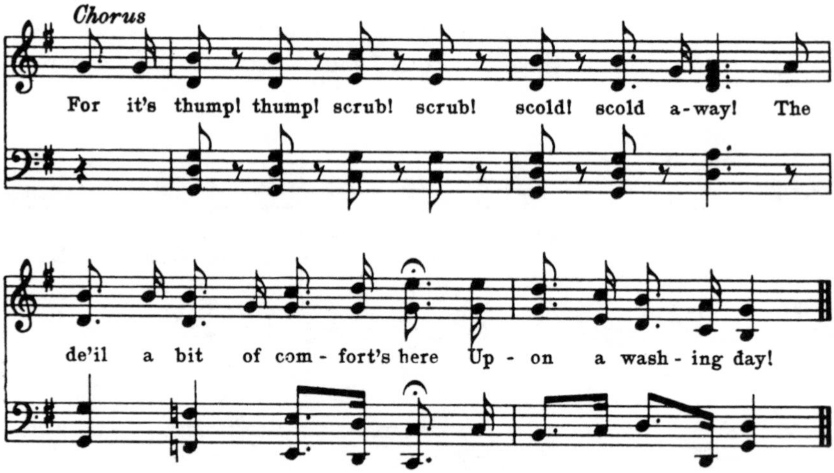

3

A friend of mine once asked me
How long poor Jenny's dead.
Lamenting the good creature,
And sorry I was wed
To such a scolding vixen,
Whilst he had been at sea.
The real truth was, he chanced to come
Upon a washing day. *(Chorus.)*

4

I asked him to come and dine.
"Come, come," sez I, "oddsbuds!
Now no denial take shall I,
Though Kate is in the suds."
But what he had to dine upon,
In faith, I shall not say;
I'll wager he'll not come again
Upon a washing day. *(Chorus.)*

5

Oh, that sad morning when I rise,
I make a fervent prayer
Unto the gods that it may be
Throughout the day quite fair;
That not a gown or handkerchief
May in the ditch be laid,
For, should it happen so, egad!
I should catch a broken head. *(Chorus.)*

WILL YOU WEAR THE RED?
or
JENNIE JENKINS

This song was sung to Mrs. Frances Merrow Horn of Wolfeboro, New Hampshire, when she was three years old, by her grandmother, Olive Merrow, of Newfield, Maine, then an old lady of ninety years.

The earliest printed text of this song is called "Jane Jenkins" and is found in *The Green Mountain Songster,* Sandgate, Vermont, 1823. The symbolism recalls both the old English ballad "Hind Horn" and the game song "Jennia Jones." Undoubtedly there is a connection between the song "Jennie Jenkins" and the game song "Jennia Jones." The song as sung in the Merrow family is called "Will You Wear the Red?"*

*Add verses with colors and rhymes to suit the singer.

Will you wear the red, Jen - ny Jen - kins? "Oh, I
Will you wear the white, Jen - ny Jen - kins? "Oh, I
will not wear the red, for the col - or it will fade, So con -
will not wear the white, for the white is much too light, So con -
fine me the doub - le rose, Sal - ly wears a sin - gle, Jen - ny
fine me the doub - le rose, Sal - ly wears a sin - gle, Jen - ny
a green gown, Tal - ly a brown bay." Jen - ny Jen - kins, oh!
a green gown, Tal - ly a brown bay." Jen - ny Jen - kins, oh!

WILLIKINS AND HIS DINAH

This was sung to her children by Mrs. Elizabeth Wheeler Hubbard, who learned it from her father, Dr. Edward Reed Wheeler of Spencer, Massachusetts. The text of the ballad was so moving to one small girl that when the tragic end was finally reached, her mother could always be induced to linger in the nursery for "just one more song."

The earliest record of a variant of this song is sung with a text of "Lord Randall." This would seem to give the ballad a Scotch background. The record was made by Joyce in 1848 in county Limerick, Ireland. The ballad is one of the most popular and is generally known in the British Isles.

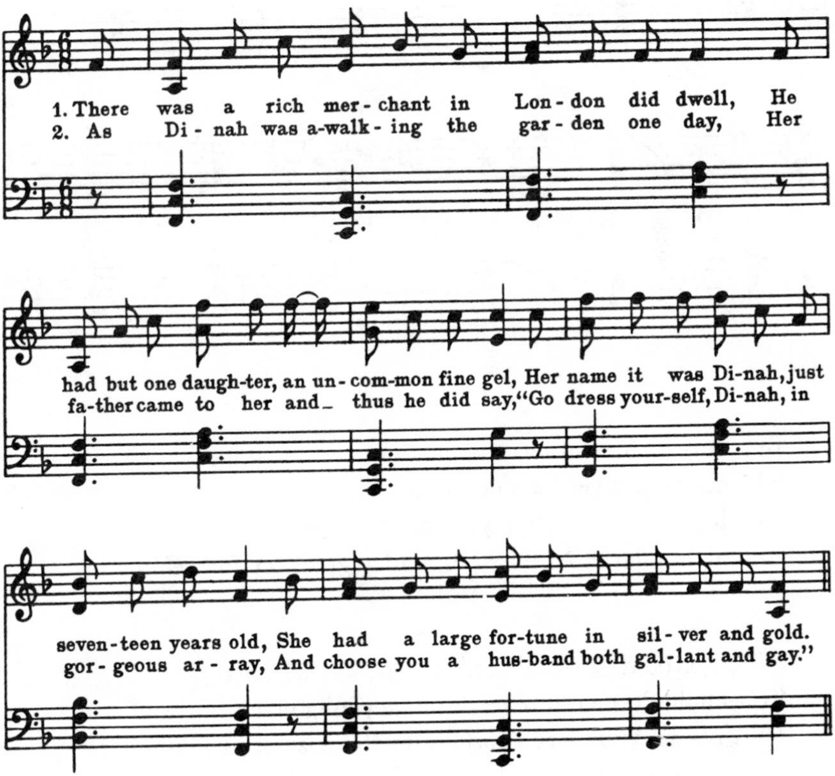

3

But thus to her father Dinah spoke up her mind,
"To marry just yet I am not quite inclined,
Just let me live single a year or two more,
And all my large fortune I'll gladly give o'er." *(Chorus.)*

4

"Go, go, boldest daughter," the parent he cried,
"If you don't consent to be this here young man's bride,
I'll give all your large fortune to the nearest of kin,
And you shan't reap the benefit of one single pin." *(Chorus.)*

5

When Willikins was a-walking the garden around,
He spied his dear Dinah, all dead on the ground,
With a cup of cold pizon all down by her side,
So he knew 'twas from pizon that Dinah she died. *(Chorus.)*

6

Then he kissed her cold corpus a thousand times o'er,
And called her his Dinah, though she was no more,
Then he swallowed up the pizon and sung a short stave,
And Willikins and his Dinah were laid in one grave. *(Chorus.)*

7

Now all ye young men and ye maidens beware,
And don't disobey your old govenare,
Or else like poor Dinah some day you'll be found,
With a cup of cold pizon, all dead on the ground. *(Chorus.)*

YOUNG ALANTHIA

This very old Scotch ballad is recorded as Miss Ada F. Kelley of Harwich, Massachusetts, remembers it from the singing of her uncle seventy years ago.

The version of the text and tune given here has been traditional in the singer's family for many generations.

Better known as "Lamkin" or "Bloody Mason," the scene of the ballad has been localized by some scholars as being in the county of Northumberland, possibly near the village of Ovingham-on-Tyne. It is there that is found the tradition of Lamkin and his tower. The story was printed in the *Scots Musical Museum.*

The hero of the lullaby, "Lamkin" has been the unrivaled bogey-man of Scotch nurseries.

3

"Oh, yes, I dare to stay here, I am not afraid of young Alanthia,
or none of his kin,
I will bar up my doors and my windows pin in."

4

She barred up her doors and her windows pinned in,
All but the kitchen window, where the maid let him in.

5

"Oh, spare young Alanthia, oh, spare but an hour,
You shall have my daughter Betsey, she's queen of the tower."

6

"Call out your daughter Betsey, she may do you some good,
She may hold the silver basin to catch your heart's blood."

7

"Stay still, Betsey, wherever you may be,
So's to wait upon your father when he comes home from sea."

8

Laird Arnold came home, he opened the gate,
There lay his little baby, lying dead at his feet.

9

He went in the house, he opened the door,
There lay his loving lady, lying dead on the floor.

10

"Who's been here?" he cried. Daughter Betsey steps up,
"Young Alanthia's been here, he killed my mother."

11

Young Alanthia was burned in the fire to fry,
And the maid was hung on Billings to die.

YOUNG CHARLOTTE

This ballad is here recorded as remembered by Miss Mary Harmon, from the singing of her mother fifty years ago.

"Young Charlotte" is the second native American ballad to be discovered. It was written by Seba Smith (1792–1868), probably some time before 1833, and was first printed in *The Rover*. The ballad is found in Maine and Vermont and at nearly every point where William Carter, a blind singer, has been known to have traveled.

The familiar air is sung to "The False-hearted Knight," but the melody used here is traditional in the Ellingwood family. Only the first two verses were given by the singer; verses 3–12 are reprinted by permission of the Folksong Society of the Northeast.

3

In a village fifteen miles from home,
There's a merry ball tonight,
Although the air is freezing-cold,
Our hearts are warm and light.
Long and anxiously she watched,
Till a well known voice she hears,
And driving up to the cottage door,
Young Charles Wesley appears.

4

"Why, Charlotte, dear," her mother says,
"This blanket around you fold;
It is a dreadful night, you know,
You'll take your death of cold."
"Oh, no! Oh, no!" young Charlotte says,
She laughed like a gypsy queen,
"To ride in blankets muffled up,
I never would be seen."

5

"My silken cloak is quite enough—
It is lined, you know, throughout.
Besides, I have a silken scarf,
To tie my head about."
Gloves and bonnets being on,
They jumped into the sleigh,
And away they rode o'er the mountain side,
And the hills so far away.

6

There's music in the sound of bells,
As over the hills we go;
What a crackling noise the runners make,
As they bite the frozen snow.
With faces muffled silently for five long miles they rode,
Until at length with a few frozen words,
Young Charles the silence broke.

7

"Such a night as this I never knew,
My reins I scarce can hold."
Young Charlotte says with a feeble voice,
"I feel exceeding cold."

He cracked his whip, he urged his steed much
faster than before,
Until at length five more long miles,
In silence they rode on.

8

Young Charles he says, "I feel the air
A-gathering on my brow."
Young Charlotte says with a weaker voice,
"I'm growing warmer now."
Away they rode on the mountain side,
And through the cold starlight,
Until they entered the village,
And the ballroom hove in sight.

9

Driving up, young Charles jumps out,
And he offers his hand to her;
"Why sit you there like a monument
That hath no power to stir?"
He called her once, he called her twice,
But she uttered not a word;
He called her for her hand again,
But still she never stirred.

10

He tore the mantle from her brow,
And the cold stars on her shone,
And quickly in the lighted room,
Her lifeless form was borne.
They tried all means 'twas in their power,
Her life for to restore,
For Charlotte's was a frozen corpse,
Ne'er to speak nevermore.

11

He threw himself down on his knees,
And the bitter tears did flow,
Saying, "My young and intended bride,
No more with me you'll go."
He threw himself down by her side,
And he kissed her marble brow,
And his thought ran back to the place she says,
"I'm growing warmer now."

12

They bore her out into the sleigh,
And Charles with her rode home,
And when he reached the cottage door,
Oh, how her parents mourned!
They mourned for the loss of their daughter dear,
And Charles mourned for his bride,
Until at length his heart did break,
And they slumber side by side.

THE SINGERS

Miss Lucy Allen of West Newton, Massachusetts, is a descendant of James Allen, who came from northern England to Dedham, Massachusetts, whence he moved almost immediately to Medfield in 1639. The Allen family gathered for reunions in the homestead in Medfield for nearly three hundred years. Records of these meetings are in the possession of the family today. Part of the entertainment, in which both youngsters and grown-ups took part, was the singing of songs handed down by oral tradition. On an old register, dated September 2, 1848, the succinct lines stand, "Once more united after years of separation, in their old home, these sons and daughters joined to sing the praises of Free men, Free speech, and *God's free soil.*" Members of this family were leaders in the educational field; the singer's father, Nathaniel, was a protégé of Horace Mann. Miss Allen is principal of the Misses Allen School in West Newton, Massachusetts—founded in 1904. In her father's school, which was founded in 1853, her uncles, Joseph, James, and George, taught.

All of the family in the seventh and eighth generations were singers, and the *Allen Family Songbook* was printed by Miss Rosa G. Allen, sister of our contributor.

Henry A. Castle lives in Plainville, Connecticut, where his family are old settlers. He remembers many songs and yarns that were current when he was a boy, more than fifty years ago.

Mrs. Helen Dunham Elliott of Avon, Massachusetts, wife of Dr. R. A. Elliott, is a descendant of Captain Cornelius Dunham, who was born in Plymouth, Massachusetts. He was captain of a privateer out of Plymouth during the Revolution. He followed the sea for many years and then was at Pemaquid Lighthouse, Pemaquid, Maine. Captain Dunham's original sea chest and many old documents are in the possession of the family today.

On the ship *Bevis* in May, 1638, *John Frye* sailed from Basing, England, to Newbury, Massachusetts. From there he went to Andover, where the family was known as the "Fighting Fryes of Andover," because they were such valiant fighters in the Indian wars. Among them were sergeants, corporals, lieutenants, and colonels. Fryeburg, Maine, was named for Parson Frye, who was chaplain to the Andover Camp, called the "Flower of Essex." From these gallant soldiers *Miss Mary P. Frye* and *Miss Serena J. Frye* are descended, the former a schoolteacher in Brookline, Massachusetts, for forty years. The men as well as the women in this family were great singers.

Mrs. Mildred Miner Hadley of Fall River, Massachusetts, is a descendant of Captain Tristram Coffin, who came from England to Nantucket, Massachusetts. The family were Quakers, but an aunt of Mrs. Hadley married Mr. Clisby, who taught her many songs which the children of the singer now enjoy.

Mrs. Mary E. Harmon is a descendant of Ralph Ellwood (1610–1679), who sailed from England on the ship *Truelove,* in September, 1635, and came to Salem, Massachusetts. He added the three letters *ing* to his name when he settled in that town in 1637. In Salem and Beverly the Ellingwoods were "pretty numerous" and were known as the "Beverly Ellingwoods." Benjamin and Mary Ellingwood, ancestors of the singer, had fourteen children. All of this family were singers; and the songs of the family traditions are many and with particularly pleasing melodies.

A descendant of Nicholas Hatheway, who came in 1636 from England to Taunton, Massachusetts, was Abiah Ashley, grandmother of *Mrs. Edith Irons Kidder* and *Miss Helen Hatheway Irons.* Family tradition notes that Abiah had an unusually lovely voice and enjoyed singing to her twelve children. Her five great-great-grandchildren today sing the songs of their mother's people. It is a Yankee family of farmers and educators and the home site is still occupied by the family.

About sixty years ago, when *Mrs. Frances Merrow Horn* was three years old, her grandmother, then ninety years old, sang to her "Will You Wear the Red?" The men and women of this family of farmers settled in West Newfield, Maine, about 1830. Although they had been in this country one hundred years previously, there were no records of them before this time. The singer has a fine voice and takes part in all the local entertainments in Wolfeboro, New Hampshire, where she lives on a great farm.

Some time before 1698, Philip Hubbard sailed from the Isle of Jersey to Kittery, Maine, where he built a blockhouse and became an active leader of town affairs. His descendant, *Dr. Frank Allen Hubbard,* a practicing physician for more than fifty years, sang many songs learned when he was a boy from his mother, Harriet Ann Barrett. She was the great-granddaughter of Smith Barrett, who was fifteen years old in 1781 and was in Captain Robbins' Company, the 7th Connecticut. In both the Hubbard and the Barrett line were singers, though their work was as statesmen, farmers, and doctors.

There were in the family of *Dr. and Mrs. Frank Allen Hubbard* of Taunton, Massachusetts, three boys and three girls who grew up with music a part of their daily lives. The great open back yard was a favorite gathering place for the whole neighborhood. Many an afternoon after school or on Saturday, the mother looked out to count with her own youngsters the noisy number of fifteen or twenty visiting children. The songs and games played so persistently and commonly left an indelible mark in the memory of these boys and girls. In this home both the mother and the father sang—the mother's songs, learned from her father and his people, were sung as lullabies. It was a great privilege for these children to have the company of their father, a surgeon and physician with a large practice. He possessed a fine intelligence, and blended with the mental equipment of the scholar was a strain of homely characteristics that endeared him to every one. Though he took an active interest in city affairs and was constantly at the beck and call of the sick, it was common for him to spend part of each Sunday evening with his youngsters, telling them Bible stories, followed as a special treat by songs accompanied on the concertina. On many a long ride with the bay horse or black mare under the night sky, when the good man was called far out of the city limits to care for old Mrs. Wood's "bad turn," the sound of the clopping hooves made a fine accompaniment to the muted rolling tune of an old song. Sunday evenings in the summertime around the campfire saw the doctor finishing the "Camp sing" with a performance on the concertina. Always the audience of children and grown-ups were requested to join in the chorus. In such a home, where music was part of the emotional pattern of living, the family ties were closely knit; and today the songs which were the parents' heritage are the treasure of the grandchildren.

Mrs. Elizabeth Wheeler Hubbard, whose father was Dr. Edward Reed Wheeler of Spencer, Massachusetts, is descended from Asa Foster Reed. In the family both men and women knew many old songs, but the majority of the singers were men.

Mrs. Lucy Palmer Johnson is a descendant of Nathaniel Palmer, who, with a younger brother, came from Wales to settle in Scituate, Massachusetts, about 1748. The singer, who was a schoolteacher, recalls many of her mother's songs which had been in the family for generations.

Miss Ada Kelley is descended from David O'Killy, who sailed from Ireland to North Harwich, Massachusetts, about the middle of the seventeenth century with a load of brick to build a home in the new colony. The name was changed to Kelley when the family moved to Yarmouth. The men in the Kelley family were great singers, and Ada, our ballad singer, overheard her mischievous brother many times when she was not supposed to be around. Like all children, she remembered best the forbidden information.

Stanton L. King went to sea when he was thirteen and served six years in the merchant marine and six in the United States Navy. The ships of the merchant marine were the *Florida*, the *Queenstown*, and the *Hagarstown*, from Maine out of Richmond. These ships carried, as cargo, kerosene to Japan, with vanilla and hemp and sugar as ballast. The *Queenstown* was set on fire in the harbor of Manila by the Chinese cook, whose wife, as Captain King says, "got chummy with the mate." On the brigantine *Pearl*, from New York to Trinidad, a deck load of mules was washed overboard in one sea as a West Indian hurricane struck the ship. On a three-masted schooner from New York to Wilmington, lumber was the cargo, as on the *Maracaibo*, which carried logwood to Boston. Captain King sailed three times around the world in the *Alliance* and was gone three years and four months.

In April, 1892, Captain King came to Boston on the *Wabash*, passed his examinations, and began his work at the Sailors' Haven in Charlestown, where today he carries on for the forty-seventh year as superintendent of the home for sailors. During the World War he was given a captain's commission, and he has been the official United States Government chanteyman.

James M. Linscott, ex-seaman in the United States merchant marine, served with the American Republic Line on the steamships *West Imboden* and *Capillo* to the South American coast, and in the *Magmeric* of the South Atlantic Mail Line as quartermaster. In these ships many old chanteys were sung for entertainment.

Theophilus Hardy came from England to Berwick, Maine (then Massachusetts), about 1720. He was a hatter by trade and a Shaker by religion. He married Mary Sullivan, sister of John Sullivan (1740–1795), a major general in the Revolutionary Army. A descendant of Theophilus and Mary Sullivan Hardy, is *Mrs. Jennie Hardy Linscott*, who remembers her grandmother, Sarah Palmer Arnold, and her mother, Elizabeth Arnold Hardy, who was "a sweet singer." They were always singing about the house. In this family the music seems to have been carried on by the women. The family have been Yankee farmers, statesmen, and, of course, soldiers.

Andrew Moore came from England to Windsor, Connecticut, in 1636. The singer from this family is *Mrs. Harriet Moore Deming*, Winsted, Connecticut. Her father, from whom she learned her songs, was a singer with a fine voice.

Mrs. Addie Jackson Morse of Underhill, Vermont, is a descendant of John Jackson, who came from England about 1816. Calvin, the son of Mercy Mead and Calvin Morse, built the house in which the fifth generation is now living. Both men and women sang in this family. There is a monument in the Medfield cemetery to the seven Morse brothers who came from England.

At the time of the Great Irish Rebellion, Henry Prescott came to New Brunswick and thence to Lawrence, Massachusetts. His descendant *Henry Prescott* of Hyde Park, Massachusetts, knows several fine old ballads that his father and grandfather used to sing.

Fred Pullen left home at the age of fifteen but returned; and, when he was eighteen years old he bought from his father the home farm, where he has lived for sixty years. Mr. Pullen was road commissioner for sixteen years and has in his possession the model T Ford automobile with which he made his rounds. His remembrance of kissing parties is vivid and humorous.

Elizabeth Foster Reed, descendant of Asa Foster and wife of Major Samuel Horton Reed of Rowe, Massachusetts, kept a manuscript, now in the possession of her descendants, of songs and dance tunes; but the exact date or purpose of this record is not known.

Mrs. Asenath Slade of Fall River, Massachusetts, is a descendant of Mary Ann Buckley Tetlow, who emigrated from Heywood, England, to Providence, Rhode Island. The family moved almost immediately to Fall River in 1842, where they have since lived.

Captain Charlton L. Smith went to sea when he was fifteen years old, with the consent of his father, an importer of gems. Captain Smith made three voyages to South America in the *Mancunia* of Manchester, England, in the mahogany trade; to Chile in the *Queen Louise;* and was on the *Paul Revere,* one of the last of the wooden sailing ships, when a mutiny broke out that ended with five men in irons. As "chips," or ship's carpenter, Captain Smith spent most of his years in sailing ships, though he was in a few steamships, including the *Brambletie,* named for King Edward's horse, *McDermott,* a British ship out of the Isle of Mann, *Lucarnia, Montcalm, John Orchard,* and *Albert Crandell.* On Yankee ships, "chips" *was* somebody, says Captain Smith, for he had to be chief carpenter, blacksmith, and all-around mechanic; he ranked to eat at the second table. Captain Smith was officer during his last eight years at sea in deep-water ships. Since 1889 he has been yacht master at Marblehead. He built the first *Brutal Beast,* a small sailing boat, and today in his trim workshop this master mariner is a boat builder. He is the chanteyman for the Boston Yacht Club dogwatch dinners.

Mrs. Sarah Stuart Wilkins is the descendant of Isaac Allerton Stuart, who came from England to Plymouth, Massachusetts, on the *Mayflower* in 1620. She remembers a few of the songs from her mother's family.

Mrs. Ella M. Wright, known to all as "Auntie May," learned her songs from her father, a descendant of John Smith, a "pressed" soldier in Burgoyne's army. So "put out" was he at being shipped from England for military service, that when he landed in Plymouth, New Hampshire, he swore allegiance to the United States. He was an educated swordsman, but he would never tell where he came from; and the only information that the family has is that he was English. The singer's father possessed a fine voice, and the family have many songs that have come down through the male line. "Auntie May" sang at concerts fifty years ago and recalls that as a child she was not supposed to repeat the songs she heard, for once her father heard her singing "Old Irish Gentleman" and said, "Ella May! If *you're* going to sing my songs, *I'm* not going to sing *any more!*"

Charlie Young of Moultonboro, New Hampshire, is the son of Sam Young of North Anson, Maine, and, like his father, was a river driver and woodsman. He was guide in the Penobscot region for ten years.

When he was thirteen, *Sam Young* of North Anson, Maine, went into the woods, where for thirty years he lived in logging camps as logger and river driver and moved with the crews on all the great Maine logging waters. He has a great repertory of songs that he learned and sang in the woods, and he sings them today to his grandson on the farm where he has settled.

He sighs today that the real lumberjack has vanished forever, and scoffs at the weaklings who can stay but a week in the woods, there to be pampered with radio and fancy grub. With a light in his eye he tells of the days when five hundred loggers roared into town for a blow-in, their pockets full of pay, their calked boots scarring the tavern floors and plank sidewalks while they shouted and pounded at the bars. Sam Young is a vigorous and magnificent specimen of the Maine woodsman, one of the last of the real pioneers.

FIDDLERS AND PROMPTERS

Harry E. Brigham of Marlboro, Massachusetts, is leader of his own orchestra, and has played and called for old dances for over sixty years. He plays the bass viol while prompting and twirls it with gusto as he calls the changes.

Edson H. Cole of Freedom, New Hampshire, has been fiddler, caller, and dancing master for more than thirty years. When he was a boy he was sent to Boston to study the violin; but he had acquired his taste for music and his prompting from his uncle, Jim Cole, famous in the section as a past master in these arts for fifty years. Edson Cole, an old-time dancing master, conducted his own dancing school for seventeen years. Today he is caretaker of two large farms—one his own—tax collector, takes an active part in town and county affairs, and with two of his children to carry on his music, he still plays and calls the changes for the old dances.

Happy Hale of Hinsdale, New Hampshire, was chosen champion caller of New England for 1937 at the Eastern States Exposition in Springfield, Massachusetts. He says he is "known from Maine to California." One of the innovations in which he took part was calling the changes for some of the old dances presented by the Gay Blades, a traveling ice-skating carnival. Two of the dances for which Happy sang his calls in the Boston Garden were "Hull's Victory" and a plain quadrille. As he is one of the few prompters who make up their own rhymes for the dance changes and sing them in time to the rhythm of the air, he is one of the best known. He has called dance changes as a special feature on radio programs.

Lewis L. Jillson of Bernardston, Massachusetts, is a fiddler and caller who plays for the most part around Putney, Vermont. Very often he will be leader of the orchestra when Happy Hale calls the changes.

Dennis McClure is a fiddler and caller of Willimantic, Connecticut, and plays with the orchestra known as the Connecticut Hayshakers. Although he is blind, he is one of the most popular and versatile of the old-time fiddlers.

Ralph Merrill of Cumberland Mills, Maine, is a prompter, particularly for the orchestra of the Singing Smiths of South Parsonsfield, Maine. He began calling several years ago for the country dances at East Limington, Maine, when no caller was present to direct the old dances. He has a fine voice for prompting, and his favorite dances are "Haymaker's Jig" and "Green Mountain Volunteers."

Smith Paine of Wolfeboro, New Hampshire, has been fiddler and caller for over thirty years and began playing for the old dances when he was a very young man. On a small farm in Pleasant Valley he practices his trade of carpenter and is in charge of a large neighboring estate. Mr. Paine is known as a maker of fine fiddles, and many violins are brought to him for intricate repair. From the top of a mellow maple table he has made a violin with a lovely tone, exquisite workmanship, and delicate inlay.

Cassius Radford of Pembroke, New Hampshire, has traveled all over New England and New York State, calling the changes and fiddling for the old dances. In 1936 he was chosen champion fiddler of New Hampshire. Today he is ninety-three years old, and his fingers are crippled; but though they can no longer hold a bow, Cash can whistle any merry tune in the same rhythm that he played it.

The Singing Smiths are a family of five musicians, led by the father, Mr. R. V. Smith, who plays the fiddle. The youngest, a boy five years old, plays the drums, and at the old dances Mrs. Smith does her share as ticket taker at the door. Many of the instruments used by this family orchestra are homemade. The family plays for the old dances within a fifty-mile radius of Limerick, Maine.

Willie Woodward of Bristol, New Hampshire, plays an accordion for the old dances and is a fine prompter. Bill is only twenty-three and is in great demand in his section. He says he doesn't know where he learned the dance changes, because "I have always known them." He has called dance changes as a special feature on radio programs.

REFERENCES

This is a condensed reference list.
Abbreviations used:

JAFL: Journal of American Folk Lore
JEFSS: Journal of English Folk Song Society
JEFDS: Journal of English Folk Dance Society
ESPB: English and Scottish Popular Ballads (Francis J. Child)
FSSNE: Folk Song Society of the North East

SINGING GAMES

Counting-Out Rhymes

Ref. Henry C. Bolton, *Counting-Out Rhymes*, pp. 49, 58, 102, 107.

Did You Ever See a Lassie

Ref. Alice B. Gomme, *Children's Singing Games*, p. 14.
JEFDS, Vol. II.
Farnsworth and Sharp, *Folksongs, Chanteys and Singing Games*, p. 87.

The Farmer in the Dell

Ref. Alice E. Gillington, *Old Isle of Wight Singing Games*, p. 4.
Alice B. Gomme, *Dictionary of British Folklore*, Vol. II, p. 420.
W. W. Newell, *Games and Songs of American Children*, p. 29.
James O. Phillips-Halliwell, *Nursery Rhymes of England*, No. 352.
JAFL, Vol. III, p. 253; Vol. XXXI, pp. 51, 160.

Go In and Out the Windows

Ref. W. W. Newell, *Games and Songs of American Children*, p. 128.
Alice B. Gomme, *Dictionary of British Folklore*, Vol. II, p. 122.
JAFL, Vol. VIII, p. 253; Vol. XV, p. 114.

Green Gravel

Ref. W. W. Newell, *Games and Songs of American Children*, p. 71.
Alice B. Gomme, *Dictionary of British Folklore*, Vol. I, p. 182.

Green Grow the Rushes, Oh

Ref. W. W. Newell, *Games and Songs of American Children*, p. 56.
Alice B. Gomme, *Dictionary of British Folklore*, Vol. II, p. 231.

Here Come Three Dukes a-Riding

Ref. Alice B. Gomme, *Children's Singing Games*, p. 67.
——, *Dictionary of British Folklore*, Vol. II, p. 233.
G. L. Gomme, *Folklore Relics of Early Village Life*, pp. 190, 197, 203–5, 221.
W. W. Newell, *Games and Songs of American Children*, p. 47.
James O. Phillips-Halliwell, *Popular Rhymes and Nursery Tales*, p. 123.
Robert Chambers, *Popular Rhymes of Scotland*, p. 66.
Henry Bett, *Games of Children*, p. 11.
JAFL, Vol. VIII, p. 254; Vol. XII, p. 75; Vol. XXXI, p. 52.

Here Stands an Old Maid Forsaken

Ref. W. W. Newell, *Games and Songs of American Children*, p. 70.
Alice B. Gomme, *Dictionary of British Folklore*, Vol. I, pp. 204, 205.

Here We Go Gathering Nuts in May

Ref. Alice B. Gomme, *Dictionary of British Folklore*, Vol. I, p. 425.
G. L. Gomme, *Folklore Relics of Early Village Life*, pp. 207, 210, 221.
W. W. Newell, *Games and Songs of American Children*, pp. 14, 15, 89.
JAFL, Vol. VIII, p. 253; Vol. XXXI, pp. 47, 178.
Henry Bett, *Games of Children*, p. 16.

How Many Miles to London Town?

Ref. John Mactaggart, *Gallovidian Encyclopedia*, p. 300.
Henry Bett, *Games of Children*, p. 47.
W. W. Newell, *Games and Songs of American Children*, pp. 153–54.
James O. Phillips-Halliwell, *Popular Rhymes and Nursery Tales*, p. 118.
Alice B. Gomme, *Dictionary of British Folklore*, Vol. I, p. 231.
Alice E. Gillington, *Old Isle of Wight Singing Games*, p. 30.
Robert Chambers, *Popular Rhymes of Scotland*, p. 63.

I Am a Rich Widow

Ref. W. W. Newell, *Games and Songs of American Children*, p. 57.
Alice B. Gomme, *Dictionary of British Folklore*, Vol. I, pp. 315, 380.
JAFL, Vol. XIV, p. 298.

I'll Give to You a Paper of Pins

Ref. W. W. Newell, *Games and Songs of American Children*, pp. 51–54.
G. L. Gomme, *Folklore Relics of Early Village Life*, pp. 217, 230.
JAFL, Vol. XXXI, p. 49.

Alice B. Gomme, *Dictionary of British Folklore*, Vol. II, pp. 437, 450.
JEFSS, Vol. VIII, p. 151.

I Put My Little Hand In

Ref. Alice B. Gomme, *Dictionary of British Folklore*, Vol. I, p. 353.
W. W. Newell, *Games and Songs of American Children*, p. 131.
James O. Phillips-Halliwell, *Popular Rhymes and Nursery Tales*, p. 128.
——, *Nursery Rhymes of England.*
JEFDS, No. 4, Second Series, p. 222.
Robert Chambers, *Popular Rhymes of Scotland*, p. 65.
FSSNE, Bulletin No. 4, 1932, p. 17.

Jennia Jones

Ref. W. W. Newell, *Games and Songs of American Children*, p. 63.
Alice B. Gomme, *Children's Singing Games*, p. 22.
——, *Dictionary of British Folklore*, Vol. I, p. 260.
William Chappell, *Roxburghe Ballads*, Vol. I, pp. 186–89.
Robert Chambers, *Popular Rhymes of Scotland*, pp. 66, 140.
JAFL, Vol. III, p. 171; Vol. XXXI, p. 50.
Henry Bett, *Games of Children*, p. 31.

King's Land

Ref. Alice B. Gomme, *Dictionary of British Folklore*, Vol. I, p. 300.
W. W. Newell, *Games and Songs of American Children*, p. 221.

Lazy Mary

Ref. James O. Phillips-Halliwell, *Nursery Rhymes of England*, p. 119.
W. W. Newell, *Games and Songs of American Children*, p. 96.

London Bridge

Ref. Alice E. Gillington, *Old Isle of Wight Singing Games*, p. 18.
W. W. Newell, *Games and Songs of American Children*, pp. 204 ff.
Alice B. Gomme, *Dictionary of British Folklore*, Vol. I, p. 333.
G. L. Gomme, *Folklore Relics of Early Village Life*, pp. 25, 28–36.
Henry Bett, *Games of Children*, p. 100.

Lucy Locket

Ref. James O. Phillips-Halliwell, *Nursery Rhymes of England*, p. 165.
——, *Popular Rhymes and Nursery Tales*, p. 130.
Henry Bett, *Games of Children*, pp. 16, 29.
JAFL, Vol. XXIX, p. 165; Vol. XXXI, p. 57.
Alice B. Gomme, *Dictionary of British Folklore*, Vol. I, p. 305.

Mulb'ry Bush

Ref. W. W. Newell, *Games and Songs of American Children*, pp. 16, 17, 86.
Alice B. Gomme, *Dictionary of British Folklore*, Vol. I, p. 404.
James O. Phillips-Halliwell, *Popular Rhymes and Nursery Tales*, p. 216.
Henry Bett, *Games of Children*, p. 42.
JAFL, Vol. XXXI, pp. 54, 178.

My Fairey and My Forey

Ref. Alice B. Gomme, *Children's Singing Games*, pp. 56, 69.
——, *Dictionary of British Folklore*, Vol. II, p. 343.
Alice E. Gillington, *Old Isle of Wight Singing Games*, p. 19.
JAFL, Vol. XVII.
JEFS, Vol. IV, p. 67.

The Needle's Eye

Ref. W. W. Newell, *Games and Songs of American Children*, p. 91.
Alice B. Gomme, *Dictionary of British Folklore*, Vol. II, pp. 229, 230.

On the Green Carpet

Ref. Alice B. Gomme, *Dictionary of British Folklore*, Vol. I, pp. 153, 322.
G. L. Gomme, *Folklore Relics of Early Village Life*, p. 199.
W. W. Newell, *Games and Songs of American Children*, p. 60.
JAFL, Vol. XIV, p. 297; Vol. XXXI, pp. 48, 55, 160.

Old Woman All Skin and Bone

Ref. Alice B. Gomme, *Children's Singing Games*, p. 68.
G. L. Gomme, *Folklore Relics of Early Village Life*, p. 113.
JAFL, Vol. XXVI, pp. 16, 142.
Gammer Gurton's Garland, p. 180.

Poor Mary Sits a-Weeping

Ref. Alice B. Gomme, *Children's Singing Games*, p. 70.
——, *Dictionary of British Folklore*, Vol. II, p. 46.
G. L. Gomme, *Folklore Relics of Early Village Life*, p. 82.
JAFL, Vol. XII, p. 74.

Ring Around o' Rosies

Ref. Alice B. Gomme, *Dictionary of British Folklore*, Vol. I, p. 205; Vol. II, p. 108.
W. W. Newell, *Games and Songs of American Children*, p. 127.
Henry Bett, *Games of Children*, p. 89.
JAFL, Vol. XXXI, p. 57 n.

Shall I Show You How the Farmer?

Ref. Alice B. Gomme, *Dictionary of British Folklore*, Vol. I, pp. 399–401.
G. L. Gomme, *Folklore Relics of Early Village Life*, p. 128.
JAFL, Vol. XII, p. 74.

The Twelve Days of Christmas

Ref. Alice B. Gomme, *Dictionary of British Folklore*, Vol. II, p. 315.

Water, Water, Wild Flower

Ref. Robert Ford, *Harp of Perthshire.*
W. W. Newell, *Games and Songs of American Children*, pp. 8, 68.
Alice E. Gillington, *Old Hampshire Folksongs*, p. 15.
Alice B. Gomme, *Dictionary of British Folklore*, Vol. I, p. 99; Vol. II, p. 330.
JAFL, Vol. XII, p. 292.

THE COUNTRY DANCE

Bonaparte Crossing the Rhine (March)

Ref. Elizabeth Foster Reed's *Manuscript Copybook.*

Boston Fancy, or **Lady Walpole's Reel**

Ref. Henry Ford, *Good Morning*, p. 104.
Tolman and Page, *Country Dance Book*, p. 111.
Elias Howe, *Musician's Omnibus*, No. 1, p. 45

Chorus Jig

Ref. P. W. Joyce, *Old Irish Folk Music and Songs*, p. 36.
Edward Bunting, *Collection of Ancient Irish Music*, p. 76.
Elizabeth Burchenal, *American Country Dances*, p. 25.

Devil's Dream

Ref. John Playford, *The Dancing Master*, p. 72.

The Duchess

Ref. John Playford, *The Dancing Master*, p. 179.

Fishers' Hornpipe

Ref. Elizabeth Burchenal, *American Country Dances*, p. 47.

French Four

Ref. John Playford, *The Dancing Master*, p. 44.
William Chappell, *Popular Music of the Olden Time*, p. 82.

The Girl I Left Behind Me

Ref. Cecil J. Sharp, *The Country Dance Book,* Vol. I, p. 33.

Green Mountain Volunteers

Ref. E. Benjamin Andrews, *History of the United States,* Vol. II, p. 86.

Haymakers' Jig

Ref. Duncan Edmonstone, *Minstrelsy of England,* p. 307.
William Chappell, *Old English Popular Music,* Vol. II, p. 51.
William Chappell, *Later Popular Music,* Vol. II, p. 128.
Elizabeth Burchenal, *American Country Dances,* pp. 4, 5.
Moffatt and Kidson, *Dances of the Olden Times,* p. 17.

High, Betty Martin

Ref. Tolman and Page, *The Country Dance Book,* p. 62.

Hull's Victory

Ref. E. Benjamin Andrews, *History of the United States,* Vol. II, p. 343.
Elizabeth Foster Reed's *Manuscript Copybook.*
Elizabeth Burchenal, *American Country Dances,* p. 30.

Lady of the Lake

Ref. *Collection of National English Airs,* p. 129, No. CLXIII.
JEFSS, Vol. VII, p. 222.
William Chappell, *Old English Popular Music,* Vol. I, p. 276 (1893).
Grigg and Elliot, *Southern and Western Songster,* p. 23.
Elias Howe, *Musician's Companion,* Part II, p. 77; Part III, p. 242.

The London Lanciers

Ref. Henry Ford, *Good Morning,* p. 83.
Encyclopædia Britannica, 11th ed., Vol. VII, p. 800.

Maid in the Pump Room

Ref. Elizabeth Burchenal, *American Country Dances,* p. 24.
John Playford, *The Dancing Master,* p. 32.
Cecil J. Sharp, *The Country Dance Book,* Part II, p. 66.
——, *Folkdance Airs,* p. 26.
Elias Howe, *Musician's Companion,* Part II, p. 35; Part III, p. 238.
JEFS, Vol. I, p. 27.

The Merry Dance

Ref. Cecil J. Sharp, *Country Dance Tunes, from the English Dancing Master,* p. 16.

Cecil J. Sharp, *The Country Dance Book*, Part IV, p. 68.
P. W. Joyce, *Old Irish Folkmusic and Songs*, p. 65.

Miss Brown's Reel

Ref. John Glen, *Collection of Scottish Dance Music*, p. 6.

Money Musk

Ref. Alfred Moffatt, *Dance Music of the North*, p. 10.
John Glen, *Collection of Scottish Dance Music*, p. 31.
Elizabeth Burchenal, *American Country Dances*, p. 55.

Morning Star

Ref. P. W. Joyce, *Ancient Irish Music and Songs*, p. 262.
Elias Howe, *Musician's Companion*, Part III, p. 297.

Ninepin Quadrille, or **The Cheat**

Ref. Tolman and Page, *The Country Dance*, p. 59.
Elizabeth Foster Reed's *Manuscript Copybook.*

Petronella

Ref. Cecil J. Sharp, *Country Dance Tunes*, Set II, p. 12.

Plain Quadrille

Ref. Elizabeth Foster Reed's *Manuscript Copybook.*
William Chappell, *Introduction to the Country Dance.*

Pop! Goes the Weasel

Ref. Alice B. Gomme, *Dictionary of British Folklore*, p. 63.
Cecil J. Sharp, *The Country Dance Book*, Vol. I, p. 40.
Elizabeth Burchenal, *American Country Dances*, p. 22.

Portland Fancy

Ref. Elizabeth Burchenal, *American Country Dances*, p. 7.

Sicilian Circle

Ref. *JEFDS*, Vol. I.
Elizabeth Burchenal, *American Country Dances*, pp. 1, 2, 3.
Elias Howe, *Musician's Companion*, Part II, p. 164.

Soldier's Joy

Ref. *JEFSS*, Vol. I, p. 81.
Elizabeth Burchenal, *American Country Dances*, p. 6.

Speed the Plough

Ref. John Brand, *Popular Antiquities of Great Britain*, p. 472.
Cecil J. Sharp, *The Country Dance Book*, p. 39.
Alfred Moffatt, *Dance Music of the North*, p. 19.
JEFSS, Vol. I, pp. 18, 19.
Elizabeth Burchenal, *American Country Dances*, p. 37.

Steamboat Quickstep

Ref. E. Benjamin Andrews, *History of the United States*, Vol. II, p. 290.
Elizabeth Foster Reed's *Manuscript Copybook.*

The Tempest

Ref. John Playford, *The Dancing Master.*
Elias Howe, Jr., *Preceptor for the Accordion*, p. 19.
Edward Bunting, *Collection of Ancient Irish Music.*

Twin Sisters

Ref. John Playford, *The Dancing Master*, p. 33.
Edward Bunting, *Collection of Ancient Irish Music.*

Virginia Reel

Ref. Thomas Croker, *Popular Songs of Ireland.*
Alfred Moffatt, *Minstrelsy of Ireland.*
Alfred Moffatt, *Minstrelsy of England.*
William Chappell, *Country Dance*, p. 672.
Grigg and Elliot, *Southern and Western Songster*, p. 95.

The Waltz

Ref. *Encyclopædia Britannica*, 11th ed., Vol. VII, p. 799.
Cecil J. Sharp, *Introduction to the Country Dance.*

Washington Grand March

Ref. *Brown Collection*, Boston Public Library; Firth and Hall, New York.

The White Cockade

Ref. *Encyclopædia Britannica*, 11th ed., Vol. VI, CHA-CON.

SEA CHANTEYS AND FO'CASTLE SONGS

Amsterdam

Ref. Captain W. B. Whall, *Sea Songs and Shanties*, p. 58.
Joanna Colcord, *Roll and Go*, p. 37.

D. W. Bone, *Capstan Bars*, p. 99.
Farnsworth and Sharp, *Folk Songs, Chanteys, and Singing Games*, p. 100.

A Long Time Ago

Ref. Joanna Colcord, *Roll and Go*, p. 20.

Blow, Boys, Blow

Ref. Joanna Colcord, *Roll and Go*, p. 7.
Captain W. B. Whall, *Sea Songs and Shanties*, p. 68.
D. W. Bone, *Capstan Bars*, p. 57.
Eckstorm and Smyth, *Minstrelsy of Maine*, p. 238.

Blow the Man Down

Ref. Captain W. B. Whall, *The Shanty Book*, Part I, p. 34.
Robert Frothingham, *Songs of the Sea and Sailor's Chanteys*, p. 245.
D. W. Bone, *Capstan Bars*, p. 75ff.
Eckstorm and Smyth, *Minstrelsy of Maine*, pp. 243–44.

Captain Kidd

Ref. Knapp and Baldwin, *Newgate Calendar* (verses 3, 6, 12, 13).
Mrs. Lucy Johnson (verses 1, 2, 16, 17).
Forget-Me-Not Songster, published by Locke and Bubier (remaining verses).
Eckstorm and Smyth, *Minstrelsy of Maine*, p. 247.

The Gallant Victory, or Lowlands Low

Ref. F. J. Child, 286 *ESPB*, pp. 611–613.
Broadwood and Mason, *English County Songs*, p. 54.
Alfred Moffatt, *Minstrelsy of England*, p. 300.
Singer's Journal, Vol. II, p. 686.
JAFL, Vol. XVIII, pp. 125–127; Vol. XXX, p. 331.
Cecil J. Sharp, *One Hundred Folksongs*, p. 23.
——, *English County Songs*, p. 182.

The Dead Horse

Ref. Captain W. B. Whall, *Sea Songs and Shanties*, p. 119.
Joanna Colcord, *Roll and Go*, p. 19.
D. W. Bone, *Capstan Bars*, p. 48
Farnsworth and Sharp, *Folksongs, Chanteys, and Singing Games*, p. 107.

Haul Away, Joe

Ref. Captain W. B. Whall, *Sea Songs and Shanties*, p. 85.
Joanna Colcord, *Roll and Go*, p. 3.

Haul the Bowline

Ref. Robert Frothingham, *Songs of the Sea and Sailor's Chanteys*, p. 257.
Captain W. B. Whall, *The Shanty Book*, Part I, p. 58.
D. W. Bone, *Capstan Bars*, p. 38.

Homeward Bound

Ref. Captain W. B. Whall, *Sea Songs and Shanties*, p. 6.
D. W. Bone, *Capstan Bars*, p. 116.

Johnny Boker

Ref. Joanna Colcord, *Roll and Go*, p. 5.
Captain W. B. Whall, *Sea Songs and Shanties*, p. 95.

Old Horse

Ref. Eckstorm and Smyth, *Minstrels of Maine*, p. 223.
Richard Henry Dana, *Two Years Before the Mast.*

Reuben Renzo

Ref. Captain W. B. Whall, *Sea Songs and Shanties*, p. 60.
Joanna Colcord, *Roll and Go*, p. 23.
D. W. Bone, *Capstan Bars*, p. 54.
Farnsworth and Sharp, *Folksongs, Chanteys and Singing Games*, p. 104.

Rio Grande

Ref. Captain W. B. Whall, *Sea Songs and Shanties*, p. 54.
Joanna Colcord, *Roll and Go*, p. 35.
D. W. Bone, *Capstan Bars*, p. 114.

Shenandoah, or **The Wide Missouri**

Ref. Joanna Colcord, *Roll and Go*, p. 33.
D. W. Bone, *Capstan Bars*, pp. 104ff.
Eckstorm and Smyth, *Minstrelsy of Maine*, p. 243.

Tommy's Gone to Hilo

Ref. Captain W. B. Whall, *Sea Songs and Shanties*, p. 53.
Joanna Colcord, *Roll and Go*, p. 25.
D. W. Bone, *Capstan Bars*, p. 61.
Farnsworth and Sharp, *Folksongs, Chanteys and Singing Games*, p. 105.

Whisky Johnnie

Ref. Joanna Colcord, *Roll and Go*, p. 19.
D. W. Bone, *Capstan Bars*, p. 82.

BALLADS, FOLK SONGS, AND DITTIES

All Bound 'Round with a Woolen String

Ref. Alice Gillington, *Songs of the Open Road*, p. 34.
JEFSS, Vol. VIII, p. 202.
P. W. Joyce, *Old Irish Folkmusic*, p. 90.

Away Down East

Ref. Hutchinson Family Songbook.

The Bailiff's Daughter of Islington

Ref. F. J. Child, 105, *ESPB*, pp. 220–21.
William Chappell, *Popular Music of the Olden Times*, Vol. I, p. 203.
J. O. Phillips-Halliwell, *Norfolk Anthology*, p. 53.

Barb'ry Ellen, or Barbara Allen

Ref. F. J. Child, *ESPB*, pp. 180, 181.
Percy's Reliques of Ancient Poetry, 1847, Vol. III, pp. 169–71.
W. W. Newell, *Games and Songs of American Children*, p. 78.

A Bear Went over the Mountain

Ref. W. Tappert, *Wandernde Meloden.*
Cecil J. Sharp, *The Country Dance Book*, p. 38.
——, *Country Dance Tunes*, p. 6.

Billy Boy

Ref. J. O. Phillips-Halliwell, *Nursery Rhymes of England*, pp. 226, 227.
Robert Chambers, *Popular Rhymes of Scotland*, p. 53.
The Golden Wreath, p. 136.
JAFL, Vol. XXVI, p. 357; Vol. XXXI, pp. 73, 78, 160.

Bingo

Ref. A. B. Gomme, *Dictionary of British Folklore*, Vol. I, p. 29.
William Shakespeare, *King Henry VI*, Act I, Scene 4, line 21.
JAFL, Vol. VI, p. 39. Appendix.
Alice Gillington, *Old Isle of Wight Songs*, p. 6.

Blow, Ye Winds, Blow, or **The Elfin Knight**

Ref. JAFL, Vol. VII, pp. 228, 232; Vol. XXVI, p. 174; Vol. XIX, pp. 130, 223, 430.
William Motherwell, *Minstrelsy,* Appendix, p. 1.
F. J. Child, 19, *ESPB,* p. 84.
G. R. Kinloch, *Ancient Scottish Ballads,* p. 145.

Bold Dickie

Ref. JAFL, Vol. VIII, pp. 256, 257.

The Brookfield Murder

Ref. Records of the town clerk of Brookfield, New Hampshire; Documents of indictments filed in Carroll County Courthouse, Ossipee, N. H.

The Bunnit of Straw

Ref. Encyclopedia Americana, Vol. S.

The Butcher Boy

Ref. Cecil J. Sharp, *Folksongs of England,* p. 29.
JAFL, Vol. XXXI, p. 73.
Kelley family (verses 1, 4).
J. H. Johnson, *Broadside Ballads* (verses 2, 3).

Canaday-I-O

Ref. FSSNE, Bulletin No. 6, 1933, p. 10.
Eckstorm and Smyth, *Minstrelsy of Maine,* pp. 22ff.
Stewart H. Holbrook, *Holy Old Mackinaw,* p. 140.

Caroline of Edinboro Town

Ref. JAFL, Vol. XXXV, p. 362.

The Carrion Crow

Ref. JEFDS, Vol. I, p. 136.
JAFL, Vol. I, No. 3, p. 136.
J. O. Phillips-Halliwell, *Popular Rhymes and Nursery Tales,* p. 12.
Percy Society, *Early English Poetry and Ballads,* Vol. IV, pp. 42, 47.

Common Bill

Ref. Broadwood and Maitland, *English County Songs,* p. 52.

The Devil and the Farmer's Wife

Ref. Kittredge and Sargent, *English and Scottish Popular Ballads,* p. 605.
Percy Society, *Early English Poetry and Ballads,* Vol. XVII, p. 210.

JAFL, Vol. XXX, p. 329; Vol. XII, p. 126.
James Johnson, *Scots Musical Museum*, p. 392.
JEFSS, Vol. VIII, p. 131.

Dirante, My Son, or **Lord Randall**

Ref. F. J. Child, 12, *ESPB*, pp. 12–24.
JAFL, Vol. XXVI, p. 352.
James Johnson, *Scots Musical Museum*, 1787, p. 337.
Gavin Greig, *Border Minstrelsy*, Vol. II, p. 291.
Barry, Eckstorm, and Smyth, *British Ballads from Maine*, pp. 69–72, 492–95.
G. R. Kinloch, *Ancient Scottish Ballads*, p. 115.

Fair Rosamond, or **Rosamond's Downfall**

Ref. *Collection of Old Ballads*, London, 1723, 4–17.
Percy Society, *Reliques of Ancient Poetry*, 1847; Vol. II, p. 151 ff.
F. J. Child, 156, *ESPB*, pp. 372–74.

The Farmington Canal Song

Ref. Lois Lenski, *Phebe Fairchild*, p. 288.

Fiddle Dee Dee

Ref. Percy B. Greene, *History of Nursery Rhymes*, p. 85.

First Families of Fall River

Ref. S. Baring-Gould, *English Minstrelsy*, Introduction, p. 12.

A Fox Went Out on a Starry Night

Ref. J. O. Phillips-Halliwell, *Popular Rhymes and Nursery Tales*, p. 84.
F. E. Bryant, *History of English Ballads*, p. 123.

A Frog He Would a-Wooing Go

Ref. J. O. Phillips-Halliwell, *Nursery Rhymes of England*, p. 70.
JAFL, Vol. XXXV, p. 394.
Robert Ford, *Children's Rhymes, Games, Songs and Stories*, p. 122.

Frog in the Well

Ref. Robert Chambers, *Popular Rhymes of Scotland*, p. 54.
Thomas D'Urfey, *Pills to Purge Melancholy*, Vol. V.
Robert Ford, *Song Histories*, p. 121.
Four Books of Choice Scotch Ballads, Book I, p. 86.
JAFL, Vol. XXVI, p. 135.
Kittredge and Sargent, *English and Scottish Popular Ballads*, p. 605.
Percy Society, *Early English Poetry and Ballads*, Vol. IV, p. 70.

Go Tell Aunt Rhody

Ref. *JAFL,* Vol. XXVI, p. 130.

Gypsy Daisy

Ref. F. J. Child, 200 *ESPB,* pp. 482–85.
Gallovidian Encyclopedia, p. 284.
Kittredge and Sargent, *English and Scottish Popular Ballads,* p. 483.
William Motherwell, *Minstrelsy,* p. 360.

Here We Go Up

Ref. James Johnson, *Scots Musical Museum,* p. 577.
J. O. Halliwell, *Nursery Rhymes of England,* p. 208.
William Chappell, *Later Popular Music,* p. 74.
——, *Collection of National English Arts,* p. 33; Notes III.

I Had a Little Nut Tree

Ref. J. O. Phillips-Halliwell, *Nursery Rhymes of England,* p. 10.

I'll Not Marry at All

Ref. F. J. Child, *ESPB,* pp. 277, 278.

In Good Old Colony Times

Ref. Campbell and Sharp, *Songs from Somersetshire,* p. 130.
JAFL, Vol. XXIX, p. 167; Vol. XXXV, p. 350.
Maguire's Comic Variety Songster.
Collegensia Carmensia.

Jack Haggerty, or **The Flat River Girl**

Ref. Franz Rickaby, *Ballads and Songs of the Shanteyboy,* p. 3.
Eckstorm and Smyth, *Minstrelsy of Maine,* p. 124 ff.
Stewart H. Holbrook, *Holy Old Mackinaw,* pp. 136–37.

The Jam on Gerry's Rocks

Ref. *FSSNE,* Bulletin, No. 10, 1935, pp. 18, 19; No. 12, p. 21.
Franz Rickaby, *Ballads and Songs of the Shanteyboy,* p. 11.
Eckstorm and Smyth, *Minstrelsy of Maine,* pp. 82 ff.
Stewart H. Holbrook, *Holy Old Mackinaw,* p. 131.

The Jolly Miller

Ref. Thomas D'Urfey, *Pills to Purge Melancholy.*
Cecil J. Sharp, *One Hundred English Folksongs.*
——, *Collection of National English Airs,* p. 43; Note XXIII.

William Chappell, *Later Popular Music*, Vol. II, p. 124.
Alfred Moffatt, *Minstrelsy of England*, p. 44.
Alice B. Gomme, *Dictionary of British Folklore*, Vol. II, p. 436.
Alice E. Gillington, *Old Isle of Wight Singing Games*, p. 7.

Jolly Old Roger

Ref. Percy Society, *Early English Poetry and Ballads*, Vol. I, p. 155.
Broadwood and Maitland, *English County Songs*, p. 54.
Thomas D'Urfey, *Songs Compleat*, p. 9.

Julia Grover

Ref. None.

Katy Cruel

Ref. *Allen Family Songs*, No. 1 (reprinted here by courtesy of Miss Lucy G. Allen).
Flanders and Brown, *Vermont Folksongs and Ballads*, p. 123.

The Ladle Song

Ref. Frank Kidson, *Traditional Tunes*, p. 92.
P. W. Joyce, *Old Irish Folkmusic and Songs*, p. 111.

Lavender's Blue

Ref. J. O. Phillips-Halliwell, *Nursery Rhymes of England*, p. 237.
W. W. Newell, *Games and Songs of American Children*, p. 120.

Let's Go to the Woods, or **The Hunting of the Wren**

Ref. Robert Chambers, *Popular Rhymes of Scotland*, p. 48.
Gammer Gurton's Garland.
Donald A. Mackenzie, *Tales from the Moors and Mountains*, p. 23.
JEFDS, Vol. III, p. 36.

Lord Lovell

Ref. Barry, Eckstorm, and Smyth, *British Ballads from Maine*, pp. 145, 149, 482.
F. J. Child, 75 *ESPB*, Vol. II, pp. 159–62.
M. W. Disher, *The Cowells in America*, Chap. XLVIII, p. 112.
JEFSS, Vol. I, p. 134; Vol. VI, pp. 31, 32.
G. R. Kinloch, *Ancient Scottish Ballads*, p. 31.
Kittredge and Sargent, *English and Scottish Popular Ballads*, p. 159.
Cecil J. Sharp, *Folksongs of England*, p. 26.

The Lumberman's Alphabet

Ref. Eckstorm and Smyth, *Minstrelsy of Maine*, p. 30.
Franz Rickaby, *Ballads and Songs of the Shanteyboy*, p. 34; Notes p. 198.

Maple Sweet

Ref. P. B. Fish, *The Palm* (published in Keene, N. H., by G. U. Tilden Company).

The Monkey's Wedding

Ref. Elias Howe, *One Hundred Comic Songs* (verses 3, 4), p. 120.

My Grandmother Lived on Yonder Little Green

Ref. William Chappell, *Later English Popular Music.*
——, *Old English Popular Music.*
Grigg and Elliot, *Southern and Western Songster*, p. 95.

Old Pod-Auger Times

Ref. Comical Brown's Song Book.

The Old Woman in Dover

Ref. F. J. Child, *ESPB*, Vol. II, p. 216.
Gavin Gregg, XII.
JAFL, Vol. XXV, p. 160; Vol. XXIX, pp. 178, 179; Vol. XXXV, p. 385.
Louise Pound, *American Ballads and Songs*, p. 179.

The Old Sow Song

Ref. Farnsworth and Sharp, *Folksongs, Chanteys, and Singing Games*, p. 46.
Story Parade 1938.

The Old Woman Who Went to Market

Ref. Percy Society, *Early English Poetry and Ballads*, Vol. IV, p. 45.

Our Goodman

Ref. F. J. Child, 274 *ESPB*, pp. 597–600.
James Johnson, *Scots Musical Museum*, p. 466.
David Herd, *Ancient and Modern Scottish Songs*, Vol. II, p. 172.
Percy Society, *Early English Poetry and Ballads*, Vol. XVII, p. 212.

Over the Water to Charlie

Ref. James Johnson, *Scots Musical Museum*, p. 489.
W. W. Newell, *Games and Songs of American Children*, p. 171.
Percy Society, *Early English Poetry and Ballads*, Vol. IV, p. 11.

The Oxen Song

Ref. Eckstorm and Smyth, *Minstrelsy of Maine*, p. 79.
Stewart H. Holbrook, *Holy Old Mackinaw*, pp. 63, 163.

Perrie, Merrie, Dixi, Domini

Ref. W. W. Newell, *Games and Songs of American Children*, p. 66.
J. O. Phillips-Halliwell, *Popular Rhymes and Nursery Tales*, p. 150.

Peter Emily

Ref. *FSSNE*, Bulletin No. 2, 1931, pp. 13, 14.
Stewart H. Holbrook, *Holy Old Mackinaw*, p. 138.
Eckstorm and Smyth, *Minstrelsy of Maine*, pp. 98 ff.

Polly Oliver

Ref. Bebbington Broadwise, No. 262.
John Harland, *Ancient Ballads and Songs of Lancashire*, p. 61.
Granville Bantock, *One Hundred Songs of England*, No. 20.
William Chappell, *Popular Music of the Olden Times*, p. 676.
P. W. Joyce, *Old Irish Folkmusic and Songs*, pp. 291, 324.

Polly Van

Ref. *Allen Family Songs* (reprinted here by courtesy of Miss Lucy Allen).
Jamieson, *Popular Ballads*, Vol. I, p. 194.
JEFSS, Vol. VII, p. 17.
Cecil J. Sharp, *Folksongs from Somersetshire*, p. 32.
FSSNE, No. 10, p. 13.
FAFL, Vol. 30, p. 358.

The Quaker's Wooing

Ref. W. W. Newell, *Games and Songs of American Children*, p. 95.
Alice B. Gomme, *Dictionary of British Folklore*, Vol. II, p. 437.
JAFL, Vol. III, p. 49.
JEFSS, Vol. VII, p. 92.

The Rolling of the Stones, or **The Twa Brothers**

Ref. William Motherwell, *Minstrelsy*, p. 211.
F. J. Child, *English and Scottish Popular Ballads*, Vol. I, p. 434.
Folksong Society of the Northeast, Bul. No. 5, p. 6.

The Sawmill Song

Ref. Stewart H. Holbrook, *Holy Old Mackinaw*, p. 39.

A Ship a-Sailing

Ref. Alice B. Gomme, *Dictionary of British Folklore*, Vol. I, p. 113.
J. O. Phillips-Halliwell, *Nursery Rhymes of England*, No. CCCLXXVII, p. 203.
Northamptonshire, *Revue Celtique*, Vol. IV, p. 200.

Springfield Mountain, or The Black Sarpent

Ref. *Bulletin of the Folksong Society of the Northeast*, Vol. II, p. 10.
JAFL, Vol. XXIX.
Wendell Collection, Harvard University Library.

Sweet Kitty Clover

Ref. Copybook of Elizabeth Foster Reed.

Three Blind Mice

Ref. Percy Society, *Early English Poetry and Ballads*, Vol. XIV, p. 43.
J. O. Phillips-Halliwell, *Nursery Rhymes of England*, p. 110.

Three Children Sliding on the Ice

Ref. J. O. Phillips-Halliwell, *History of Nursery Rhymes*, p. 57.
——, *Nursery Rhymes of England*, p. 197.
JEFSS, Vol. IV, p. 35.
Percy Society, *Early English Poetry and Ballads*, Vol. IV, p. 19.

Three Crows

Ref. Alfred Moffatt, *Minstrelsy of England*, p. 32.
William Chappell, *Collection of National English Airs*, Vol. I, p. 59.
James Johnson, *Scots Musical Museum*, p. 387.
Robert Ford, *Auld Scots Ballads*, p. 232.
Cecil J. Sharp, *English County Songs*, p. 232.
Frank Kidson, *Traditional Tunes*, p. 18.
William Motherwell, *Minstrelsy*, p. 7.
Kittredge and Sargent, *English and Scottish Popular Ballads*, p. 45.
JAFL, Vol. XX, p. 154; Vol. XXXI, p. 273.

Three Jovial Huntsmen

Ref. Caldecotte, Vol. II, pp. 1 ff.
W. W. Newell, *Games and Songs of American Children*, p. 97.
Percy Society, *Early English Poetry and Ballads*, Vol. IV, p. 118.
J. O. Phillips-Halliwell, *Nursery Rhymes of England*, p. 161.

Tittery Nan

Ref. *Bulletin of the Folksong Society of the Northeast*, No. 7, 1934, p. 13.
FSSNE, 1933, No. 6, p. 13.

Too-ril-Te-Too

Ref. Alfred Moffatt, *Minstrelsy of Ireland*, p. 336.

Tyburn Hill

Ref. Charles Gordon, *Old Bailey and Newgate.*
Gallovidian Encyclopedia, p. 60.
Collegensia Carmensia.

Washing Day

Ref. *Harp of Renfrewshire* (published by William Turnbull, 1820), Essay, p. LXVII.
Chap Book of Ballads.
Gallovidian Encyclopedia, p. 244.
James Johnson, *Scots Musical Museum*, p. 615.
Copybook of Elizabeth Foster Reed.
Nathaniel March, *New England Songster*, p. 35.

Will You Wear the Red? or **Jennie Jenkins**

Ref. F. J. Child, 7 *ESPB*, pp. 31–33.
Green Mountain Songster, Sandgate, Vermont, 1823.
Flanders and Brown, *Vermont Folksongs and Ballads*, pp. 166–67.
W. W. Newell, *Games and Songs of American Children*, p. 63.

Willikins and His Dinah

Ref. Wendell Collection, Harvard University Library (verses 4 and 6).
JEFSS, Vol. VIII, p. 146.

Young Alanthia

Ref. James Johnson, *Scots Musical Museum.*
William Motherwell, *Minstrelsy*, p. 290.
JEFSS, Vol. I, No. 1.
Cecil J. Sharp, *Folksongs from Various Counties*, p. 38.
F. J. Child, 93, *ESPB.*
Kittredge and Sargent, *English and Scottish Popular Ballads*, p. 196.
Four Books of Choice Old Scotch Ballads, Book IV, p. 73.
Broadwood and Mason, *Northumberland County Songs*, p. 126.

Young Charlotte

Ref. *FSSNE*, No. 12, 1937, p. 26.
FSSNE, No. 8, p. 18.
JAFL, Vol. XXV, p. 160.
The Rover, Vol. II, p. 225.

ADDENDA AND CORRIGENDA

(p. 1) SINGING GAMES. One of the gentle recreations of old New England was the "Singing School" which was conducted by a "master"—he with the urge to sing and a smattering of talent—who summoned a group of young folk to some accepted family hearth. Each singer brought his own book and candle.

(p. 20) Second verse, *I Am A Rich Widow:*

"I've married off my daughter
I've given her away;
I've married off my daughter
She's bound to obey;
Bound to obey and
She'll never disagree
So as we go 'round kiss her
One, two, three!"

(p. 59) Line five from bottom, for "country" read "county".

(p. 67) The drawings are by Charles Baker Wilbar.

(pp. 71-2) *Chorus Jig.* Three movements, each with its own air, are usually played for this dance. The traditional key for the first phrase is D. To play the melody as printed, the musical symbols read Segno sign at the beginning of second movement and DS *al fine* at end of tune. At the end of the first movement, symbol should be *fine*. Thus the two airs here can be made for the three phases of the dance. Here is the version of the *Chorus Jig* played by Ed Lewis of Durham, New Hampshire, Ed Larkin of Chelsea, Vermont, and Aunt Carrie B. Grover of Gorham, Maine.

CHORUS JIG

(p. 82) The melody of this jig for *Green Mountain Volunteers* is known as "St. Patrick's Day in the Morning".

(p. 83) The traditional key for the *Arkansas Traveler* is D.

(p. 84) Thirty-two bars of music will take the dance pattern of *Haymaker's Jig* through.

(p. 87) Line nine should read: "The Capture of Carrickfergus", written by Thurot, a French admiral who captured Carrick.

(p. 89) The last eight measures are the tune *Lady Of The Lake* (or *The Fairy Dance)*. The last bar may be omitted and two quarter notes used in place of the half note printed, and a rest symbol placed to end the tune.

(p. 98) *Morning Star*. Dance changes called by Happy Hale of Hinsdale, New Hampshire.

(p. 99) Thirty-two bars of music should be played for the dance.

(p. 102) *Old Zip Coon*. The first version of the dance directions are known as "Sweet Ellen".

(p. 103) The last measure of the first line should have a double bar to close the phrase.

(p. 108) *Pop! Goes The Weasel*. When playing the violin, use the key of G for special fingering to make the "pop". Here is the version of the tune as played by Edson H. Cole of Freedom, New Hampshire.

POP! GOES THE WEASEL

(p. 109) Line two, for "quardrille" read "quadrille".

(p. 110) This is the way Ed Lewis of Durhám, New Hampshire, plays *Soldier's Joy*.

SOLDIER'S JOY

(p. 114) *Twin Sisters*. Another name is "Ladies Triumph". The thirteenth edition of Playford's *The Dancing Master* was published in London in 1707. "Farewell to Whiskey" is possibly not an Irish tune.

(p. 116) *Virginia Reel*. Beginning with line four, directions for the dance should read:

First gentleman turn foot lady in center with right hand	4 bars
First lady turn foot gentleman in center with left hand	4 bars
First gentleman turn foot lady in center with left hand	4 bars
First lady turn foot gentleman in center with both hands	4 bars
First gentleman turn foot lady in center with both hands	4 bars
First lady meets foot gentleman in center and Do-si-do	4 bars
First gentleman meets foot lady in center and Do-si-do	4 bars
First lady gives right hand to partner and they reel down the set	8 bars

To Reel:—

(p. 118) *The Waltz*. For more than half a century an indigenous tune called "*That Waltz*" was played by Arthur Colburn, Wallace Ladd, and Burney Plummer for the dances in the region of Weld, Maine. In spite of its popularity no one recalls it by any other than its local title. It can still be heard at the country dance.

THAT WALTZ

(p. 121) Paragraph two. The town of Popham, Maine, claims the distinction of building the first ship in the New England colonies.

(p. 126) Top line. The third note of the third measure should be "D". *Blow, Boys, Blow!* sung by James M. Linscott II.

(p. 128) *Blow The Man Down* sung by James M. Linscott II.

(p. 138) *Haul Away, Joe!* The chord in the upper clef of the third measure should read "D, A, F".

(p. 114) *Johnny Boker.* James M. Linscott II.

(p. 142) *Old Horse.* James M. Linscott II.

(p. 147) *Rio Grande.* "*Rio*" should be pronounced "Ry-o" throughout the song.

(p. 148) *Shenandoah.* James M. Linscott II.

(p. 150) *Tommy's Gone To Hilo.* James M. Linscott II.

(p. 153) BALLADS, FOLK SONGS, AND DITTIES. The songs that were sung or hummed to the time of the spinning loom were hymns; very lively spirituals they were too, since religion was an active and passionate thing. It is said that these were the foundation of the Negro spiritual in the southern states, as one can easily imagine in the lively cadence of many of those tunes.

(p. 160) The last line of the third verse should read: "He had not yet begun to get *Away Down East!*".

(p. 182) In the fifth verse, "route" is pronounced "rout".

(p. 194) In the second line of the air, the 6th note should read "B" and the 12th note "A".

(p. 207) *Gypsy Daisy* is sometimes called "Gypsy Davey".

(p. 209) Verse 4:

"Last night I lay with my own true love,
Last night I lay with my baby,
Tonight I lie on the cold, cold ground
In the arms of the gypsy daisy."

(p. 222) *Jolly Old Roger.* This was sung by John A. Moore of Colebrook, Connecticut, father of Mrs. Deming and six other children. A brother of Mrs. Deming, Ira W. Moore, says "My sister couldn't sing a note nor could my mother, but Father was always singing and we seven children 'sang' with him."

(p. 224) The third line of the fourth verse should read: "And down in the churchyard they trampled him in."

(p. 248) *The Old Man.* In the second verse, "tiny" should read "Tiny", since it is the cow's name.

(p. 239) The rest sign should be omitted in the sixth measure.

(p. 261) The last line of the second verse should read: "But a saddle upon a brindle cow I never saw before."

(p. 264) For good harmony, the third chord in the fourth measure should read "F, G" in the upper clef and "E, B, E" in the base clef.

(p. 296) The chord after the 6th note should be half notes, not quarter notes.

(p. 297) The melody to *Washing Day* was known to Llewellyn Powers as "I Can't Untie the Knot" and he with other fiddlers used it for a dance tune.

(p. 299) *Will You Wear The Red.* This song was sung to Mrs. Frances E. Horn . . . by her grandmother, Olive Merrow Goodwin . . . .

(p. 300) The second verse should read:

"Will you wear the white . . .
Oh, I will wear the white
For the color is just right. . . ."

(p. 306) In both measures nine and thirteen the rest should be omitted; in both measures the accompaniment should read "D, F, B, D".

(p. 314) Paragraph three: James M. Linscott II.

A CATALOG OF SELECTED

DOVER BOOKS

IN ALL FIELDS OF INTEREST

HOW TO WRITE, Gertrude Stein. Gertrude Stein claimed anyone could understand her unconventional writing—here are clues to help. Fascinating improvisations, language experiments, explanations illuminate Stein's craft and the art of writing. Total of 414pp. 4⅜ × 6⅜. 23144-5 Pa. $6.95

ADVENTURES AT SEA IN THE GREAT AGE OF SAIL: Five Firsthand Narratives, edited by Elliot Snow. Rare true accounts of exploration, whaling, shipwreck, fierce natives, trade, shipboard life, more. 33 illustrations. Introduction. 353pp. 5⅜ × 8½. 25177-2 Pa. $9.95

THE HERBAL OR GENERAL HISTORY OF PLANTS, John Gerard. Classic descriptions of about 2,850 plants—with over 2,700 illustrations—includes Latin and English names, physical descriptions, varieties, time and place of growth, more. 2,706 illustrations. xlv + 1,678pp. 8½ × 12¼. 23147-X Cloth. $75.00

DOROTHY AND THE WIZARD IN OZ, L. Frank Baum. Dorothy and the Wizard visit the center of the Earth, where people are vegetables, glass houses grow and Oz characters reappear. Classic sequel to *Wizard of Oz*. 256pp. 5⅜ × 8. 24714-7 Pa. $5.95

SONGS OF EXPERIENCE: Facsimile Reproduction with 26 Plates in Full Color, William Blake. This facsimile of Blake's original "Illuminated Book" reproduces 26 full-color plates from a rare 1826 edition. Includes "The Tyger," "London," "Holy Thursday," and other immortal poems. 26 color plates. Printed text of poems. 48pp. 5¼ × 7. 24636-1 Pa. $3.95

SONGS OF INNOCENCE, William Blake. The first and most popular of Blake's famous "Illuminated Books," in a facsimile edition reproducing all 31 brightly colored plates. Additional printed text of each poem. 64pp. 5¼ × 7. 22764-2 Pa. $3.95

PRECIOUS STONES, Max Bauer. Classic, thorough study of diamonds, rubies, emeralds, garnets, etc.: physical character, occurrence, properties, use, similar topics. 20 plates, 8 in color. 94 figures. 659pp. 6⅛ × 9¼. 21910-0, 21911-9 Pa., Two-vol. set $15.90

ENCYCLOPEDIA OF VICTORIAN NEEDLEWORK, S. F. A. Caulfeild and Blanche Saward. Full, precise descriptions of stitches, techniques for dozens of needlecrafts—most exhaustive reference of its kind. Over 800 figures. Total of 679pp. 8⅛ × 11. 22800-2, 22801-0 Pa., Two-vol. set $23.90

THE MARVELOUS LAND OF OZ, L. Frank Baum. Second Oz book, the Scarecrow and Tin Woodman are back with hero named Tip, Oz magic. 136 illustrations. 287pp. 5⅜ × 8½. 20692-0 Pa. $5.95

WILD FOWL DECOYS, Joel Barber. Basic book on the subject, by foremost authority and collector. Reveals history of decoy making and rigging, place in American culture, different kinds of decoys, how to make them, and how to use them. 140 plates. 156pp. 7⅞ × 10¾. 20011-6 Pa. $8.95

HISTORY OF LACE, Mrs. Bury Palliser. Definitive, profusely illustrated chronicle of lace from earliest times to late 19th century. Laces of Italy, Greece, England, France, Belgium, etc. Landmark of needlework scholarship. 266 illustrations. 672pp. 6⅛ × 9¼. 24742-2 Pa. $16.95

SUNDIALS, Albert Waugh. Far and away the best, most thorough coverage of ideas, mathematics concerned, types, construction, adjusting anywhere. Over 100 illustrations. 230pp. 5⅜ × 8½. 22947-5 Pa. $5.95

PICTURE HISTORY OF THE NORMANDIE: With 190 Illustrations, Frank O. Braynard. Full story of legendary French ocean liner: Art Deco interiors, design innovations, furnishings, celebrities, maiden voyage, tragic fire, much more. Extensive text. 144pp. 8⅜ × 11¾. 25257-4 Pa. $10.95

THE FIRST AMERICAN COOKBOOK: A Facsimile of "American Cookery," 1796, Amelia Simmons. Facsimile of the first American-written cookbook published in the United States contains authentic recipes for colonial favorites—pumpkin pudding, winter squash pudding, spruce beer, Indian slapjacks, and more. Introductory Essay and Glossary of colonial cooking terms. 80pp. 5⅜ × 8½. 24710-4 Pa. $3.50

101 PUZZLES IN THOUGHT AND LOGIC, C. R. Wylie, Jr. Solve murders and robberies, find out which fishermen are liars, how a blind man could possibly identify a color—purely by your own reasoning! 107pp. 5⅜ × 8½. 20367-0 Pa. $2.95

ANCIENT EGYPTIAN MYTHS AND LEGENDS, Lewis Spence. Examines animism, totemism, fetishism, creation myths, deities, alchemy, art and magic, other topics. Over 50 illustrations. 432pp. 5⅜ × 8½. 26525-0 Pa. $8.95

ANTHROPOLOGY AND MODERN LIFE, Franz Boas. Great anthropologist's classic treatise on race and culture. Introduction by Ruth Bunzel. Only inexpensive paperback edition. 255pp. 5⅜ × 8½. 25245-0 Pa. $6.95

THE TALE OF PETER RABBIT, Beatrix Potter. The inimitable Peter's terrifying adventure in Mr. McGregor's garden, with all 27 wonderful, full-color Potter illustrations. 55pp. 4¼ × 5½. (Available in U.S. only) 22827-4 Pa. $1.75

THREE PROPHETIC SCIENCE FICTION NOVELS, H. G. Wells. *When the Sleeper Wakes, A Story of the Days to Come* and *The Time Machine* (full version). 335pp. 5⅜ × 8½. (Available in U.S. only) 20605-X Pa. $8.95

APICIUS COOKERY AND DINING IN IMPERIAL ROME, edited and translated by Joseph Dommers Vehling. Oldest known cookbook in existence offers readers a clear picture of what foods Romans ate, how they prepared them, etc. 49 illustrations. 301pp. 6⅛ × 9¼. 23563-7 Pa. $7.95

SHAKESPEARE LEXICON AND QUOTATION DICTIONARY, Alexander Schmidt. Full definitions, locations, shades of meaning of every word in plays and poems. More than 50,000 exact quotations. 1,485pp. 6½ × 9¼. 22726-X, 22727-8 Pa., Two-vol. set $31.90

THE WORLD'S GREAT SPEECHES, edited by Lewis Copeland and Lawrence W. Lamm. Vast collection of 278 speeches from Greeks to 1970. Powerful and effective models; unique look at history. 842pp. 5⅜ × 8½. 20468-5 Pa. $12.95

PLANTS OF THE BIBLE, Harold N. Moldenke and Alma L. Moldenke. Standard reference to all 230 plants mentioned in Scriptures. Latin name, biblical reference, uses, modern identity, much more. Unsurpassed encyclopedic resource for scholars, botanists, nature lovers, students of Bible. Bibliography. Indexes. 123 black-and-white illustrations. 384pp. 6 × 9. 25069-5 Pa. $8.95

FAMOUS AMERICAN WOMEN: A Biographical Dictionary from Colonial Times to the Present, Robert McHenry, ed. From Pocahontas to Rosa Parks, 1,035 distinguished American women documented in separate biographical entries. Accurate, up-to-date data, numerous categories, spans 400 years. Indices. 493pp. 6½ × 9¼. 24523-3 Pa. $10.95

THE FABULOUS INTERIORS OF THE GREAT OCEAN LINERS IN HISTORIC PHOTOGRAPHS, William H. Miller, Jr. Some 200 superb photographs capture exquisite interiors of world's great "floating palaces"—1890s to 1980s: *Titanic, Ile de France, Queen Elizabeth, United States, Europa,* more. Approx. 200 black-and-white photographs. Captions. Text. Introduction. 160pp. 8⅞ × 11¾. 24756-2 Pa. $9.95

THE GREAT LUXURY LINERS, 1927–1954: A Photographic Record, William H. Miller, Jr. Nostalgic tribute to heyday of ocean liners. 186 photos of *Ile de France, Normandie, Leviathan, Queen Elizabeth, United States,* many others. Interior and exterior views. Introduction. Captions. 160pp. 9 × 12. 24056-8 Pa. $10.95

A NATURAL HISTORY OF THE DUCKS, John Charles Phillips. Great landmark of ornithology offers complete detailed coverage of nearly 200 species and subspecies of ducks: gadwall, sheldrake, merganser, pintail, many more. 74 full-color plates, 102 black-and-white. Bibliography. Total of 1,920pp. 8⅝ × 11¼. 25141-1, 25142-X Cloth., Two-vol. set $100.00

THE SEAWEED HANDBOOK: An Illustrated Guide to Seaweeds from North Carolina to Canada, Thomas F. Lee. Concise reference covers 78 species. Scientific and common names, habitat, distribution, more. Finding keys for easy identification. 224pp. 5⅜ × 8½. 25215-9 Pa. $6.95

THE TEN BOOKS OF ARCHITECTURE: The 1755 Leoni Edition, Leon Battista Alberti. Rare classic helped introduce the glories of ancient architecture to the Renaissance. 68 black-and-white plates. 336pp. 8⅜ × 11¼. 25239-6 Pa. $14.95

MISS MACKENZIE, Anthony Trollope. Minor masterpieces by Victorian master unmasks many truths about life in 19th-century England. First inexpensive edition in years. 392pp. 5⅜ × 8½. 25201-9 Pa. $8.95

THE RIME OF THE ANCIENT MARINER, Gustave Doré, Samuel Taylor Coleridge. Dramatic engravings considered by many to be his greatest work. The terrifying space of the open sea, the storms and whirlpools of an unknown ocean, the ice of Antarctica, more—all rendered in a powerful, chilling manner. Full text. 38 plates. 77pp. 9¼ × 12. 22305-1 Pa. $4.95

THE EXPEDITIONS OF ZEBULON MONTGOMERY PIKE, Zebulon Montgomery Pike. Fascinating firsthand accounts (1805–6) of exploration of Mississippi River, Indian wars, capture by Spanish dragoons, much more. 1,088pp. 5⅜ × 8½. 25254-X, 25255-8 Pa., Two-vol. set $25.90

A CONCISE HISTORY OF PHOTOGRAPHY: Third Revised Edition, Helmut Gernsheim. Best one-volume history—camera obscura, photochemistry, daguerreotypes, evolution of cameras, film, more. Also artistic aspects—landscape, portraits, fine art, etc. 281 black-and-white photographs. 26 in color. 176pp. 8⅜ × 11¼.
25128-4 Pa. $14.95

THE DORÉ BIBLE ILLUSTRATIONS, Gustave Doré. 241 detailed plates from the Bible: the Creation scenes, Adam and Eve, Flood, Babylon, battle sequences, life of Jesus, etc. Each plate is accompanied by the verses from the King James version of the Bible. 241pp. 9 × 12. 23004-X Pa. $9.95

WANDERINGS IN WEST AFRICA, Richard F. Burton. Great Victorian scholar/adventurer's invaluable descriptions of African tribal rituals, fetishism, culture, art, much more. Fascinating 19th-century account. 624pp. 5⅜ × 8½. 26890-X Pa. $12.95

FLATLAND, E. A. Abbott. Intriguing and enormously popular science-fiction classic explores the complexities of trying to survive as a two-dimensional being in a three-dimensional world. Amusingly illustrated by the author. 16 illustrations. 103pp. 5⅜ × 8½. 20001-9 Pa. $2.50

THE HISTORY OF THE LEWIS AND CLARK EXPEDITION, Meriwether Lewis and William Clark, edited by Elliott Coues. Classic edition of Lewis and Clark's day-by-day journals that later became the basis for U.S. claims to Oregon and the West. Accurate and invaluable geographical, botanical, biological, meteorological and anthropological material. Total of 1,508pp. 5⅜ × 8½.
21268-8, 21269-6, 21270-X Pa., Three-vol. set $29.85

LANGUAGE, TRUTH AND LOGIC, Alfred J. Ayer. Famous, clear introduction to Vienna, Cambridge schools of Logical Positivism. Role of philosophy, elimination of metaphysics, nature of analysis, etc. 160pp. 5⅜ × 8½. (Available in U.S. and Canada only) 20010-8 Pa. $3.95

MATHEMATICS FOR THE NONMATHEMATICIAN, Morris Kline. Detailed, college-level treatment of mathematics in cultural and historical context, with numerous exercises. For liberal arts students. Preface. Recommended Reading Lists. Tables. Index. Numerous black-and-white figures. xvi + 641pp. 5⅜ × 8½.
24823-2 Pa. $11.95

HANDBOOK OF PICTORIAL SYMBOLS, Rudolph Modley. 3,250 signs and symbols, many systems in full; official or heavy commercial use. Arranged by subject. Most in Pictorial Archive series. 143pp. 8⅛ × 11. 23357-X Pa. $7.95

INCIDENTS OF TRAVEL IN YUCATAN, John L. Stephens. Classic (1843) exploration of jungles of Yucatan, looking for evidences of Maya civilization. Travel adventures, Mexican and Indian culture, etc. Total of 669pp. 5⅜ × 8½.
20926-1, 20927-X Pa., Two-vol. set $11.90

DEGAS: An Intimate Portrait, Ambroise Vollard. Charming, anecdotal memoir by famous art dealer of one of the greatest 19th-century French painters. 14 black-and-white illustrations. Introduction by Harold L. Van Doren. 96pp. 5⅜ × 8½.
25131-4 Pa. $4.95

PERSONAL NARRATIVE OF A PILGRIMAGE TO AL-MADINAH AND MECCAH, Richard F. Burton. Great travel classic by remarkably colorful personality. Burton, disguised as a Moroccan, visited sacred shrines of Islam, narrowly escaping death. 47 illustrations. 959pp. 5⅜ × 8½.
21217-3, 21218-1 Pa., Two-vol. set $19.90

PHRASE AND WORD ORIGINS, A. H. Holt. Entertaining, reliable, modern study of more than 1,200 colorful words, phrases, origins and histories. Much unexpected information. 254pp. 5⅜ × 8½. 20758-7 Pa. $5.95

THE RED THUMB MARK, R. Austin Freeman. In this first Dr. Thorndyke case, the great scientific detective draws fascinating conclusions from the nature of a single fingerprint. Exciting story, authentic science. 320pp. 5⅜ × 8½. (Available in U.S. only) 25210-8 Pa. $6.95

AN EGYPTIAN HIEROGLYPHIC DICTIONARY, E. A. Wallis Budge. Monumental work containing about 25,000 words or terms that occur in texts ranging from 3000 B.C. to 600 A.D. Each entry consists of a transliteration of the word, the word in hieroglyphs, and the meaning in English. 1,314pp. 6⅞ × 10.
23615-3, 23616-1 Pa., Two-vol. set $35.90

THE COMPLEAT STRATEGYST: Being a Primer on the Theory of Games of Strategy, J. D. Williams. Highly entertaining classic describes, with many illustrated examples, how to select best strategies in conflict situations. Prefaces. Appendices. xvi + 268pp. 5⅜ × 8½. 25101-2 Pa. $6.95

THE ROAD TO OZ, L. Frank Baum. Dorothy meets the Shaggy Man, little Button-Bright and the Rainbow's beautiful daughter in this delightful trip to the magical Land of Oz. 272pp. 5⅜ × 8. 25208-6 Pa. $5.95

POINT AND LINE TO PLANE, Wassily Kandinsky. Seminal exposition of role of point, line, other elements in nonobjective painting. Essential to understanding 20th-century art. 127 illustrations. 192pp. 6½ × 9¼. 23808-3 Pa. $5.95

LADY ANNA, Anthony Trollope. Moving chronicle of Countess Lovel's bitter struggle to win for herself and daughter Anna their rightful rank and fortune—perhaps at cost of sanity itself. 384pp. 5⅜ × 8½. 24669-8 Pa. $8.95

EGYPTIAN MAGIC, E. A. Wallis Budge. Sums up all that is known about magic in Ancient Egypt: the role of magic in controlling the gods, powerful amulets that warded off evil spirits, scarabs of immortality, use of wax images, formulas and spells, the secret name, much more. 253pp. 5⅜ × 8½. 22681-6 Pa. $4.50

THE DANCE OF SIVA, Ananda Coomaraswamy. Preeminent authority unfolds the vast metaphysic of India: the revelation of her art, conception of the universe, social organization, etc. 27 reproductions of art masterpieces. 192pp. 5⅜ × 8½.
24817-8 Pa. $6.95

THE ART NOUVEAU STYLE BOOK OF ALPHONSE MUCHA: All 72 Plates from "Documents Decoratifs" in Original Color, Alphonse Mucha. Rare copyright-free design portfolio by high priest of Art Nouveau. Jewelry, wallpaper, stained glass, furniture, figure studies, plant and animal motifs, etc. Only complete one-volume edition. 80pp. $9\frac{3}{8} \times 12\frac{1}{4}$. 24044-4 Pa. $10.95

ANIMALS: 1,419 Copyright-Free Illustrations of Mammals, Birds, Fish, Insects, Etc., edited by Jim Harter. Clear wood engravings present, in extremely lifelike poses, over 1,000 species of animals. One of the most extensive pictorial sourcebooks of its kind. Captions. Index. 284pp. 9×12. 23766-4 Pa. $10.95

OBELISTS FLY HIGH, C. Daly King. Masterpiece of American detective fiction, long out of print, involves murder on a 1935 transcontinental flight—"a very thrilling story"—*NY Times*. Unabridged and unaltered republication of the edition published by William Collins Sons & Co. Ltd., London, 1935. 288pp. $5\frac{3}{8} \times 8\frac{1}{2}$. (Available in U.S. only) 25036-9 Pa. $5.95

VICTORIAN AND EDWARDIAN FASHION: A Photographic Survey, Alison Gernsheim. First fashion history completely illustrated by contemporary photographs. Full text plus 235 photos, 1840–1914, in which many celebrities appear. 240pp. $6\frac{1}{2} \times 9\frac{1}{4}$. 24205-6 Pa. $8.95

THE ART OF THE FRENCH ILLUSTRATED BOOK, 1700–1914, Gordon N. Ray. Over 630 superb book illustrations by Fragonard, Delacroix, Daumier, Doré, Grandville, Manet, Mucha, Steinlen, Toulouse-Lautrec and many others. Preface. Introduction. 633 halftones. Indices of artists, authors & titles, binders and provenances. Appendices. Bibliography. 608pp. $8\frac{3}{8} \times 11\frac{1}{4}$. 25086-5 Pa. $24.95

THE WONDERFUL WIZARD OF OZ, L. Frank Baum. Facsimile in full color of America's finest children's classic. 143 illustrations by W. W. Denslow. 267pp. $5\frac{3}{8} \times 8\frac{1}{2}$. 20691-2 Pa. $7.95

FOLLOWING THE EQUATOR: A Journey Around the World, Mark Twain. Great writer's 1897 account of circumnavigating the globe by steamship. Ironic humor, keen observations, vivid and fascinating descriptions of exotic places. 197 illustrations. 720pp. $5\frac{3}{8} \times 8\frac{1}{2}$. 26113-1 Pa. $15.95

THE FRIENDLY STARS, Martha Evans Martin & Donald Howard Menzel. Classic text marshalls the stars together in an engaging, nontechnical survey, presenting them as sources of beauty in night sky. 23 illustrations. Foreword. 2 star charts. Index. 147pp. $5\frac{3}{8} \times 8\frac{1}{2}$. 21099-5 Pa. $3.95

FADS AND FALLACIES IN THE NAME OF SCIENCE, Martin Gardner. Fair, witty appraisal of cranks, quacks, and quackeries of science and pseudoscience: hollow earth, Velikovsky, orgone energy, Dianetics, flying saucers, Bridey Murphy, food and medical fads, etc. Revised, expanded In the Name of Science. "A very able and even-tempered presentation."—*The New Yorker*. 363pp. $5\frac{3}{8} \times 8$. 20394-8 Pa. $6.95

ANCIENT EGYPT: Its Culture and History, J. E. Manchip White. From predynastics through Ptolemies: society, history, political structure, religion, daily life, literature, cultural heritage. 48 plates. 217pp. $5\frac{3}{8} \times 8\frac{1}{2}$. 22548-8 Pa. $5.95

SIR HARRY HOTSPUR OF HUMBLETHWAITE, Anthony Trollope. Incisive, unconventional psychological study of a conflict between a wealthy baronet, his idealistic daughter, and their scapegrace cousin. The 1870 novel in its first inexpensive edition in years. 250pp. 5⅜ × 8½. 24953-0 Pa. $6.95

LASERS AND HOLOGRAPHY, Winston E. Kock. Sound introduction to burgeoning field, expanded (1981) for second edition. Wave patterns, coherence, lasers, diffraction, zone plates, properties of holograms, recent advances. 84 illustrations. 160pp. 5⅜ × 8¼. (Except in United Kingdom) 24041-X Pa. $3.95

INTRODUCTION TO ARTIFICIAL INTELLIGENCE: Second, Enlarged Edition, Philip C. Jackson, Jr. Comprehensive survey of artificial intelligence—the study of how machines (computers) can be made to act intelligently. Includes introductory and advanced material. Extensive notes updating the main text. 132 black-and-white illustrations. 512pp. 5⅜ × 8½. 24864-X Pa. $10.95

HISTORY OF INDIAN AND INDONESIAN ART, Ananda K. Coomaraswamy. Over 400 illustrations illuminate classic study of Indian art from earliest Harappa finds to early 20th century. Provides philosophical, religious and social insights. 304pp. 6⅝ × 9⅝. 25005-9 Pa. $11.95

THE GOLEM, Gustav Meyrink. Most famous supernatural novel in modern European literature, set in Ghetto of Old Prague around 1890. Compelling story of mystical experiences, strange transformations, profound terror. 13 black-and-white illustrations. 224pp. 5⅜ × 8½. (Available in U.S. only) 25025-3 Pa. $6.95

PICTORIAL ENCYCLOPEDIA OF HISTORIC ARCHITECTURAL PLANS, DETAILS AND ELEMENTS: With 1,880 Line Drawings of Arches, Domes, Doorways, Facades, Gables, Windows, etc., John Theodore Haneman. Sourcebook of inspiration for architects, designers, others. Bibliography. Captions. 141pp. 9 × 12. 24605-1 Pa. $7.95

BENCHLEY LOST AND FOUND, Robert Benchley. Finest humor from early 30s, about pet peeves, child psychologists, post office and others. Mostly unavailable elsewhere. 73 illustrations by Peter Arno and others. 183pp. 5⅜ × 8½. 22410-4 Pa. $4.95

ERTÉ GRAPHICS, Erté. Collection of striking color graphics: *Seasons, Alphabet, Numerals, Aces* and *Precious Stones*. 50 plates, including 4 on covers. 48pp. 9⅜ × 12¼. 23580-7 Pa. $7.95

THE JOURNAL OF HENRY D. THOREAU, edited by Bradford Torrey, F. H. Allen. Complete reprinting of 14 volumes, 1837–61, over two million words; the sourcebooks for *Walden*, etc. Definitive. All original sketches, plus 75 photographs. 1,804pp. 8½ × 12¼. 20312-3, 20313-1 Cloth., Two-vol. set $130.00

CASTLES: Their Construction and History, Sidney Toy. Traces castle development from ancient roots. Nearly 200 photographs and drawings illustrate moats, keeps, baileys, many other features. Caernarvon, Dover Castles, Hadrian's Wall, Tower of London, dozens more. 256pp. 5⅜ × 8¼. 24898-4 Pa. $6.95

CATALOG OF DOVER BOOKS